PERSIAN STUDIES SERIES NO. 5

SHI'ITE ISLAM

ʿAllāmah Sayyid Muḥammad Husayn Ṭabāṭabāʾī

PERSIAN STUDIES SERIES
General Editor: Ehsan Yar-Shater, *Columbia University*

SHI'ITE ISLAM

by
'Allāmah Sayyid Muḥammad Husayn Ṭabāṭabā'ī

Translated from the Persian
and Edited with an Introduction and Notes
by Seyyed Hossein Nasr

STATE UNIVERSITY OF NEW YORK PRESS
Albany 1975

The Persian Studies Series is published under the auspices of the Pahlavi Foundation's Royal Institute of Translation and Publication

Published with assistance from
The Fund for the Study of the Great Religions
at Colgate University

Second Edition 1977

First published in 1975 by
State University of New York Press
99 Washington Avenue, Albany, New York 12210

Printed in the United States of America

Library of Congress Cataloging in Publication Data

al-Ṭabāṭabā'ī, Muḥammad Ḥusayn, 1903 or 4–
Shī'ite Islām.

(The Persian studies series, no. 5)
Translation of Shī'ah dar Islām.
Bibliography: p.
1. Shiites. I. Title.

BP193.5.T3213   297'.82   74-8289

ISBN 0-87395-272-3

ISBN 0-87395-273-1 (microfiche)

PERSIAN STUDIES MONOGRAPHS

The Persian Studies Monographs are devoted to works of scholarship which explore and elucidate various aspects of Iranian culture. Initiated with the encouragement of H.I.M. the Shahanshah of Iran, the series is published under the auspices of the Pahlavi Foundation.

CONTENTS

PART II: SHIʿITE RELIGIOUS THOUGHT

PART III:
ISLAMIC BELIEFS FROM THE SHI'ITE POINT OF VIEW

Transliteration

Arabic Letters

symbol	transliteration
ء	'
ب	b
ت	t
ث	th
ج	j
ح	ḥ
خ	kh
د	d
ذ	dh
ر	r
ز	z
س	s
ش	sh
ص	ṣ
ض	ḍ
ط	ṭ
ظ	ẓ
ع	'
غ	gh
ف	f
ق	q

Long Vowels

ای	ā
و	ū
ي	ī

Short Vowels

َ	a
ُ	u
ِ	i

Diphthongs

ـَو	au
ـَي	ai
ـيّ	īy (Final Form ī)
ـوّ	uww (Final Form ū)

Persian Letters

پ	p
چ	ch

symbol	transliteration	Persian Letters	
ك	k	ژ	zh
ل	l	گ	g
م	m		
ن	n		
ه	h		
و	w		
ي	y		
ة	ah; at (*construct state*, and in certain words where the Persian pronunciation has been retained)		
ال	(*article*) al- and ’l (*even before the antepalatals*)		

IN THE NAME OF ALLAH MOST MERCIFUL AND COMPASSIONATE

PREFACE

Seyyed Hossein Nasr

The Study of Shiʿism

Despite the vast amount of information and the number of factual details assembled during the past century by Western scholarship in the fields of orientalism and comparative religion, many gaps still exist in the knowledge of the various religions of the world, even on the level of historical facts. Moreover, until recently most of the studies carried out within these fields have suffered from a lack of metaphysical penetration and sympathetic insight. One of the most notable omissions in Western studies of the religions of the East, and of Islam in particular, has occurred in the case of Shiʿism. Until now Shiʿism has received little attention; and when it has been discussed, it has usually been relegated to the secondary and peripheral status of a religio-political "sect," a heterodoxy or even a heresy. Hence its importance in both the past and the present has been belittled far more than a fair and objective study of the matter would justify.

The present work hopes to redress partially the lack of accessible and reliable English-language material pertaining to Shiʿism. It is the first of a series of books designed to bring to the English-speaking world accurate information about Shiʿism through the translation of writings by authentic Shiʿite representatives and of some of the traditional sources which, along with the Quran, form the foundation of Shiʿite Islam. The purpose of this series is to present Shiʿism as a living reality as it has been and as it is, in both its doctrinal and historical aspects. Thereby we can reveal yet another dimension of the Islamic tradition and make better known the richness of the Islamic revelation in its historical unfolding, which could have been willed only by Providence.

This task, however, is made particularly difficult in a European language and for a predominantly non-Muslim audience by the fact that to explain Shiʿism and the causes for its coming into being is to fall immediately into polemics with Sunni Islam. The issues which thus arise, in turn, if presented without the proper safeguards and without taking into account the audience involved could only be detrimental to the sympathetic understanding of Islam itself. In the traditional Islamic atmosphere where faith in the revelation is naturally very strong, the Sunni-Shiʿite polemics which have gone on for over thirteen centuries, and which have become especially accentuated since the Ottoman-Safavid rivalries dating from the tenth/sixteenth century, have never resulted in the rejection of Islam by anyone from either camp. In the same way the bitter medieval theological feuds among different Christian churches and schools never caused anyone to abandon Christianity itself, for the age was one characterized by faith. But were Christianity to be presented to Muslims beginning with a full description of all the points that separated, let us say, the Catholic and Orthodox churches in the Middle Ages, or even the branches of the early church, and all that the theologians of one group wrote against the other, the effect upon the Muslims' understanding of the Christian religion itself could only be negative. In fact a Muslim might begin to wonder how anyone could have remained Christian or how the Church could have survived despite all these divisions and controversies. Although the divisions within Islam are far fewer than those in Christianity, one would expect the same type of effect upon the Western reader faced with the Shiʿite-Sunni polemics. These controversies would naturally be viewed by such a reader from the outside and without the faith in Islam itself which has encompassed this whole debate since its inception and has provided its traditional context as well as the protection and support for the followers of both sides.

Despite this difficulty, however, Shiʿism must of necessity be studied and presented from its own point of view as well as from within the general matrix of Islam. This task is made necessary first of all because Shiʿism exists as an important historical reality within Islam and hence it must be studied as an objective religious fact. Secondly, the very attacks made against Islam and its unity by certain Western authors (who point to the Sunni-Shiʿite division and often fail to remember the similar divisions within every other world religion) necessitate a detailed and at the same time authentic study of Shiʿism within the total context of Islam. Had not such a demand existed it would not even have been necessary to present to the world outside Islam all the polemical arguments that have separated Sunnism and Shiʿism. This is especially true at a time when many among the Sunni and Shiʿite *ʿulamā'* are seeking in every way possible to avoid confrontation with each other in order to safeguard the unity of Islam in a secularized world which threatens Islam from both the outside and the inside.

The attitude of this group of ulama is of course in a sense reminiscent of the ecumenism among religions, and also within a given religion, that is so often discussed today in the West. Most often, however, people search in these ecumenical movements for a common denominator which, in certain instances, sacrifices divinely ordained qualitative differences for the sake of a purely human and often quantitative egalitarianism. In such cases the so-called "ecumenical" forces in question are no more than a concealed form of the secularism and humanism which gripped the West at the time of the Renaissance and which in their own turn caused religious divisions within Christianity. This type of ecumenism, whose hidden motive is much more worldly than religious, goes hand in hand with the kind of charity that is willing to forego the love of God for the love of the neighbor and in fact insists upon the love of the neighbor in spite of a total lack of the love for God and the Transcendent. The mentality which advocates this kind of "charity" affords one more example of the loss of the transcendent dimension and the reduction of all things to the purely worldly. It is yet another manifestation of the secular character of modernism which in this case has penetrated into the supreme Christian virtue of charity and, to the extent that it has been successful, has deprived this virtue of any spiritual significance.

From the point of view of this type of ecumenical mentality, to speak approvingly of the differences between religions, or of the different orthodox schools within a single religion, is tantamount to betraying man and his hope for salvation and peace. A secular and humanistic ecumenism of this kind fails to see that real peace or salvation lies in Unity *through* this divinely ordained diversity and not in its rejection, and that the diversity of religions and also of the orthodox schools within each religion are signs of the Divine compassion, which seeks to convey the message of heaven to men possessing different spiritual and psychological qualities. True ecumenism would be a search in depth after Unity, essential and Transcendent Unity, and not the quest after a uniformity which would destroy all qualitative distinctions. It would accept and honor not only the sublime doctrines but even the minute details of every tradition, and yet see the Unity which shines through these very outward differences. And within each religion true ecumenism would respect the other orthodox schools and yet remain faithful to every facet of the traditional background of the school in question. It would be less harmful to oppose other religions, as has been done by so many religious authorities throughout history, than to be willing to destroy essential aspects of one's own religion in order to reach a common denominator with another group of men who are asked to undergo the same losses. To say the least, a league of religions could not guarantee religious peace, any more than the League of Nations guaranteed political peace.

Different religions have been necessary in the long history of mankind because there have been different "humanities" or human collectivities on earth. There having been different recipients of the Divine message, there has been more than one echo of the Divine Word. God has said "I" to each of these "humanities" or communities; hence the plurality of religions.[1] Within each religion as well, especially within those that have been destined for many ethnic groups, different orthodox interpretations of the tradition, of the one heavenly message, have been necessary in order to guarantee the integration of the different psychological and ethnic groupings into a single spiritual perspective. It is difficult to imagine how the Far Eastern peoples could have become Buddhist without the Mahayana school, or some of the Eastern peoples Muslim without Shiʿism. The presence of such divisions within the religious tradition in question does not contradict its inner unity and transcendence. Rather it has been the way of ensuring spiritual unity in a world of diverse cultural and ethnic backgrounds.

Of course, since the exoteric religious perspective relies on outward forms, it always tends in every religion to make its own interpretation the only interpretation. That is why a particular school in any religion chooses a single aspect of the religion and attaches itself so intensely to that one aspect that it forgets and even negates all other aspects. Only on the esoteric level of religious experience can there be understanding of the inherent limitation of being bound to only one aspect of the total Truth; only on the esoteric level can each religious assertion be properly placed so as not to destroy the Transcendent Unity which is beyond and yet dwells within the outward forms and determinations of a particular religion or religious school.

Shiʿism in Islam should be studied in this light: as an affirmation of a particular dimension of Islam which is made central and in fact taken by Shiʿites to be Islam as such. It was not a movement that in any way destroyed the Unity of Islam, but one that added to the richness of the historical deployment and spread of the Quranic message. And despite its exclusiveness, it contains within its forms the Unity which binds all aspects of Islam together. Like Sunnism, Sufism and everything else that is genuinely Islamic, Shiʿism was already contained as a seed in the Holy Quran and in the earliest manifestations of the revelation, and belongs to the totality of Islamic orthodoxy.[2]

Moreover, in seeking to draw closer together in the spirit of a true ecumenism in the above sense, as is advocated today by both the Sunni and Shiʿite religious authorities, Shiʿism and Sunnism must not cease to be what they are and what they have always been. Shiʿism, therefore, must be presented in all its fullness, even in those aspects which contradict Sunni interpretations of certain events in Islamic history, which in any case are open to various interpretations. Sunnism and Shiʿism must first of all remain faithful to themselves and to their own traditional foundations before they can engage in a discourse for the sake of Islam or, more generally speaking, religious values as such. But if they are to sacrifice their integrity for a common denominator which would of necessity fall below the fullness of each, they will only have succeeded in destroying the traditional foundation which has preserved both schools and guaranteed their vitality over the centuries. Only Sufism or gnosis (*ʿirfān*) can reach that Unity which embraces these two facets of Islam and yet transcends their outward differences. Only Islamic esotericism can see the legitimacy and meaning of each and the real significance of the interpretation each has made of Islam and of Islamic history.

Without, therefore, wanting to reduce Shiʿism to a least common denominator with Sunnism or to be apologetic, this book presents Shiʿism as a religious reality and an important aspect of the Islamic tradition. Such a presentation will make possible a more intimate knowledge of Islam in its multidimensional reality but at the same time it will pose certain difficulties of a polemical nature which can be resolved only on the level which transcends polemics altogether. As already mentioned, the presentation of Shiʿism in its totality and therefore including its polemical aspects, while nothing new for the Sunni world, especially since the intensification of Sunni-Shiʿite polemics during the Ottoman and Safavid periods, would certainly have an adverse effect upon the non-Muslim reader if the principles mentioned above were to be forgotten.

In order to understand Islam fully it must always be remembered that it, like other religions, contained in itself from the beginning the possibility of different types of interpretation: (1) that Shiʿism and Sunnism, while opposed to each other on certain important aspects of sacred history, are united in the acceptance of the Quran as the Word of God and in the basic principles of the faith; (2) that Shiʿism bases itself on a particular dimension of Islam and on an aspect of the nature of the Prophet as continued later in the line of the *Imāms* and the Prophet's Household to the exclusion of, and finally in opposition to, another aspect which is contained in Sunnism; (3) and finally, that the Shi'ite-Sunni polemics can be put aside and the position of each of these schools explained only on the level of esotericism, which transcends their differences and yet unites them inwardly.

Fundamental Elements of Shi'ism

Although in Islam no political or social movement has ever been separated from religion, which from the point of view of Islam necessarily embraces all things, Shi'ism was not brought into existence *only* by the question of the political succession to the Prophet of Islam—upon whom be blessings and peace—as so many Western works claim (although this question was of course of great importance). The problem of political succession may be said to be the element that crystallized the Shi'ites into a distinct group, and political suppression in later periods, especially the martyrdom of Imam Ḥusayn—upon whom be peace—only accentuated this tendency of the Shi'ites to see themselves as a separate community within the Islamic world. The principal cause of the coming into being of Shi'ism, however, lies in the fact that this possibility existed within the Islamic revelation itself and so had to be realized. Inasmuch as there were exoteric and esoteric interpretations from the very beginning, from which developed the schools (*madhhab*) of the *Sharī'ah* and Sufism in the Sunni world, there also had to be an interpretation of Islam which would combine these elements in a single whole. This possibility was realized in Shi'ism, for which the Imam is the person in whom these two aspects of traditional authority are united and in whom the religious life is marked by a sense of tragedy and martyrdom. There had to be the possibility, we might say, of an esotericism—at least in its aspect of love rather than of pure gnosis—which would flow into the exoteric domain and penetrate into even the theological dimension of the religion, rather than remain confined to its purely inward aspect. Such a possibility was

Shiʿism. Hence the question which arose was not so much who should be the successor of the Holy Prophet as what the function and qualifications of such a person would be.

The distinctive institution of Shiʿism is the Imamate and the question of the Imamate is inseparable from that of *walāyat*, or the esoteric function of interpreting the inner mysteries of the Holy Quran and the Shariʿah.[3] According to the Shiʿite view the successor of the Prophet of Islam must be one who not only rules over the community in justice but also is able to interpret the Divine Law and its esoteric meaning. Hence he must be free from error and sin (*maʿṣūm*) and he must be chosen from on high by divine decree (*naṣṣ*) through the Prophet. The whole ethos of Shiʿism revolves around the basic notion of walayat, which is intimately connected with the notion of sancitity (*wilāyah*) in Sufism. At the same time walayat contains certain implications on the level of the Shariʿah inasmuch as the Imam, or he who administers the function of walayat, is also the interpreter of religion for the religious community and its guide and legitimate ruler.

It can be argued quite convincingly that the very demand of ʿAlī for allegiance (*bayʿah*) from the whole Islamic community at the moment that he became caliph implies that he accepted the method of selecting the caliph by the voice of the majority which had been followed in the case of the three *khulafā' rāshidūn* or "rightly-guided caliphs" before him, and that thereby he accepted the previous caliphs insofar as they were rulers and administrators of the Islamic community. What is also certain from the Shiʿite point of view, however, is that he did not accept their function as Imams in the Shiʿite sense of possessing the power and function of giving the esoteric interpretations of the inner mysteries of the Holy Quran and the Shariʿah, as is seen by his insistence from the beginning that he was the heir and inheritor (*waṣī*) of the Prophet and the Prophet's legitimate successor in the Shiʿite sense of "succession." The Sunni-Shiʿite dispute over the successors to the Holy Prophet could be resolved if it were recognized that in one case there is the question of administering a Divine Law and in the other of also revealing and interpreting its inner mysteries. The very life of Ali and his actions show that he accepted the previous caliphs as understood in the Sunni sense of *khalīfah* (the ruler and the administrator of the Shariʿah), but confined the function of walayat, after the Prophet, to himself. That is why it is perfectly possible to respect him as a caliph in the Sunni sense and as an Imam in the Shiʿite sense, each in its own perspective.

The five principles of religion (*uṣūl al-dīn*) as stated by Shiʿism include: *tawḥīd* or belief in Divine Unity; *nubuwwah* or prophecy; *maʿād* or ressurrection; *imāmah* or the Imamate, belief in the Imams as successors of the Prophet; and *ʿadl* or Divine Justice. In the three basic principles—Unity, prophecy, and resurrection—Sunnism and Shiʿism agree. It is only in the other two that they differ. In the question of the Imamate, it is the insistence on the esoteric function of the Imam that distinguishes the Shiʿite perspective from the Sunni; in the question of justice it is the emphasis placed upon this attribute as an intrinsic quality of the Divine Nature that is particular to Shiʿism. We might say that in the exoteric formulation of Sunni theology, especially as contained in Ashʿarism, there is an emphasis upon the will of God. Whatever God wills is just, precisely because it is willed by God; and intelligence (*ʿaql*) is in a sense subordinated to this will and to the "voluntarism" which characterizes this form of theology.[4] In Shiʿism, however, the quality of justice is considered as innate to the Divine Nature. God cannot act in an unjust manner because it is His Nature to be just. For Him to be unjust would violate His own Nature, which is impossible. Intelligence can judge the justness or unjustness of an act and this judgment is not completely suspended in favor of a pure voluntarism on the part of God. Hence, there is a greater emphasis upon intelligence (ʿaql) in Shiʿite theology and a greater emphasis upon will (*irādah*) in Sunni *kalām*, or theology, at least in the predominant Ashʿarite school. The secret of the greater affinity of Shiʿite theology for the "intellectual sciences" (*al-ʿulūm al-ʿaqlīyah*) lies in part in this manner of viewing Divine Justice.[5]

Shiʿism also differs from Sunnism in its consideration of the means whereby the original message of the Quranic revelation reached the Islamic community, and thereby in certain aspects of the sacred history of Islam. There is no disagreement on the Quran and the Prophet, that is, on what constitutes the origin of the Islamic religion. The difference in view begins with the period immediately following the death of the Prophet. One might say that the personality of the Prophet contained two dimensions which were later to become crystallized into Sunnism and Shiʿism. Each of these two schools was later to reflect back upon the life and personality of the Prophet solely from its own point of view, thus leaving aside and forgetting or misconstruing the other dimension excluded from its own perspective. For Shiʿism the "dry" (in the alchemical sense) and "austere" aspect of the Prophet's personality as reflected in his successors in the Sunni world was equated with worldliness, while his "warm" and "compassionate" dimension was emphasized as his whole personality and as the essence of the nature of the Imams, who were considered to be a continuation of him.[6]

For the vast majority of the Islamic community, which supported the original caliphate, the companions (*ṣaḥābah*) of the Prophet represent the Prophet's heritage and the channel through which his message was transmitted to later generations. Within the early community the companions occupied a favored position and among them the first four caliphs stood out as a distinct group. It is through the companions that the sayings (*ḥadīth*) and manner of living (*sunnah*) of the Prophet were transmitted to the second generation of Muslims. Shiʿism, however, concentrating on the question of walayat and insisting on the esoteric content of the prophetic message, saw in Ali and the Household of the Prophet (*ahl-i bayt*), in its Shiʿite sense, the sole channel through which the original message of Islam was transmitted, although, paradoxically enough the majority of the descendants of the Prophet belonged to Sunnism and continue to do so until today. Hence, although most of the hadith literature in Shiʿism and Sunnism is alike, the chain of transmission in many instances is not the same. Also, inasmuch as the Imams constitute for Shiʿism a continuation of the spiritual authority of the Prophet—although not of course his law-bringing function—their sayings and actions represent a supplement to the prophetic hadith and sunnah. From a purely religious and spiritual point of view the Imams may be said to be for Shiʿism an extension of the personality of the Prophet during the succeeding centuries. Such collections of the sayings of the Imams as the *Nahj al-balāghah* of Ali and the *Uṣūl al-kāfī*, containing sayings of all the Imams, are for the Shiʿites a continuation of the hadith collections concerned with the sayings of the Prophet himself. In many Shiʿite collections of hadith, the sayings of the Prophet and of the Imams are combined. The grace (*barakah*[7]) of the Quran, as conveyed to the world by the Prophet, reached the Sunni community through the companions (foremost among them were Abū Bakr, ʿUmar, ʿUthmān, Ali, and a few others such as Anas and Salmān), and during succeeding generations through the ulama and the Sufis, each in his own world. This barakah, however, reached the Shiʿite community especially through Ali and the Household of the Prophet—in its particular Shiʿite sense as referred to above and not simply in the sense of any Alid.

It is the intense love for Ali and his progeny through Fāṭimah that compensates for the lack of attention towards, and even neglect of, the other companions in Shiʿism. It might be said that the light of Ali and the Imams was so intense that it blinded the Shiʿites to the presence of the other companions, many of whom were saintly men and also had remarkable human qualities. Were it not for that intense love of Ali, the Shiʿite attitude towards the companions would hardly be conceivable and would appear unbalanced, as it surely must when seen from the outside and without consideration for the intensity of devotion to the Household of the Prophet. Certainly the rapid spread of Islam, which is one of the most evident extrinsic arguments for the divine origin of the religion, would have been inconceivable without the companions and foremost among them the caliphs. This fact itself demonstrates how the Shiʿite views concerning the companions and the whole of early Sunnism were held within the context of a religious family (that of the whole of Islam) whose existence was taken for granted. If Islam had not spread through the Sunni caliphs and leaders many of the Shiʿite arguments would have had no meaning. Sunnism and its very success in the world must therefore be assumed as a necessary background for an understanding of Shiʿism, whose minority role, sense of martyrdom and esoteric qualities could only have been realized in the presence of the order which had previously been established by the Sunni majority and especially by the early companions and their entourage. This fact itself points to the inner bond relating Sunnism and Shiʿism to their common Quranic basis despite the outward polemics.

The barakah present in both Sunnism and Shiʿism has the same origin and quality, especially if we take into consideration Sufism, which exists in both segments of the Islamic community. The barakah is everywhere that which has issued from the Quran and the Prophet, and it is often referred to as the "Muhammadan barakah" (*al-barakat al-muḥammadīyah*).

Shiʿism and the general esoteric teachings of Islam which are usually identified with the essential teachings of Sufism have a very complex and intricate relationship.[8] Shiʿism must not be equated simply with Islamic esotericism as such. In the Sunni world Islamic esotericism manifests itself almost exclusively as Sufism, whereas in the Shiʿite world, in addition to a Sufism similar to that found in the Sunni world, there is an esoteric element based upon love (*maḥabbah*) which colors the whole structure of the religion. It is based on love (or in the language of Hinduism, *bhakta*) rather than on pure gnosis or *maʿrifah*, which by definition is always limited to a small number. There are, of course, some who would equate original Shiʿism purely and simply with esotericism.[9] Within the Shiʿite tradition itself the proponents of "Shiʿite gnosis" (*ʿirfān-i shīʿī*) such as Sayyid Ḥaydar Āmulī speak of the equivalence of Shiʿism and Sufism. In fact in his major work, the *Jāmiʿ al-asrār* (*Compendium of Divine Mysteries*), Āmulī's main intention is to show that real Sufism and Shiʿism are the same.[10] But if we consider the whole of Shiʿism, then there is of course in addition to the esoteric element the exoteric side, the law which governs a human community. Ali ruled over a human society and the sixth Imam, Jaʿfar al-Ṣādiq, founded the Twelve-Imam Shiʿite school of law. Yet, as mentioned above, esotericism, especially in the form of love, has always occupied what might be called a privileged position within Shiʿism, so that even the Shiʿite theology and creed contain formulations that are properly speaking more mystical than strictly theological.

In addition to its law and the esoteric aspect contained in Sufism and gnosis, Shiʿism contained from the beginning a type of Divine Wisdom, inherited from the Prophet and the Imams, which became the basis for the *ḥikmah* or *sophia* that later developed extensively in the Muslim world and incorporated into its structure suitable elements of the Graeco-Alexandrian, the Indian, and the Persian intellectual heritages. It is often said that Islamic philosophy came into being as a result of the translation of Greek texts and that after a few centuries Greek philosophy died out in the Muslim world and found a new home in the Latin West. This partially true account leaves out other basic aspects of the story, such as the central role of the Quran as the source of knowledge and truth for the Muslims; the fundamental role of the spiritual hermeneutics (*ta'wīl*) practiced by Sufis and Shiʿites alike, through which all knowledge became related to the inner levels of meaning of the Sacred Book; and the more than one thousand years of traditional Islamic philosophy and theosophy which has continued to our day in Shiʿite Persia and in adjacent areas.[11] When we think of Shiʿism we must remember that, in addition to the law and the strictly esoteric teachings, Shiʿism possesses a "theosophy" or hikmah which made possible the vast development of later Islamic philosophy and the intellectual sciences from the beginning, enabling it to have a role in the intellectual life of Islam far outweighing its numerical size.

The respect accorded to the intellect as the ladder to Divine Unity, an element that is characteristic of all of Islam and especially emphasized by Shiʿism, helped create a traditional educational system in which rigorous training in logic went hand in hand with the religious and also the esoteric sciences. The traditional curriculum of the Shiʿite universities (*madrasahs*) includes to this day courses ranging from logic and mathematics to metaphysics and Sufism. The hierarchy of knowledge has made of logic itself a ladder to reach the suprarational. Logical demonstration, especially *burhān*—or demonstration in its technical sense, which has played a role in Islamic logic that differs from its use in Western logic—came to be regarded as a reflection of the Divine Intellect itself, and with the help of its certainties the Shiʿite metaphysicians and theologians have sought to demonstrate with rigor the most metaphysical teachings of the religion. We see many examples of this method in the present book, which is itself the result of such a traditional madrasah education. It may present certain difficulties to the Western reader who is accustomed to the total divorce of mysticism and logic and for whom the certainty of logic has been used, or rather misused, for so long as a tool to destroy all other certainties, both religious and metaphysical. But the method itself has its root in a fundamental aspect of Islam—in which the arguments of religion are based not primarily on the miraculous but on the intellectually evident[12]—an aspect which has been strongly emphasized in Shiʿism and is reflected in both the content and the form of its traditional expositions.

Present State of Shiʿite Studies

Historical factors, such as the fact that the West never had the same direct political contact with Shiʿite Islam that it did with Sunni Islam, have caused the Occident to be less aware until now of Shiʿite Islam than of Sunnism. And Sunni Islam also has not always been understood properly or interpreted sympathetically by all Western scholars. The West came into direct contact with Islam in Spain, Sicily, and Palestine in the Middle Ages and in the Balkans during the Ottoman period. These encounters were all with Sunni Islam with the exception of limited contacts with Ismaʿilism during the Crusades. In the colonial period India was the only large area in which a direct knowledge of Shiʿism was necessary for day-to-day dealings with Muslims. For this reason the few works in English dealing with Twelve-Imam Shiʿism are mostly connected with the Indian subcontinent.[13] As a result of this lack of familiarity many of the early Western orientalists brought the most fantastic charges against Shi'ism, such as that its views were forged by Jews disguised as Muslims. One of the reasons for this kind of attack, which can also be seen in the case of Sufism, is that this type of orientalist did not want to see in Islam any metaphysical or eschatological doctrines of an intellectual content, which would make of it something more than the famous "simple religion of the desert." Such writers therefore had to reject as spurious any metaphysical and spiritual doctrines found within the teachings of Shi'ism or Sufism. One or two works written during this period and dealing with Shi'ism were composed by missionaries who were particularly famous for their hatred of Islam.[14]

It is only during the last generation that a very limited number of Western scholars have sought to make a more serious study of Shi'ism. Chief among them are L. Massignon, who devoted a few major studies to early Arab Shi'ism, and H. Corbin, who has devoted a lifetime to the study of the whole of Shi'ism and its later intellectual development especially as centered in Persia, and who has made known to the Western world for the first time some of the metaphysical and theosophical richness of this as yet relatively unknown aspect of Islam.[15] Yet, despite the efforts of these and a few other scholars, much of Shi'ism remains to this day a closed book, and there has not appeared as yet an introductory work in English to present the whole of Shi'ism to one who is just beginning to delve into the subject.

The Present Book

It was to overcome this deficiency that in 1962 Professor Kenneth Morgan of Colgate University, who pursues the laudable goal of presenting Oriental religions to the West from the point of view of the authentic representatives of these religions, approached me with the suggestion that I supervise a series of three volumes dealing with Shi'ism and written from the Shi'ite point of view. Aware of the difficulty of such an undertaking, I accepted because of the realization of the importance which the completion of such a project might have upon the future of Islamic studies and even of comparative religion as a whole. The present work is the first in that series; the others will be a volume dealing with the Shi'ite view of the Quran, written also by 'Allāmah[16] Ṭabāṭabā'ī, and an anthology of the sayings of the Shi'ite Imams.

During the summer of 1963 when Professor Morgan was in Tehran we visited 'Allāmah Sayyid Muḥammad Ḥusayn Ṭabāṭabā'ī in Darakah, a small village by the mountains near Tehran, where the venerable Shi'ite authority was spending the summer months away from the heat of Qum where he usually resides. The meeting was dominated by the humble presence of a man who has devoted his whole life to the study of religion, in whom humility and the power of intellectual analysis are combined. As we walked back from the house through the winding and narrow roads of the village, which still belongs to a calm and peaceful traditional world not as yet perturbed by the sound and fury of modernism, Professor Morgan proposed that 'Allāmah Ṭabāṭabā'ī write the general volume on Shi'ism in the series and also the volume on the Quran. Later I was able to gain the consent of this celebrated Shi'ite authority that he put aside his monumental Quranic commentary, *al-Mīzān*, to devote some of his time to these volumes. Having studied for years with him in the fields of traditional philosophy and theosophy, I knew that of the traditional Shi'ite authorities he was the one most qualified to write such a work, a work which would be completely authentic from the Shi'ite point of view and at the same time based upon an intellectual foundation. I realized of course the innate difficulty of finding a person who would be a reputable religious authority, respected by the Shi'ite community and untainted by the influence of Western modes of thought, and at the same time well enough conversant with the Western world and the mentality of the Western reader to be able to address his arguments to them. Unfortunately, no ideal solution could be found to this problem, for in Persia, as elsewhere in the Muslim world, there are today usually two types of men concerned with religious questions: (1) the traditional authorities, who are as a rule completely unaware of the nature of the psychological and mental structure of modern man, or at best have a shallow knowledge of the modern world, and (2) the modernized so-called "intellectuals," whose attachment to Islam is often only sentimental and apologetic and who usually present a version of Islam which would not be acceptable to the traditional authorities or to the Muslim community (*ummah*). Only during the past few years has a new class of scholars, still extremely small in number, come into being which is both orthodox and traditional in the profound sense of these terms and at the same time knows well the modern world and the language necessary to reach the intelligent Western reader.

In any case, since the aim of Professor Morgan was to have a description of Shiʿism by one of the respected traditional Shiʿite scholars, the ulama, it was necessary to turn to the first class, of which ʿAllāmah Ṭabāṭabāʾī is an eminent example. Of course one could not expect in such a case the deep understanding of the Western audience for whom the work is intended. Even his knowledge of Sunni Islam moves within the orbit of the traditional polemics between Sunnism and Shiʿism, which has been taken for granted until now by him as by so many other of the prominent ulama of both sides. There are several types of Muslim and in particular of Shiʿite ulama and among them some are not well-versed in theosophy and gnosis and limit themselves to the exoteric sciences. ʿAllāmah Ṭabāṭabāʾī represents that central and intellectually dominating class of Shiʿite ulama who have combined interest in jurisprudence and Quranic commentary with philosophy, theosophy, and Sufism and who represent a more universal interpretation of the Shiʿite point of view. Within the class of the traditional ulama, ʿAllāmah Ṭabāṭabāʾī possesses the distinction of being a master of both the Shariʿite and esoteric sciences and at the same time he is an outstanding *ḥakīm* or traditional Islamic philosopher (or more exactly, "theosopher"). Hence he was asked to perform this important task despite all the difficulties inherent in the presentation of the polemical side of Shiʿism to a world that does not believe in the Islamic revelation to start with and for whom the intense love of Ali and his Household, held by the Shiʿites, simply does not exist. Certain explanations, therefore, are demanded that would not occur to a person writing and thinking solely within the Shiʿite world view.

Six years of collaboration with 'Allāmah Ṭabāṭabā'ī and many journeys to Qum and even Mashhad, which he often visits in the summer, helped me to prepare the work gradually for translation into English—a task which requires a translation of meaning from one world to another, to a world that begins without the general background of knowledge and faith which the usual audience of 'Allāmah Ṭabāṭabā'ī possesses. In editing the text so that it would make possible a thorough and profound understanding of the structure of Islam, I have sought to take into full consideration the differences existing between traditional and modern scholarship, and also the particular demands of the audience to which this work is addressed.[17] But putting aside the demands made by these two conditions, I have tried to remain as faithful to the original as possible so as to enable the non-Muslim reader to study not only the message but also the form and intellectual style of a traditional Muslim authority.

The reader must therefore always remember that the arguments presented in this book are not addressed by 'Allāmah Ṭabāṭabā'ī to a mind that begins with doubt but to one that is grounded in certainty and is moreover immersed in the world of faith and religious dedication. The depth of the doubt and nihilism of certain types of modern man would be inconceivable to him. His arguments, therefore, may at times be difficult to grasp or unconvincing to some Western readers; they are only so, however, because he is addressing an audience whose demand for causality and whose conception of the levels of reality is not identical with that of the Western reader. Also there may be explanations in which too much is taken for granted, or repetitions which appear to insult the intelligence of the perspicacious Western reader in whom the analytical powers of the mind are usually more developed than among most Orientals.[18] In these cases, the characteristic manner of his presentation and the only world known to him, that of contemporary Islam in its traditional aspect, must be kept in mind. If the arguments of St. Anselm and St. Thomas for the proof of the existence of God do not appeal to most modern men, it is not because modern men are more intelligent than the medieval theologians, but because the medieval masters were addressing men of different mentalities with different needs for the explanation of causality. Likewise, 'Allāmah Ṭabāṭabā'ī offers arguments addressed to the audience he knows, the traditional Muslim intelligentsia. If all of his arguments do not appeal to the Western reader, this should not be taken as proof of the contention that his conclusions are invalid.

To summarize, this book may be said to be the first general introduction to Shi'ism in modern times written by an outstanding contemporary Shi'ite authority. While meant for the larger world outside of Shi'ism, its arguments and methods of presentation are those of traditional Shi'ism, which he represents and of which he is a pillar. 'Allāmah Ṭabāṭabā'ī has tried to present the traditional Shi'ite point of view as it is and as it has been believed in and practiced by generations of Shi'ites. He has sought to be faithful to Shi'ite views without regard for the possible reactions of the outside world and without brushing aside the particular features of Shi'ism that have been controversial. To transcend the polemical level, two religious schools would either have to put aside their differences in the face of a common danger, or the level of discourse would have to be shifted from the level of historical and theological facts and dogmas to purely metaphysical expositions. 'Allāmah Ṭabāṭabā'ī has not taken either path but has remained content with describing Shi'ism as it is. He has sought to do full justice to the Shi'ite perspective in the light of the official position that he holds in the Shi'ite religious world as he is a master of both the exoteric (*ẓāhir*) and the esoteric (*bāṭin*) sciences. For those who know the Islamic world well it is easy to discern the outward difficulties that such an authority faces in expounding the total view of things and especially in exposing the esoteric doctrines which alone can claim true universality. He is seen in this book as the expositor and defender of Shi'ism in both its exoteric and esoteric aspects, to the extent that his position in the Shi'ite world has allowed him to speak openly of the esoteric teachings. But all that is uttered carries with it the voice of authority, which tradition alone provides. Behind the words of 'Allāmah Ṭabāṭabā'ī stand fourteen centuries of Shi'ite Islam and the continuity and transmission of a sacred and religious knowledge made possible by the continuity of the Islamic tradition itself.

The Author

ʿAllāmah Sayyid Muḥammad Ḥusayn Ṭabāṭabāʾī[19] was born in Tabriz in A.H. (lunar) 1321 or A.H. (solar) 1282, (A.D. 1903)[20] in a family of descendants of the Holy Prophet which for fourteen generations has produced outstanding Islamic scholars.[21] He received his earliest education in his native city, mastering the elements of Arabic and the religious sciences, and at about the age of twenty set out for the great Shiʿite University of Najaf to continue more advanced studies. Most students in the madrasahs follow the branch of "transmitted sciences" (*al-ʿulūm al-naqlīyah*), especially the sciences dealing with the Divine Law, *fiqh* or jurisprudence, and *uṣūl al-fiqh* or the principles of jurisprudence. ʿAllāmah Ṭabāṭabāʾī, however, sought to master both branches of the traditional sciences: the transmitted and the intellectual. He studied Divine Law and the principles of jurisprudence with two of the great masters of that day, Mīrzā Muḥammad Ḥusayn Nāʾīnī and Shaykh Muḥammad Ḥusayn Iṣfahānī. He became such a master in this domain that had he kept completely to these fields he would have become one of the foremost *mujtahids* or authorities on Divine Law and would have been able to wield much political and social influence.

But such was not his destiny. He was more attracted to the intellectual sciences, and he studied assiduously the whole cycle of traditional mathematics with Sayyid Abu'l-Qāsim Khwānsārī, and traditional Islamic philosophy, including the standard texts of the *Shifāʾ* of Ibn Sīnā, the *Asfār* of Ṣadr al-Dīn Shīrāzī and the *Tamhīd al-qawāʿid* of Ibn Turkah, with Sayyid Ḥusayn Bādkūbaʾī, himself a student of two of the most famous masters of the school of Tehran, Sayyid Abu'l-Ḥasan Jilwah and Āqā ʿAlī Mudarris Zunūzī.[22]

In addition to formal learning, or what the traditional Muslim sources call "acquired science" (*ʿilm-i ḥuṣūlī*), ʿAllāmah Ṭabāṭabā'ī sought after that "immediate science" (*'ilm-i ḥuḍūrī*) or gnosis through which knowledge turns into vision of the supernal realities. He was fortunate in finding a great master of Islamic gnosis, Mīrzā 'Alī Qāḍī, who initiated him into the Divine mysteries and guided him in his journey toward spiritual perfection. 'Allāmah Ṭabāṭabā'ī once told me that before meeting Qāḍī he had studied the *Fuṣūṣ al-ḥikam* of Ibn 'Arabī and thought that he knew it well. When he met this master of real spiritual authority he realized that he knew nothing. He also told me that when Mirza Ali Qadi began to teach the *Fuṣūṣ* it was as if all the walls of the room were speaking of the reality of gnosis and participating in his exposition. Thanks to this master the years in Najaf became for 'Allāmah Ṭabāṭabā'ī not only a period of intellectual attainment but also one of asceticism and spiritual practices, which enabled him to attain that state of spiritual realization often referred to as becoming divorced from the darkness of material limitations (*tajrīd*). He spent long periods in fasting and prayer and underwent a long interval during which he kept absolute silence. Today his presence carries with it the silence of perfect contemplation and concentration even when he is speaking.

'Allāmah Ṭabāṭabā'ī returned to Tabriz in A.H. (solar) 1314 (A.D. 1934) and spent a few quiet years in that city teaching a small number of disciples, but he was as yet unknown to the religious circles of Persia at large. It was the devastating events of the Second World War and the Russian occupation of Persia that brought 'Allāmah Ṭabāṭabā'ī from Tabriz to Qum in A.H. (solar) 1324 (A.D. 1945) Qum was then, and continues to be, the center of religious studies in Persia. In his quiet and unassuming manner 'Allāmah Ṭabāṭabā'ī began to teach in this holy city, concentrating on Quranic commentary and traditional Islamic philosophy and theosophy, which had not been taught in Qum for many years. His magnetic personality and spiritual presence soon attracted some of the most intelligent and competent of the students to him, and gradually he made the teachings of Mullā Ṣadrā once again a cornerstone of the traditional curriculum. I still have a vivid memory of some of the sessions of his public lectures in one of the mosque-madrasahs of Qum where nearly four hundred students sat at his feet to absorb his wisdom.

The activities of 'Allāmah Ṭabāṭabā'ī since he came to Qum have also included frequent visits to Tehran. After the Second World War, when Marxism was fashionable among some of the youth in Tehran, he was the only religious scholar who took the pains to study the philosophical basis of Communism and supply a response to dialectical materialism from the traditional point of view. The fruit of this effort was one of his major works, *Uṣūl-i falsafah wa rawish-i ri'ālīsm* (*The Principles of Philosophy and the Method of Realism*), in which he defended realism—in its traditional and medieval sense—against all dialectical philosophies. He also trained a number of disciples who belong to the community of Persians with a modern education.

Since his coming to Qum, 'Allāmah Ṭabāṭabā'ī has been indefatigable in his efforts to convey the wisdom and intellectual message of Islam on three different levels: to a large number of traditional students in Qum, who are now scattered throughout Persia and other Shi'ite lands; to a more select group of students whom he has taught gnosis and Sufism in more intimate circles and who have usually met on Thursday evenings at his home or other private places; and also to a group of Persians with a modern education and occasionally non-Persians with whom he has met in Tehran. During the past ten or twelve years there have been regular sessions in Tehran attended by a select group of Persians, and in the fall season by Henry Corbin, sessions in which the most profound and pressing spiritual and intellectual problems have been discussed, and in which I have usually had the role of translator and interpreter. During these years we have studied with 'Allāmah Ṭabāṭabā'ī not only the classical texts of divine wisdom and gnosis but also a whole cycle of what might be called comparative gnosis, in which in each session the sacred texts of one of the major religions, containing mystical and gnostic teachings, such as the *Tao Te-Ching*, the *Upanishads* and the *Gospel of John*, were discussed and compared with Sufism and Islamic gnostic doctrines in general.

'Allāmah Ṭabāṭabā'ī has therefore exercised a profound influence in both the traditional and modern circles in Persia. He has tried to create a new intellectual elite among the modern educated classes who wish to be acquainted with Islamic intellectuality as well as with the modern world. Many among his traditional students who belong to the class of ulama have tried to follow his example in this important endeavor. Some of his students, such as Sayyid Jalāl al-Dīn Āshtiyānī of Mashhad University and Murtaḍā Muṭahharī of Tehran University, are themselves scholars of considerable reputation. 'Allāmah Ṭabāṭabā'ī often speaks of others among his students who possess great spiritual qualities but do not manifest themselves outwardly.

In addition to a heavy program of teaching and guidance, 'Allāmah Ṭabāṭabā'ī has occupied himself with writing many books and articles which attest to his remarkable intellectual powers and breadth of learning within the world of the traditional Islamic sciences.[23]

Today at his home in Qum the venerable authority devotes nearly all of his time to his Quranic commentary and the direction of some of his best students. He stands as a symbol of what is most permanent in the long tradition of Islamic scholarship and science, and his presence carries a fragrance which can only come from one who has tasted the fruit of Divine Knowledge. He exemplifies in his person the nobility, humility and quest after truth which have characterized the finest Muslim scholars over the ages. His knowledge and its exposition are a testimony to what real Islamic learning is, how profound and how metaphysical, and how different from so many of the shallow expositions of some of the orientalists or the distorted caricatures of so many Muslim modernists. Of course he does not have the awareness of the modern mentality and the nature of the modern world that might be desired, but that could hardly be expected in one whose life experience has been confined to the traditional circles in Persia and Iraq.

* * *

A word must be added about the system of transliteration of Arabic and Persian words and the manner in which reference is made to Islamic sources. In the question of transliteration I have followed the standard system used in most works on Islam (see the table on p. vii), but in making reference to Islamic books I have sought to remain completely faithful to the original manuscript. The author, like most other Persian writers, refers to the very well-known Arabic works in the Persian-speaking world in their Persian form and to the less well-known in the original Arabic. For example, the history of al-Ṭabarī is referred to by the author as *Tārīkh-i Ṭabarī*, using the *iḍāfah* construction in Persian, which gives the same meaning as the word "of" in English. This may appear somewhat disconcerting to one who knows Arabic but no Persian, but it conveys a feeling for the spiritual and religious climate of Persia where the two languages are used side by side. In any case such references by the author have been transliterated according to the original. I have only sought to make them uniform and to give enough indication in the bibliography to make clear which author and which work is in question.

In the bibliography also, only the works referred to by ʿAllāmah Ṭabāṭabāʾī as his sources have been included, and not any secondary or even other primary ones which I could have added myself. Also the entry in the bibliography is according to the name of the book and not the author, which has always been the method used in Islamic circles.

For technical reasons diacritical marks on Arabic words which have become common in English, and italics in the case of all Arabic words appearing in the text, have been employed only in the index and at the first appearance of the word.

In the end I should like to thank Professor Kenneth Morgan, whose keen interest and commendable patience in this project has made its achievement possible, and Mr. William Chittick, who has helped me greatly in preparing the manuscript for publication.

Seyyed Hossein Nasr

Tehran
Rabi al-awwal, 1390
Urdibihisht, 1350
May, 1971

NOTES

PREFACE

1. See F. Schuon, *Light on the Ancient Worlds*, translated by Lord Northbourne, London, 1965, especially Ch. IX, "Religio Perennis."
2. See S. H. Nasr, *Ideals and Realities of Islam*, London, 1966, Ch. IV, "Sunnism and Shi'ism."
3. On walayat see S. H. Nasr, *Ideals*, pp. 161–162, and the many writings of H. Corbin on Shi'ism, which nearly always turn to this major theme.
4. For a profound analysis and criticism of Ash'arite theology see F. Schuon, "Dilemmas of Theological Speculation," *Studies in Comparative Religion*, Spring, 1969, pp. 66–93.
5. See S. H. Nasr, *An Introduction to Islamic Cosmological Doctrines*, Cambridge (U.S.A.), 1964, Introduction; also S. H. Nasr, *Science and Civilization in Islam*, Cambridge (U.S.A.), 1968, Chapter II.
6. This idea was first formulated in an as yet unpublished article of F. Schuon entitled "Images d'Islam," some elements of which can be found in the same author's *Das Ewige im Vorgänglichkeit*, translated by T. Burckhardt, Weilheim/Oberbayern, 1970, in the Chapter entitled "Blick auf den Islam," pp. 111–129.
7. This term is nearly impossible to translate into English, the closest to an equivalent being the word "grace," if we do not oppose grace to the natural order as is done in most Christian theological texts. See S. H. Nasr, *Three Muslim Sages*, Cambridge (U.S.A.), 1964, pp. 105–106.
8. See our study "Shi'ism and Sufism: Their Relationship in Essence and in History," *Religious Studies*, October 1970, pp. 229–242; also in our *Sufi Essays*, Albany, 1972.
9. This position is especially defended by H. Corbin, who has devoted so many penetrating studies to Shi'ism.
10. See H. Corbin's introduction to Sayyīd Ḥaydar Āmulī, *La Philosophie Shi'ite*, Tehran-Paris, 1969.
11. The only history of philosophy in Western languages which takes these elements into account is H. Corbin (with the collaboration of S. H. Nasr and O. Yahaya), *Histoire de la philosophie islamique*, vol. I, Paris, 1964.
12. This question has been treated with great lucidity in F. Schuon, *Understanding Islam*, translated by D. M. Matheson, London, 1963.
13. See for example J. N. Hollister, *The Shi'a of India*, London, 1953; A. A. A. Fyzee, *Outlines of Muhammadan Law*, London, 1887; and N. B. Baillie, *A Digest of Moohummudan Law*, London, 1887. Of course in Iraq also the British were faced with a mixed Sunni-Shi'ite population but perhaps because of the relatively small

size of the country this contact never gave rise to serious scholarly concern with Shi'ite sources as it did in India.

14. We especially have in mind D. M. Donaldson's *The Shi'ite Religion*, London, 1933, which is still the standard work on Shi'ism in Western universities. Many of the works written on the Shi'ites in India are also by missionaries who were severely opposed to Islam.

15. Some of the works of Corbin dealing more directly with Twelve-Imam Shi'ism itself include: "Pour une morphologie de la spiritualité shi'ite," *Eranos-Jahrbuch*, XXIX, 1960; "Le combat spirituel du shi'isme," *Eranos-Jahrbuch*, XXX, 1961; and "Au 'pays' de l'Imam caché, "*Eranos-Jahrbuch*, XXXII, 1963. Many of Corbin's writings on Shi'ism have been brought together in his forthcoming *En Islam iranien*.

16. 'Allāmah is an honorific term in Arabic, Persian and other Islamic languages meaning "very learned."

17. For my own views on the relationships between Sunnism and Shi'ism see *Ideals and Realities of Islam*, Ch. VI.

18. On this important question of the difference between the Oriental and Western dialectic see F. Schuon, "La dialectique orientale et son enracinement dans la foi," *Logique et Transcendence*, Paris, 1970, pp. 129–169.

19. An account in Persian of 'Allāmah Ṭabāṭabā'ī by one of his outstanding students, Sayyid Jalāl al-Dīn Āshtiyānī, can be found in *Ma'ārif-i islāmī*, vol. V, 1347 (A. H. solar), pp. 48–50.

20. Since the beginning of the reign of Reza Shah the Persians have been using even more than before the solar hegira calendar in addition to the lunar, the former for civil and daily purposes and the latter for religious functions. In the present work all Islamic dates are lunar unless otherwise specified.

21. The title "Sayyid" in 'Allāmah Ṭabāṭabā'ī's name is itself an indication of his being a descendant of the Prophet. In Persia the term *sayyid* (or *seyyed*) is used exclusively in this sense while in the Arab world it is usually used as the equivalent of "gentleman" or "Mr."

22. On these figures see S. H. Nasr, "The School of Ispahan," "Sadr al-Dīn Shīrāzī" and "Sabziwārī" in M. M. Sharif (ed), *A History of Muslim Philosophy*, vol. II, Wiesbaden, 1966.

23. See the bibliography for a complete list of the writings of 'Allāmah Ṭabāṭabā'ī.

IN THE NAME OF ALLAH MOST MERCIFUL AND COMPASSIONATE

INTRODUCTION

This book, which we have called *Shi'ite Islam*,[1] seeks to clarify the true identity of Shi'ism which is one of the two major branches of Islam—the other being Sunnism. It deals in particular with the way Shi'ism originated and later developed, with the type of religious thought present in Shi'ism, and with Islamic sciences and culture as seen from the Shi'ite point of view.

The Meaning of Religion (dīn),[2] Islam, and Shi'ism

Religion. There is no doubt that each member of the human race is naturally drawn to his fellow-men and that in his life in society he acts in ways which are interrelated and interconnected. His eating, drinking, sleeping, keeping awake, talking, listening, sitting, walking, his social intercourse and meetings, at the same time that they are formally and externally distinct, are invariably connected with each other. One cannot perform just any act in any place or after any other act. There is an order which must be observed.

There is, therefore, an order which governs the actions man performs in the journey of this life, an order against which his actions cannot rebel. In reality, these acts all originate from a distinct source. That source is man's desire to possess a felicitous life, a life in which he can reach to the greatest extent possible the objects of his desire, and be gratified. Or, one could say that man wishes to provide in a more complete way for his needs in order to continue his existence.

This is why man continually conforms his actions to rules and laws either devised by himself or accepted from others, and why he selects a particular way of life for himself among all the other existing possibilities. He works in order to provide for his means of livelihood and expects his activities to be guided by laws and regulations that must be followed. In order to satisfy his sense of taste and overcome hunger and thirst, he eats and drinks, for he considers eating and drinking necessary for the continuation of his own happy existence. This rule could be multiplied by many other instances.

The rules and laws that govern human existence depend for their acceptance on the basic beliefs that man has concerning the nature of universal existence, of which he himself is a part, and also upon his judgment and evaluation of that existence. That the principles governing man's actions depend on his conception of being as a whole becomes clear if one meditates a moment on the different conceptions that people hold as to the nature of the world and of man.

Those who consider the Universe to be confined only to this material, sensible world, and man himself to be completely material and therefore subject to annihilation when the breath of life leaves him at the moment of death, follow a way of life designed to provide for their material desires and transient mundane pleasures. They strive solely on this path, seeking to bring under their control the natural conditions and factors of life.

Similarly, there are those who, like the common people among idol-worshipers, consider the world of nature to be created by a god above nature who has created the world specially for man and provided it with multiple bounties so that man may benefit from his goodness. Such men organize their lives so as to attract the pleasure of the god and not invite his anger. They believe that if they please the god he will multiply his bounty and make it lasting and if they anger him he will take his bounty away from them.

On the other hand, such men as Zoroastrians, Jews, Christians, and Muslims follow the "high path" in this life for they believe in God and in man's eternal life, and consider man to be responsible for his good and evil acts. As a result they accept as proven the existence of a day of judgment (*qiyāmat*) and follow a path that leads to felicity in both this world and the next.

The totality of these fundamental beliefs concerning the nature of man and the Universe, and regulations in conformity with them which are applied to human life, is called religion (*dīn*). If there are divergences in these fundamental beliefs and regulations, they are called schools such as the Sunni and Shi'ite schools in Islam and the Nestorian in Christianity. We can therefore say that man, even if he does not believe in the Deity, can never be without religion if we recognize religion as a program for life based on firm belief. Religion can never be separated from life and is not simply a matter of ceremonial acts.

The Holy Quran asserts that man has no choice but to follow religion, which is a path that God has placed before man so that by treading it man can reach Him. However, those who have accepted the religion of the truth (Islam)[3] march in all sincerity upon the path of God, while those who have not accepted the religion of the truth have been diverted from the divine path and have followed the wrong road.[4]

Islam etymologically means surrender and obedience. The Holy Quran calls the religion which invites men toward this end "Islam" since its general purpose is the surrender of man to the laws governing the Universe and men, with the result that through this surrender he worships only the One God and obeys only His commands.[5] As the Holy Quran informs us, the first person who called this religion "Islam" and its followers "Muslims" was the Prophet Abraham, upon whom be peace.[6]

Shī'ah, which means literally partisan or follower, refers to those who consider the succession to the Prophet—may God's peace and benediction be upon him[7]—to be the special right of the family of the Prophet and who in the field of the Islamic sciences and culture follow the school of the Household of the Prophet.[8]

NOTES

INTRODUCTION

1. *Editor's note:* The original title given by ʿAllāmah Ṭabāṭabāʾī to the book is *Shīʿah dar Islām* (*Shiʿism in Islam*). What the author intends by the title is Islam as seen and interpreted by Shiʿism. Therefore we have chosen to call it *Shiʿite Islam.*

2. *Editor's note:* Although we have rendered the word din by religion, its meaning is more universal than that usually given to religion today. Din is the set of transcendent principles and their applications in every domain of life which concern man in his journey on earth and his life beyond this world. It could properly be translated as tradition as understood by the traditional authors in the West such as F. Schuon, R. Guénon, and A. K. Coomaraswamy.

3. *Editor's note:* Speaking as a Muslim religious authority the author has mentioned Islam in parentheses as "the religion of the truth" without, however, in any way negating the universality of revelation asserted in the Quran. For a Muslim quite naturally the "religion of the truth" *par excellence* is Islam without this belief detracting from the verity of other religions to some of which the author himself has referred in this and other works. See S. H. Nasr, "Islam and the Encounter of Religions," *The Islamic Quarterly*, vol. X, nos. 3 and 4, July and December 1966, pp. 47–68.

4. "The curse of Allah is on evil-doers, who debar (men) from the path of Allah and would have it crooked, . . ." (Quran, VII, 44–45) (This and all subsequent citations of the Quran are from *The Meaning of the Glorious Koran, An Explanatory Translation* by Mohammed Marmaduke Pickthall, New York, New American Library, 1953).

5. "Who is better in religion than he who surrendereth his purpose to Allah while doing good (to men) and followeth the tradition of Abraham, the upright?" (Quran, IV, 125). "Say: O People of the Scripture! Come to an agreement between us and you: that we shall worship none but Allah, and that we shall ascribe no partner unto Him, and that none of us shall take others for lords beside Allah. And if they turn away, then say: Bear witness that we are they who have surrendered (unto Him) [*muslimūn*]." (Quran, III, 64). "O ye who believe! Come all of you, into submission (unto Him) . . ." (Quran, II, 208).

6. "Our Lord! And make us submissive unto Thee and of our seed a nation submissive unto Thee . . ." (Quran, II, 128). "The faith of your father Abraham (is yours). He hath named you Muslims . . ." (Quran, XXII, 78).

7. *Editor's note:* In all Islamic languages whenever the name of one of the prophets, and in Shiʿism also the Imams, is cited the honorific phrase *ʿalayhi*

al-salām (May Peace be upon him) follows. In the case of the Prophet of Islam, the phrase *ṣall allāhu ʿalayhi wa sallam* (May God's peace and benediction be upon him) is added. In this translation, inasmuch as it is in a European language we have usually abstained from using these terms which appear in the original Persian. Also in this work whenever the term Prophet is used with a capital "P" it refers to the Prophet of Islam.

8. A group of Zaydis who accept two caliphs before Ali and in jurisprudence follow Abū Ḥanīfah are also called Shiʿite because in contrast to the Umayyads and Abbasids they consider the later caliphate as belonging solely to Ali and his descendants.

PART I: THE HISTORICAL BACKGROUND OF SHIʿISM

CHAPTER I THE ORIGIN AND GROWTH OF SHI'ISM

Shi'ism began with a reference made for the first time to the partisans of Ali (*shī'ah-i 'Alī*), the first leader of the Household of the Prophet, during the lifetime of the Prophet himself.[1] The course of the first manifestation and the later growth of Islam during the twenty-three years of prophecy brought about many conditions which necessitated the appearance of a group such as the Shi'ites among the companions of the Prophet.

The Holy Prophet during the first days of his prophecy, when according to the text of the Quran he was commanded to invite his closer relatives to come to his religion,[2] told them clearly that whoever would be the first to accept his invitation would become his successor and inheritor. Ali was the first to step forth and embrace Islam. The Prophet accepted Ali's submission to the faith and thus fulfilled his promise.[3]

From the Shi'ite point of view it appears as unlikely that the leader of a movement, during the first days of his activity, should introduce to strangers one of his associates as his successor and deputy but not introduce him to his completely loyal and devout aides and friends. Nor does it appear likely that such a leader should accept someone as his deputy and successor and introduce him to others as such, but then throughout his life and religious call deprive his deputy of his duties as deputy, disregard the respect due to his position as successor, and refuse to make any distinctions between him and others.

The Prophet, according to many unquestioned and completely

authenticated hadiths, both Sunni and Shiʿite, clearly asserted that Ali was preserved from error and sin in his actions and sayings. Whatever he said and did was in perfect conformity with the teachings of religion[4] and he was the most knowledgeable of men in matters pertaining to the Islamic sciences and injunctions.[5]

During the period of prophecy Ali performed valuable services and made remarkable sacrifices. When the infidels of Mecca decided to kill the Prophet and surrounded his house, the Holy Prophet decided to emigrate to Medina. He said to Ali, "Will you sleep in my bed at night so that they will think that I am asleep and I will be secure from being pursued by them?" Ali accepted this dangerous assignment with open arms. This has been recounted in different histories and collections of hadith. (The emigration from Mecca to Medina marks the date of origin of the Islamic calendar, known as the *hijrah.*) Ali also served by fighting in the battles of Badr, Uḥud, Khaybar, Khandaq, and Ḥunayn in which the victories achieved with his aid were such that if Ali had not been present the enemy would most likely have uprooted Islam and the Muslims, as is recounted in the usual histories, lives of the Prophet, and collections of hadith.

For Shiʿites, the central evidence of Ali's legitimacy as successor to the Prophet is the event of Ghadīr Khumm[6] when the Prophet chose Ali to the "general guardianship" (*walāyat-i ʿāmmah*) of the people and made Ali, like himself, their "guardian" (*walī*).[7]

It is obvious that because of such distinctive services and recognition, because of Ali's special virtues which were acclaimed by all,[8] and because of the great love the Prophet showed for him,[9] some of the companions of the Prophet who knew Ali well, and who were champions of virtue and truth, came to love him. They assembled around Ali and followed him to such an extent that many others began to consider their love for him excessive and a few perhaps also became jealous of him. Besides all these elements, we see in many sayings of the Prophet reference to the "shiʿah of Ali" and the "shiʿah of the Household of the Prophet."[10]

The Cause of the Separation of the Shiʿite Minority from the Sunni Majority

The friends and followers of Ali believed that after the death of the Prophet the caliphate and religious authority (*marjaʿīyat-i ʿilmī*) belonged to Ali. This belief came from their consideration of Ali's position and station in relation to the Prophet, his relation to the chosen among the companions, as well as his relation to Muslims in general. It was only the events that occurred during the few days of the Prophet's final illness that indicated that there was opposition to their view.[11] Contrary to their expectation, at the very moment when the Prophet died and his body lay still unburied, while his household and a few companions were occupied with providing for his burial and funeral service, the friends and followers of Ali received news of the activity of another group who had gone to the mosque where the community was gathered faced with this sudden loss of its leader. This group, which was later to form the majority, set forth in great haste to select a caliph for the Muslims with the aim of ensuring the welfare of the community and solving its immediate problems. They did this without consulting the Household of the Prophet, his relatives or many of his friends, who were busy with the funeral, and without providing them with the least information. Thus Ali and his companions were presented with a *fait accompli*.[12]

Ali and his friends—such as ʿAbbās, Zubayr, Salmān, Abū Dharr, Miqdād and ʿAmmār—after finishing with the burial of the body of the Prophet became aware of the proceedings by which the caliph had been selected. They protested against the act of choosing the caliph by consultation or election, and also against those who were responsible for carrying it out. They even presented their own proofs and arguments, but the answer they received was that the welfare of the Muslims was at stake and the solution lay in what had been done.[13]

It was this protest and criticism which separated from the majority the minority that were following Ali and made his followers known to society as the "partisans" or "shiʿah" of Ali.

The caliphate of the time was anxious to guard against this appellation being given to the Shiʿite minority and thus to have Muslim society divided into sections comprised of a majority and a minority. The supporters of the caliph considered the caliphate to be a matter of the consensus of the community (*ijmāʿ*) and called those who objected the "opponents of allegiance." They claimed that the Shiʿah stood, therefore, opposed to Muslim society. Sometimes the Shiʿah were given other pejorative and degrading names.[14]

Shiʿism was condemned from the first moment because of the political situation of the time and thus it could not accomplish anything through mere political protest. Ali, in order to safeguard the well-being of Islam and of the Muslims, and also because of lack of sufficient political and military power, did not endeavor to begin an uprising against the existing political order, which would have been of a bloody nature. Yet those who protested against the established caliphate refused to surrender to the majority in certain questions of faith and continued to hold that the succession to the Prophet and religious authority belonged by right to Ali.[15] They believed that all spiritual and religious matters should be referred to him and invited people to become his followers.[16]

The Two Problems of Succession and Authority in Religious Sciences

In accordance with the Islamic teachings which form its basis, Shiʿism believed that the most important question facing Islamic society was the elucidation and clarification of Islamic teachings and the tenets of the religious sciences.[17] Only after such clarifications were made could the application of these teachings to the social order be considered. In other words, Shiʿism believed that, before all else, members of society should be able to gain a true vision of the world and of men based on the real nature of things. Only then could they know and perform their duties as human beings—in which lay their real welfare—even if the performance of these religious duties were to be against their desires. After carrying out this first step a religious government should preserve and execute real Islamic order in society in such a way that man would worship none other than God, would possess personal and social freedom to the extent possible, and would benefit from true personal and social justice.

These two ends could be accomplished only by a person who was inerrant and protected by God from having faults. Otherwise people could become rulers or religious authorities who would not be free from the possibility of distortion of thought or the committing of treachery in the duties placed upon their shoulders. Were this to happen, the just and freedom-giving rule of Islam could gradually be converted to dictatorial rule and a completely autocratic government. Moreover, the pure religious teachings could become, as can be seen in the case of certain other religions, the victims of change and distortion in the hands of selfish scholars given to the satisfaction of their carnal desires. As confirmed by the Holy Prophet, Ali followed perfectly and completely the Book of God and the tradition of the Prophet in both words and deeds.[18] As Shiʿism sees it, if, as the majority say, only the Quraysh[19] opposed the rightful caliphate of Ali, then that majority should have answered the Quraysh by asserting what was right. They should have quelled all opposition to the right cause in the same way that they fought against the group who refused to pay the religious tax (*zakāt*). The majority should not have remained indifferent to what was right for fear of the opposition of the Quraysh.

What prevented the Shiʿah from accepting the elective method of choosing the caliphate by the people was the fear of the unwholesome consequences that might result from it: fear of possible corruption in Islamic government and of the destruction of the solid basis for the sublime religious sciences. As it happened, later events in Islamic history confirmed this fear (or prediction), with the result that the Shiʿites became ever firmer in their belief. During the earliest years, however, because of the small number of its followers, Shiʿism appeared outwardly to have been absorbed into the majority, although privately it continued to insist on acquiring the Islamic sciences from the Household of the Prophet and to invite people to its cause. At the same time, in order to preserve the power of Islam and safeguard its progress, Shiʿism did not display any open opposition to the rest of Islamic society. Members of the Shiʿite community even fought hand in hand with the Sunni majority in holy wars (*jihād*) and participated in public affairs. Ali himself guided the Sunni majority in the interest of the whole of Islam whenever such action was necessary.[20]

The Political Method of the Selection of the Caliph by Vote and Its Disagreement with the Shiʿite View

Shiʿism believes that the Divine Law of Islam (Shariʿah), whose substance is found in the Book of God and in the tradition (Sunnah)[21] of the Holy Prophet, will remain valid to the Day of Judgment and can never, nor will ever, be altered. A government which is really Islamic cannot under any pretext refuse completely to carry out the Shariʿah's injunctions.[22] The only duty of an Islamic government is to make decisions by consultation within the limits set by the Shariʿah and in accordance with the demands of the moment.

The vow of allegiance to Abu Bakr at Saqīfah, which was motivated at least in part by political considerations, and the incident described in the hadith of "ink and paper,"[23] which occurred during the last days of the illness of the Holy Prophet, reveal the fact that those who directed and backed the movement to choose the caliph through the process of election believed that the Book of God should be preserved in the form of a constitution. They emphasized the Holy Book and paid much less attention to the words of the Holy Prophet as an immutable source of the teachings of Islam. They seem to have accepted the modification of certain aspects of Islamic teachings concerning government to suit the conditions of the moment and for the sake of the general welfare.

This tendency to emphasize only certain principles of the Divine Law is confirmed by many sayings that were later transmitted concerning the companions of the Holy Prophet. For example, the companions were considered to be independent authorities in matters of the Divine Law (mujtahid),[24] being able to exercise independent judgment (*ijtihād*) in public affairs. It was also believed that if they succeeded in their task they would be rewarded by God and if they failed they would be forgiven by Him since they were among the companions. This view was widely held during the early years following the death of the Holy Prophet. Shiʿism takes a stricter stand and believes that the actions of the companions, as of all other Muslims, should be judged strictly according to the teachings of the Shariʿah. For example, there was the complicated incident involving the famous general Khālid ibn Walīd in the house of one of the prominent Muslims of the day, Mālik ibn Nuwajrah, which led to the death of the latter. The fact that Khalid was not at all taken to task for this incident because of his being an outstanding military leader[25] shows in the eyes of Shiʿism an undue lenience toward some of the actions of the companions which were below the norm of perfect piety and righteousness set by the actions of the spiritual elite among the companions.

Another practice of the early years which is criticized by Shiʿism is the cutting off of the *khums*[26] from the members of the Household of the Prophet and from the Holy Prophet's relatives.[27] Likewise, because of the emphasis laid by Shiʿism on the sayings and the Sunnah of the Holy Prophet it is difficult for it to understand why the writing down of the text of hadith was completely banned and why, if a written hadith were found, it would be burned.[28] We know that this ban continued through the caliphate of the *khulafā' rāshidūn*[29] into the Umayyad period[30] and did not cease until the period of Umar ibn ʿAbd al-ʿAzīz, who ruled from A.H. 99/A.D. 717 to A.H. 101/A.D. 719.[31]

During the period of the second caliph (13/634-25/644) there was a continuation of the policy of emphasizing certain aspects of the Shariʿah and of putting aside some of the practices which the Shiʿites believe the Holy Prophet taught and practiced. Some practices were forbidden, some were omitted, and some were added. For instance, the pilgrimage of *tamattu*ʿ (a kind of pilgrimage in which the ʿ*umrah* ceremony is utilized in place of the *hajj* ceremony) was banned by Umar during his caliphate, with the decree that transgressors would be stoned; this in spite of the fact that during his final pilgrimage the Holy Prophet—peace be upon him—instituted in the Quran, Surah II, 196, a special form for the pilgrimage ceremonies that might be performed by pilgrims coming from far away. Also, during the lifetime of the Prophet of God temporary marriage (*mutʿah*) was practiced, but Umar forbade it. And even though during the life of the Holy Prophet it was the practice to recite in the call to prayers, "Hurry to the best act" (*ḥayya ʿalā khayr el-ʿamal*), Umar ordered that it be omitted because he said it would prevent people from participating in holy war, jihad. (It is still recited in the Shiʿite call to prayers, but not in the Sunni call.) There were also additions to the Shariʿah: during the time of the Prophet a divorce was valid only if the three declarations of divorce ("I divorce thee") were made on three different occasions, but Umar allowed the triple divorce declaration to be made at one time. Heavy penalties were imposed on those who broke certain of these new regulations, such as stoning in the case of mutʿah marriage.

It was also during the period of the rule of the second caliph that new social and economic forces led to the uneven distribution of the public treasury (*bayt al-māl*) among the people,[32] an act which was later the cause of bewildering class differences and frightful and bloody struggles among Muslims. At this time Muʿawiyah was ruling in Damascus in the style of the Persian and Byzantine kings and was even given the title of the "Khusraw of the Arabs" (a Persian title of the highest imperial power), but no serious protest was made against him for his worldly type of rule.[33]

The second caliph was killed by a Persian slave in 25/644. In accordance with the majority vote of a six-man council which had assembled by order of the second caliph before his death, the third caliph was chosen. The third caliph did not prevent his Umayyad relatives from becoming dominant over the people during his caliphate and appointed some of them as rulers in the Hijaz, Iraq, Egypt, and other Muslim lands.[34] These relatives began to be lax in applying moral principles in government. Some of them openly committed injustice and tyranny, sin and iniquity, and broke certain of the tenets of firmly established Islamic laws.

Before long, streams of protest began to flow toward the capital. But the caliph, who was under the influence of his relatives—particularly Marwān ibn Ḥakam[35]—did not act promptly or decisively to remove the causes against which the people were protesting. Sometimes it even happened that those who protested were punished and driven away.

An incident that happened in Egypt illustrates the nature of the rule of the third caliph. A group of Muslims in Egypt rebelled against Uthman. Uthman sensed the danger and asked Ali for help, expressing his feeling of contrition. Ali told the Egyptians, "You have revolted in order to bring justice and truth to life. Uthman has repented saying, 'I shall change my ways and in three days will fulfill your wishes. I shall expel the oppressive rulers from their posts.'" Ali then wrote an agreement with them on behalf of Uthman and they started home. On the way they saw the slave of Uthman riding on his camel in the direction of Egypt. They became suspicious of him and searched him. On him they found a letter for the governor of Egypt containing the following words: "In the name of God. When ʿAbd al-Raḥmān ibn ʿAddīs comes to you beat him with a hundred lashes, shave his head and beard and condemn him to long imprisonment. Do the same in the case of ʿAmr ibn al-Ḥamq, Sūdā ibn Ḥamrān, and ʿUrwah ibn Nibāʿ." The Egyptians took the letter and returned with anger to Uthman, saying, "You have betrayed us!" Uthman denied the letter. They said, "Your slave was the carrier of the letter." He answered, "He has committed this act without my permission." They said, "He rode upon your camel." He answered, "They have stolen my camel." They said, "The letter is in the handwriting of your secretary." He replied, "This has been done without my permission and knowledge." They said, "In any case you are not competent to be caliph and must resign, for if this has been done with your permission you are a traitor and if such important matters take place without your permission and knowledge then your incapability and incompetence is proven. In any case, either resign or dismiss the oppressive agents from office immediately."

Uthman answered, "If I wish to act according to your will, then it is you who are the rulers. Then, what is my function?" They stood up and left the gathering in anger.[36]

During his caliphate Uthman allowed the government of Damascus, at the head of which stood Muʿawiyah, to be strengthened more than ever before. In reality, the center of gravity of the caliphate as far as political power was concerned was shifting to Damascus and the organization in Medina, the capital of the Islamic world, was politically no more than a form without the necessary power and substance to support it.[37] Finally, in the year 35/656, the people rebelled and after a few days of siege and fighting the third caliph was killed.

The first caliph was selected through the vote of the majority of the companions, the second caliph by the will and testament of the first, and the third by a six-man council whose members and rules of procedure were organized and determined by the second caliph. Altogether, the policy of these three caliphs, who were in power for twenty-five years, was to execute and apply Islamic laws and principles in society in accordance with ijtihad and what appeared as most wise at the time to the caliphs themselves. As for the Islamic sciences, the policy of these caliphs was to have the Holy Quran read and understood without being concerned with commentaries upon it or allowing it to become the subject of discussion. The hadith of the Prophet was recited and was transmitted orally without being written down. Writing was limited to the text of the Holy Quran and was forbidden in the case of hadith.[38]

After the battle of Yamānah, which ended in 12/633, many of those who had been reciters of the Holy Quran and who knew it by heart were killed. As a result Umar ibn al-Khaṭṭāb proposed to the first caliph to have the verses of the Holy Quran collected in written form, saying that if another war were to occur and the rest of those who knew the Quran by heart were to be killed, the knowledge of the text of the Holy Book would disappear among men. Therefore, it was necessary to assemble the Quranic verses in written form.[39]

From the Shiʿite point of view it appears strange that this

decision was made concerning the Quran and yet despite the fact that the prophetic hadith, which is the complement of the Quran, was faced with the same danger and was not free from corruption in transmission, addition, diminution, forgery and forgetfulness, the same attention was not paid to it. On the contrary, as already mentioned, writing it down was forbidden and all of the written versions of it that were found were burned, as if to emphasize that only the text of the Holy Book should exist in written form.

As for the other Islamic sciences, during this period little effort was made to propagate them, the energies of the community being spent mostly in establishing the new sociopolitical order. Despite all the praise and consecration which are found in the Quran concerning knowledge (*'ilm*),[40] and the emphasis placed upon its cultivation, the avid cultivation of the religious sciences was postponed to a later period of Islamic history.

Most men were occupied with the remarkable and continuous victories of the Islamic armies, and were carried away by the flood of immeasurable booty which came from all directions toward the Arabian peninsula. With this new wealth and the worldliness which came along with it, few were willing to devote themselves to the cultivation of the sciences of the Household of the Prophet, at whose head stood Ali, whom the Holy Prophet had introduced to the people as the one most versed in the Islamic sciences. At the same time, the inner meaning and purpose of the teachings of the Holy Quran were neglected by most of those who were affected by this change. It is strange that, even in the matter of collecting the verses of the Holy Quran, Ali was not consulted and his name was not mentioned among those who participated in this task, although it was known by everyone that he had collected the text of the Holy Quran after the death of the Prophet.[41]

It has been recounted in many traditions that after receiving allegiance from the community, Abu Bakr sent someone to Ali and asked for his allegiance. Ali said, "I have promised not to leave my house except for the daily prayers until I compile the Quran." And it has been mentioned that Ali gave his allegiance to Abu Bakr after six months. This itself is proof that Ali had finished compiling the Quran. Likewise, it has been recounted that after compiling the Quran he placed the pages of the Holy Book on a camel and showed it to the people. It is also recounted that the battle of Yamanah, after which the Quran was compiled, occurred during the second year of the caliphate of Abu Bakr. These facts have been mentioned in most works on history and hadith which deal with the account of the compilation of the Holy Quran.

These and similar events made the followers of Ali more firm in their belief and more conscious of the course that lay before them. They increased their activity from day to day and Ali himself, who was cut off from the possibility of educating and training the people in general, concentrated on privately training an elite.

During this twenty-five year period Ali lost through death three of his four dearest friends and associates, who were also among the companions of the Prophet: Salmān al-Fārsī, Abū Dharr al-Ghifārī, and Miqdād. They had been constant in their friendship with him in all circumstances. It was also during this same period that some of the other companions of the Holy Prophet and a large number of their followers in the Hijaz, the Yemen, Iraq, and other lands, joined the followers of Ali. As a result, after the death of the third caliph the people turned to Ali from all sides, swore allegiance to him and chose him as caliph.

The Termination of the Caliphate of ʿAlī Amīr al-mu'minīn[42] and His Method of Rule

The caliphate of Ali began toward the end of the year 35/656 and lasted about four years and nine months. During his period as caliph Ali followed the ways of the Holy Prophet[43] and brought conditions back to their original state. He forced the resignation of all the incompetent political elements who had a hand in directing affairs[44] and began in reality a major transformation of a "revolutionary" nature which caused him innumerable difficulties.[45]

On his first day as caliph, in an address to the people, Ali said, "O People, be aware that the difficulties which you faced during the apostolic period of the Prophet of God have come upon you once again and seized you. Your ranks must be turned completely around so that the people of virtue who have fallen behind should come forward and those who had come to the fore without being worthy should fall behind. There is both truth (haqq) and falsehood (*bāṭil*). Each has its followers; but a person should follow the truth. If falsehood be prevalent it is not something new, and if the truth is rare and hard to come by, sometimes even that which is rare wins the day so that there is hope of advance. Of course it does not occur often that something which has turned away from man should return to him."[46]

Ali continued his radically different type of government based more on righteousness than political efficacy but, as is necessary in the case of every movement of this kind, elements of the opposition whose interests were endangered began to display their displeasure and resisted his rule. Basing their actions on the claim that they wanted to revenge the death of Uthman, they instigated bloody wars which continued throughout almost all the time that Ali was caliph. From the Shiʿite point of view those who caused these civil wars had no end in mind other than their own personal interest. The wish to revenge the blood of the third caliph was no more than an excuse to fool the crowd. There was no question of a misunderstanding.

After the death of the Holy Prophet, a small minority, following Ali, refused to pay allegiance. At the head of the minority there were Salman, Abu Dharr, Miqdad, and Ammar. At the beginning of the caliphate of Ali also a sizable minority in disagreement refused to pay allegiance. Among the most persistent opponents were Saʿīd ibn ʿĀṣṣ, Walīd ibn ʿUqbah, Marwān ibn Ḥakam, ʿAmr ibn ʿĀṣṣ, Busr ibn Arṭāt, Samurah ibn Jundab, and Mughīrah ibn Shuʿbah.

The study of the biography of these two groups, and meditation upon the acts they have performed and stories recounted of them in history books, reveal fully their religious personality and aim. The first group were among the elite of the companions of the Holy Prophet and among the ascetics, devout worshipers and selfless devotees of Islam who struggled on the path of Islamic freedom. They were especially loved by the Prophet. The Prophet said,

"God has informed me that He loves four men and that I should love them also." They asked about their names. He mentioned Ali and then the names of Abu Dharr, Salman and Miqdad. (*Sunan* of Ibn Mājah, Cairo, 1372, vol. I, p. 66.) ʿĀ'ishah has recounted that the Prophet of God said, "If two alternatives are placed before Ammar, he will definitely choose that which is more true and right." (*Ibn Mājah*, vol. I, p. 66.) The Prophet said, "There is no one between heaven and earth more truthful than Abu Dharr." (*Ibn Mājah*, vol. I, p. 68.) There is no record of a single forbidden act committed by these men during their lifetime. They never spilled any blood unjustly, did not commit aggression against anyone, did not steal anyone's property, never sought to corrupt and misguide people.

History is, however, full of accounts of unworthy acts committed by some of the second group. The various acts committed by some of these men in opposition to explicit Islamic teachings are beyond reckoning. These acts cannot be excused in any manner except the way that is followed by certain groups among the Sunnis who say that God was satisfied with them and therefore they were free to perform whatever act they wished, and that they would not be punished for violating the injunctions and regulations existing in the Holy Book and the Sunnah.

The first war in the caliphate of Ali, which is called the "Battle of the Camel," was caused by the unfortunate class differences created during the period of rule of the second caliph as a result of the new socioeconomic forces which caused an uneven distribution of the public treasury among members of the community. When chosen to the caliphate, Ali divided the treasury evenly[47] as had been the method of the Holy Prophet, but this manner of dividing the wealth upset Talhah and Zubayr greatly. They began to show signs of disobedience and left Medina for Mecca with the alleged aim of making the pilgrimage. They persuaded "the mother of the Faithful" (*umm al-mu'minīn*), A'ishah, who was not friendly with Ali, to join them and in the name of wanting to revenge the death of the third caliph they began the bloody Battle of the Camel.[48] This was done despite the fact that this same Talhah and Zubayr were in Medina when the third caliph was besieged and killed but did nothing to defend him.[49] Furthermore, after his death they were the first to pay allegiance to Ali on behalf of the immigrants (*muhājirūn*)[50] as well as on their own.[51] Also, the "mother of the Faithful," A'ishah, did not show any opposition to those who had killed the third caliph at the moment when she received the news of his death.[52] It must be remembered that the main instigators of the disturbances that led to the death of the third caliph were those companions who wrote letters from Medina to people near and far inviting them to rebel against the caliph, a fact which is repeated in many early Muslim histories.

As for the second war, called the Battle of Ṣiffīn, which lasted for a year and a half, its cause was the covetousness of Muʿawiyah for the caliphate which for him was a worldly political instrument rather than a religious institution. But as an excuse he made the revenge of the blood of the third caliph the main issue and began a war in which more than a hundred thousand people perished without reason. Naturally, in these wars Muʿawiyah was the aggressor rather than the defender, for the protest to revenge someone's blood can never occur in the form of defense. The pretext of this war was blood revenge. During the last days of his life, the third caliph, in order to quell the uprising against him, asked Muʿawiyah for help, but the army of Muʿawiyah which set out from Damascus to Medina purposely waited on the road until the caliph was killed. Then he returned to Damascus to begin an uprising to revenge the caliph's death.[53] After the death of Ali and his gaining the caliphate himself, Muʿawiyah forgot the question of revenging the blood of the third caliph and did not pursue the matter further.

After Siffin there occurred the battle of Nahrawān in which a number of people, among whom there could be found some of the companions, rebelled against Ali, possibly at the instigation of Muʿawiyah.[54] These people were causing rebellion throughout the lands of Islam, killing the Muslims and especially the followers of Ali. They even attacked pregnant women and killed their babies. Ali put down this uprising as well, but a short while later was himself killed in the mosque of Kufa by one of the members of this group who came to be known as the Khawārij.

The opponents of Ali claim that he was a courageous man but did not possess political acumen. They claim that at the beginning of his caliphate he could have temporarily made peace with his opponents. He could have approached them through peace and friendship, thus courting their satisfaction and approval. In this way he could have strengthened his caliphate and only then turned to their extirpation and destruction. What people who hold this view forget is that the movement of Ali was not based on political opportunism. It was a radical and revolutionary religious movement (in the true sense of revolution as a spiritual movement to reestablish the real order of things and not in its current political and social sense); therefore it could not have been accomplished through compromise or flattery and forgery. A similar situation can be seen during the apostleship of the Holy Prophet. The infidels and polythesis proposed peace to him many times and swore that if he were to abstain from protesting against their gods they would not interfere with his religious mission. But the Prophet did not accept such a proposal, although he could in those days of difficulty have made peace and used flattery to fortify his own position, and then have risen against his enemies. In fact, the Islamic message never allows a right and just cause to be abandoned for the sake of strengthening another good cause, nor a falsehood to be rejected and disproven through another falsehood. There are many Quranic verses concerning this matter.[55]

The Benefit which the Shīʿah Derived from the Caliphate of Ali

During the four years and nine months of his caliphate, Ali was not able to eliminate the disturbed conditions which were prevailing throughout the Islamic world, but he was successful in three fundamental ways:

1. As a result of his just and upright manner of living he revealed once again the beauty and attractiveness of the way of life of the Holy Prophet, especially to the younger generation. In contrast to the imperial grandeur of Muʿawiyah, he lived in

simplicity and poverty like the poorest of people.[56] He never favored his friends or relatives and family above others,[57] nor did he ever prefer wealth to poverty or brute force to weakness.

2. Despite the cumbersome and strenuous difficulties which absorbed his time, he left behind among the Islamic community a valuable treasury of the truly divine sciences and Islamic intellectual disciplines.[58] Nearly eleven thousand of his proverbs and short sayings on different intellectual, religious and social subjects have been recorded.[59] In his talks and speeches he expounded the most sublime Islamic sciences in a most elegant and flowing manner. He established Arabic grammar and laid the basis for Arabic literature.[60]

He was the first in Islam to delve directly into the questions of metaphysics (*falsafah-i ilāhī*) in a manner combining intellectual rigor and logical demonstration. He discussed problems which had never appeared before in the same way among the metaphysicians of the world.[61] Moreover, he was so devoted to metaphysics and gnosis that even in the heat of battle he would carry out intellectual discourse and discuss metaphysical questions.[62]

3. He trained a large number of religious scholars and Islamic savants, among whom are found a number of ascetics and gnostics who were the forefathers of the Sufis, such men as Uways al-Qaranī, Kumayl al-Nakhaʿī, Maytham al-Tammār and Rashīd al-Ḥajarī. These men have been recognized by the later Sufis as the founders of gnosis in Islam. Others among his disciples became the first teachers of jurisprudence, theology, Quranic commentary and recitation.[63]

The Transfer of the Caliphate to Muʿawiyah and Its Transformation into a Hereditary Monarchy

After the death of Ali, his son, Hasan ibn Ali, who is recognized by the Shiʿah as their second Imam, became caliph. This designation occurred in accordance with Ali's last will and testament and also by the allegiance of the community to Hasan. But Muʿawiyah did not remain quiet before this event. He marched with his army toward Iraq, which was then the capital of the caliphate, and began to wage war against Hasan.

Through different intrigues and the payment of great sums of money, Muʿawiyah was able gradually to corrupt the aides and generals of Hasan. Finally he was able to force Hasan to hand the caliphate over to him so as to avoid bloodshed and to make peace.[64] Hasan handed the caliphate to Muʿawiyah on the condition that the caliphate would be returned to him after the death of Muʿawiyah and that no harm would come to his partisans.[65]

In the year 40/661 Muʿawiyah finally gained control of the caliphate. He then set out immediately for Iraq and in a speech to the people of that land said: "I did not fight against you for the sake of the prayers or of fasting. These acts you can perform yourself. What I wanted to accomplish was to rule over you and this end I have achieved." He also said, "The agreement I made with Hasan is null and void. It lies trampled under my feet."[66] With this declaration Muʿawiyah made known to the people the real character of his government and revealed the nature of the program he had in mind.

He indicated in his declaration that he would separate religion from politics and would not give any guarantees concerning religious duties and regulations. He would spend all his force to preserve and to keep alive his own power, whatever might be the cost. Obviously a government of such a nature is more of a sultanate and a monarchy than a caliphate and vicegerency of the Prophet of God in its traditional Islamic sense. That is why some who were admitted to his court addressed him as "king."[67] He himself in some private gatherings interpreted his government as a monarchy,[68] while in public he always introduced himself as the caliph.

Naturally any monarchy that is based on force carries with it inherently the principle of inheritance. Muʿawiyah, too, finally realized this fact, and chose his son, Yazīd, who was a heedless young man without the least religious personality,[69] as the "crown prince" and his successor. This act was to be the cause of many regrettable events in the future. Muʿawiyah had previously indicated that he would refuse to permit Hasan ibn Ali to succeed him as caliph and that he had other thoughts in mind. Therefore he had caused Hasan to be killed by poisoning,[70] thus preparing the way for his son, Yazid.

In breaking his agreement with Hasan, Mu'awiyah made it clear that he would never permit the Shi'ah of the Household of the Prophet to live in a peaceful and secure environment and continue their activity as before, and he carried into action this very intention. It has been said that he went so far as to declare that whoever would transmit a hadith in praise of the virtues of the Household of the Prophet would have no immunity or protection concerning his life, merchandise and property.[71] At the same time he ordered that whoever could recite a hadith in praise of the other companions or caliphs would be given sufficient reward. As a result a noticeable number of hadiths were recorded at this time praising the companions, some of which are of doubtful authenticity.[72] He ordered pejorative comments to be made about Ali from the pulpits of mosques throughout the lands of Islam, while he himself sought to revile Ali. This command continued to be more or less in effect until the caliphate of Umar ibn 'Abd al-'Azīz, when it was discontinued.[73] With the help of his agents and lieutenants, Mu'awiyah caused the elite and the most outstanding among the partisans of Ali to be put to death and the heads of some of them to be carried on lances throughout different cities.[74] The majority of Shi'ites were forced to disown and even curse Ali and to express their disdain for him. If they refused, they were put to death.

The Bleakest Days of Shi'ism

The most difficult period for Shi'ism was the twenty-year rule of Mu'awiyah, during which the Shi'ites had no protection and most of them were considered as marked characters, under suspicion and hunted down by the state. Two of the leaders of Shi'ism who lived at this time, Imams Hasan and Husayn, did not possess any means whatsoever to change the negative and oppressive circumstances in which they lived. Husayn, the third Imam of Shiʿism, had no possibility of freeing the Shiʿites from persecution in the ten years he was Imam during Muʿawiyah's caliphate, and when he rebelled during the caliphate of Yazid he was massacred along with all his aides and children.

Certain people in the Sunni world explain as pardonable the arbitrary, unjust and irresponsible actions carried out at this time by Muʿawiyah and his aides and lieutenants, some of whom were, like Muʿawiyah himself, among the companions. This group reasons that according to certain hadiths of the Holy Prophet all the companions could practice ijtihad, that they were excused by God for the sins they committed, and that God was satisfied with them and forgave them whatever wrong they might have performed. The Shiʿites, however, do not accept this argument for two reasons:

1. It is not conceivable that a leader of human society like the Prophet should rise in order to revivify truth, justice and freedom and to persuade a group of people to accept his beliefs—a group all of whose members had sacrificed their very existence in order to accomplish this sacred end—and then as soon as this end is accomplished give his aides and companions complete freedom to do with these sacred laws as they will. It is not possible to believe that the Holy Prophet would have forgiven the companions for whatever wrong action they might have performed. Such indifference to the type of action performed by them would have only destroyed the structure which the Holy Prophet had built with the same means that he had used to construct it.

2. Those sayings which depict the companions as inviolable and pardoned in advance for every act they might perform, even one unlawful or inadmissible, are most likely apocryphal; the authenticity of many of them has not been fully established by traditional methods. Moreover, it is known historically that the companions did not deal with one another as if they were inviolable and pardoned for all their sins and wrongdoings. Therefore, even judging by the way the companions acted and dealt with each other, it can be concluded that such sayings cannot be literally true in the way some have understood them. If they do contain an aspect of the truth it is in indicating the legal inviolability of the

companions and the sanctification which they enjoyed generally as a group because of their proximity to the Holy Prophet. The expression of God's satisfaction with the companions in the Holy Quran, because of the services they had rendered in obeying His Command,[75] refers to their past actions, and to God's satisfaction with them in the past, not to whatever action each one of them might perform in the future.

The Establishment of Umayyad Rule

In the year 60/680 Muʿawiyah died and his son Yazid became caliph, as the result of the allegiance which his father had obtained for him from the powerful political and military leaders of the community. From the testimony of historical documents it can be seen clearly that Yazid had no religious character at all and that even during the lifetime of his father he was oblivious to the principles and regulations of Islam. At that time his only interest was debauchery and frivolity. During his three years of caliphate he was the cause of calamities that had no precedent in the history of Islam, despite all the strife that had occurred before him.

During the first year of Yazid's rule Imam Husayn, the grandson of the Holy Prophet, was massacred in the most atrocious manner along with his children, relatives, and friends. Yazid even had some of the women and children of the Household of the Prophet killed and their heads displayed in different cities.[76] During the second year of his rule, he ordered a general massacre of Medina and for three days gave his soldiers freedom to kill, loot, and take the women of the city.[77] During the third year he had the sacred Kaʿbah destroyed and burned.[78]

Following Yazid, the family of Marwān gained possession of the caliphate, according to details that are recorded in the history books. The rule of this eleven-member group, which lasted for nearly seventy years, was successful politically but from the point of view of purely religious values it fell short of Islamic ideals and practices. Islamic society was dominated by the Arab element alone and non-Arabs were subordinated to the Arabs. In fact a strong Arab empire was created which gave itself the name of an Islamic caliphate. During this period some of the caliphs were indifferent to religious sentiments to the extent that one of them—who was the "vicegerent of the Holy Prophet" and was regarded as the protector of religion—decided without showing any respect for Islamic practices and the feelings of Muslims to construct a room above the Kaʿbah so that he could have a place to enjoy and amuse himself during the annual pilgrimage.[79] It is even recounted of one of these caliphs that he made the Holy Quran a target for his arrow and in a poem composed to the Quran said: "On the Day of Judgment when you appear before God tell Him 'the caliph tore me.'"[80]

Naturally the Shiʿites, whose basic differences with the Sunnis were in the two questions of the Islamic caliphate and religious authority, were passing through bitter and difficult days in this dark period. Yet in spite of the unjust and irresponsible ways of the governments of the time the asceticism and purity of the leaders of the Household of the Prophet made the Shiʿites each day ever more determined to hold on to their beliefs. Of particular importance was the tragic death of Husayn, the third Imam, which played a major role in the spread of Shiʿism, especially in regions away from the center of the caliphate, such as Iraq, the Yemen, and Persia. This can be seen through the fact that during the period of the fifth Imam, before the end of the first Islamic century, and less than forty years after the death of Husayn, the Shiʿites took advantage of the internal differences and weaknesses in the Umayyad government and began to organize themselves, flocking to the side of the fifth Imam. People came from all Islamic countries like a flood to his door to collect hadith and to learn the Islamic sciences. The first century had not yet ended when a few of the leaders who were influential in the government established the city of Qum in Persia and made it a Shiʿite settlement. But even then the Shiʿah continued to live for the most part in hiding and followed their religious life secretly without external manifestations.[81]

Several times the descendants of the Prophet (who are called in Persian *sādāt-i ʿalawī*) rebelled against the injustice of the government, but each time they were defeated and usually lost their lives. The severe and unscrupulous government of the time did not overlook any means of crushing them. The body of Zayd, the leader of Zaydī Shi'ism, was dug out of the grave and hanged; then after remaining on the gallows for three years it was brought down and burned, its ashes being thrown to the wind.[82] The Shi'ites believe that the fourth and fifth Imams were poisoned by the Umayyads as the second and third Imams had been killed by them before.[83]

The calamities brought about by the Umayyads were so open and unveiled that the majority of the Sunnis, although they believed generally that it was their duty to obey the caliphs, felt the pangs of their religious conscience and were forced to divide the caliphs into two groups. They came to distinguish between the "rightly guided caliphs" (*khulafā' rāshidūn*) who are the first four caliphs after the death of the Holy Prophet (Abu Bakr, Umar, Uthman, Ali), and the others who began with Mu'awiyah and who did not possess by any means the religious virtues of the rightly guided caliphs.

The Umayyads caused so much public hatred as a result of their injustice and heedlessness during their rule that after the definitive defeat and death of the last Umayyad caliph his two sons and a number of their family encountered great difficulties in escaping from the capital. No matter where they turned no one would give them shelter. Finally after much wandering in the deserts of Nubia, Abyssinia, and Bajāwah (between Nubia and Abyssinia) during which many of them died from hunger and thirst, they came to Bāb al-Mandab of the Yemen. There they acquired travel expenses from the people through begging and set out for Mecca dressed as porters. In Mecca they finally succeeded in disappearing among the mass of the people.[84]

Shi'ism During the 2nd/8th Century

During the latter part of the first third of the 2nd/8th century, following a series of revolutions and bloody wars throughout the

Islamic world which were due to the injustice, repressions, and wrongdoings of the Umayyads, there began an anti-Umayyad movement in the name of the Household of the Prophet in Khurasan in Persia. The leader of this movement was the Persian general, Abū Muslim Marwazī, who rebelled against Umayyad rule and advanced his cause step by step until he was able to overthrow the Umayyad government.[85]

Although this movement originated from a profound Shiʿite background and came into being more or less with the claim of wanting to avenge the blood of the Household of the Prophet, and although people were even asked secretly to give allegiance to a qualified member of the family of the Prophet, it did not rise directly as a result of the instructions of the Imams. This is witnessed by the fact that when Abu Muslim offered the caliphate to the sixth Imam in Medina he rejected it completely saying, "You are not one of my men and the time is not my time."[86]

Finally the Abbasids gained the caliphate in the name of the family of the Prophet[87] and at the beginning showed some kindness to people in general and to the descendants of the Prophet in particular. In the name of avenging the martyrdom of the family of the Prophet, they massacred the Umayyads, going to the extent of opening their graves and burning whatever they found in them.[88] But soon they began to follow the unjust ways of the Umayyads and did not abstain in any way from injustice and irresponsible action. Abū Ḥanīfah, the founder of one of the four Sunni schools of law, was imprisoned by al-Manṣūr and tortured.[89] Ibn Ḥanbal, the founder of another school of law, was whipped.[90] The sixth Imam died from poisoning after much torture and pain.[91] The descendants of the Holy Prophet were sometimes beheaded in groups, buried alive, or even placed within walls of government buildings under construction.

Hārūn al-Rashīd, the Abbasid caliph, during whose reign the Islamic empire reached the apogee of its expansion and power, occasionally would look at the sun and address it in these words: "Shine wherever thou wilt, thou shalt never be able to leave my kingdom." On the one hand his armies were advancing in the East and West, on the other hand a few steps from the palace of the caliph, and without his knowledge, officials had decided on their own to collect tolls from people who wanted to cross the Baghdad bridge. Even one day when the caliph himself wanted to cross the bridge he was stopped and asked to pay the toll.[92]

A singer, by chanting two lascivious verses, incited the passions of the Abbasid caliph, Amīn, who awarded him three million *dirhams*. The chanter in joy threw himself at the feet of the caliph saying, "Oh, leader of the faithful! You give me all this money?" The caliph answered, "It does not matter. We receive this money from an unknown part of the country."[93]

The bewildering amount of wealth that was pouring every year from all corners of the Islamic world into the public treasury in the capital helped in creating luxury and a mundane atmosphere. Much of it in fact was often spent for the pleasures and iniquities of the caliph of the time. The number of beautiful slave girls in the court of some of the caliphs exceeded thousands. By the dissolution of Umayyad rule and the establishment of the Abbasids, Shiʿism did not benefit in any way. Its repressive and unjust opponents merely changed their name.

Shiʿism in the 3rd/9th Century

At the beginning of the 3rd/9th century Shiʿism was able to breathe once again. This more favorable condition was first of all due to the fact that many scientific and philosophical books were translated from Greek, Syriac, and other languages into Arabic, and people eagerly studied the intellectual and rational sciences. Moreover, al-Ma'mūn, the Abbasid caliph from 198/813 to 218/833, had Muʿtazilite leanings and since in his religious views he favored intellectual demonstration, he was more inclined to give complete freedom to the discussion and propagation of different religious views. Shiʿite theologians and scholars took full advantage of this freedom and did their utmost to further scholarly activities and propagate Shiʿite teachings. Also, al-Ma'mun, following the demands of the political forces at the time, had made the eighth Shiʿite Imam his successor, as is recounted in most standard histories. As a result, the descendants of the Holy Prophet and their friends were to a certain extent free from pressures from the government and enjoyed some degree of liberty. Yet before long the cutting edge of the sword once again turned towards the Shiʿites and the forgotten ways of the past came upon them again. This was particularly true in the case of al-Mutawakkil (233/847-247/861) who held a special enmity towards Ali and the Shiʿites. By his order the tomb of the third Imam in Karbala was completely demolished.[94]

Shiʿism in the 4th/10th Century

In the 4th/10th century certain conditions again prevailed which aided greatly the spread and strengthening of Shiʿism. Among them were the weaknesses that appeared in the central Abbasid government and administration and the appearance of the Buyid rulers. The Buyids, who were Shiʿite, had the greatest influence not only in the provinces of Persia but also in the capital of the caliphate in Baghdad, and even upon the caliph himself. This new strength of considerable proportions enabled the Shiʿites to stand up before their opponents who previously had tried to crush them by relying upon the power of the caliphate. It also made it possible for the Shiʿites to propagate their religious views openly.

As recorded by historians, during this century most of the Arabian peninsula was Shiʿite with the exception of some of the big cities. Even some of the major cities like Hajar, Uman, and Saʿdah were Shiʿite. In Basra, which had always been a Sunni city and competed with Kufa which was considered a Shiʿite center, there appeared a notable group of Shiʿites. Also in Tripoli, Nablus, Tiberias, Aleppo, Nayshapur, and Herat there were many Shiʿites, while Ahwaz and the coast of the Persian Gulf on the Persian side were also Shiʿite.[95]

At the beginning of this century Nāṣir Uṭrūsh, after many years of propagation of his religious mission in northern Persia, gained power in Tabaristan and established a kingdom which continued for several generations after him. Before Uṭrūsh, Hasan ibn Zayd al-ʿAlawī had reigned for many years in Tabaristan.[96] Also in this period the Fatimids, who were Ismaʿili, conquered Egypt and organized a caliphate which lasted for over two centuries (296/908-567/1171).[97] Often disputation and fighting occurred in major cities like Baghdad, Cairo and Nayshapur between Shiʿites and Sunnis, in some of which the Shiʿites would gain the upper hand and come out victorious.

Shiʿism from the 5th/11th to the 9th/15th Centuries

From the 5th/11th to the 9th/15th centuries Shiʿism continued to expand as it had done in the 4th/10th century.[98] Many kings and rulers who were Shiʿite appeared in different parts of the Islamic world and propagated Shiʿism. Toward the end of the 5th/11th century the missionary activity of Ismaʿilism took root in the fort of Alamut and for nearly a century and a half the Ismaʿilis lived in complete independence in the central regions of Persia. Also the Sādāt-i Marʿashi, who were descendants of the Holy Prophet, ruled for many years in Mazandaran (Tabaristan).[99] Shāh Muḥammad Khudābandah, one of the well-known Mongol rulers, became Shiʿite and his descendants ruled for many years in Persia and were instrumental in spreading Shiʿism.[100] Mention must also be made of the kings of the Āq Qoyūnlū and Qara Qoyūnlū dynasties who ruled in Tabriz and whose domain extended to Fars and Kerman,[101] as well as of the Fatimid government which was ruling in Egypt.

Of course religious freedom and the possibility of exerting religious power by the populace differed under different rulers. For example, with the termination of Fatimid rule and coming to power of the Ayyubids the scene changed completely and the Shiʿite population of Egypt and Syria lost its religious independence. Many of the Shiʿites of Syria were killed during this period merely on the accusation of following Shiʿism. One of these was Shahīd-i awwal (the First Martyr) Muḥammad ibn Makkī, one of the great figures in Shiʿite jurisprudence, who was killed in

Damascus in 786/1384.[102] Also Shaykh al-ishrāq Shihāb al-Dīn Suhrawardī was killed in Aleppo on the accusation that he was cultivating Bāṭinī teachings and philosophy.[103] Altogether during this period Shiʿism was growing from the point of view of numbers, even though its religious power and freedom depended upon local conditions and the rulers of the time. During this period, however, Shiʿism never became the official religion of any Muslim state.

Shiʿism in the 10th/16th and 11th/17th Centuries

In the 10th/16th century Ismāʿīl, who was of the household of Shaykh Ṣafī al-Dīn Ardibīlī (d. 735/1334), a Sufi master and also a Shiʿite, began a revolt in Ardibīl, with three hundred Sufis who were disciples of his forefathers, with the aim of establishing an independent and powerful Shiʿite country. In this way he began the conquest of Persia and overcame the local feudal princes. After a series of bloody wars with local rulers and also the Ottomans who held the title of caliph, he succeeded in forming Persia piece by piece into a country and in making Shiʿism the official religion in his kingdom.[104]

After the death of Shah Ismaʿil other Safavid kings reigned in Persia until the 12th/18th century and each continued to recognize Shiʿism as the official religion of the country and further to strengthen its hold upon this land. At the height of their power, during the reign of Shāh ʿAbbās, the Safavids were able to increase the territorial expansion and the population of Persia to twice its present size.[105] As for other Muslim lands, the Shiʿite population continued the same as before and increased only through the natural growth of population.

Shiʿism from the 12th/18th to the 14th/20th Centuries

During the past three centuries Shiʿism has followed its natural rate of growth as before. At the present moment, during the latter part of the 14th/20th century, Shiʿism is recognized as the official religion of Iran, and in the Yemen and Iraq the majority of the population is Shiʿite. In nearly all lands where there are Muslims one can find a certain number of Shiʿites. It has been said that altogether in the world today there are about eighty to ninety million Shiʿites.

NOTES

CHAPTER I

1. The first designation to have appeared during the lifetime of the Holy Prophet of God was *shī'ah*, and Salmān, Abu Dharr, Miqdād and 'Ammār were known by this name. See *Hāḍir al-'ālam al-islāmī*, Cairo, 1352, vol. I, p. 188.

2. Quran, XXVI, 214.

3. According to this hadith, Ali said, "I who was the youngest of all have submitted that I am your vizier. The Prophet put his hand around my neck and said, 'This person is my brother, inheritor and vicegerent. You must obey him.' People laughed and told Abu Talib, 'He has ordered you to obey your son.'" Ṭabarī, *al-Ta'rīkh*, Cairo, 1357, vol. II, p. 63; Abu'l-Fidā', *al-Ta'rīkh*, Cairo, 1325, vol. I, p. 116; Ibn al-Athīr, *al-Bidāyah wa'l-nihāyah*, Cairo, 1358, vol. III, p. 39; Baḥrānī, *Ghāyat al-marām*, Tehran, 1272, p. 320. [*Editor's note:* The reader will notice that this hadith and certain others which are quoted more than once appear each time in a slightly different form. This is because the author has made use of different transmitted versions in each place.]

4. Umm Salmah has recounted that the Prophet said: "Ali is always with the Truth (*ḥaqq*) and the Quran, and the Truth and the Quran are always with him, and until the Day of Judgment they will not be separated from each other." This hadith has been transmitted through fifteen channels in Sunni sources and eleven in Shi'ite sources. Umm Salmah, Ibn 'Abbās, Abu Bakr, A'ishah, Ali, Abū Sa'īd Khudrī, Abū Laylā, Abū Ayyūb Anṣārī are among its transmitters. *Ghāyat al-marām*, pp. 539–540. The Prophet has also said, "God bless Ali for the Truth is always with him." *al-Bidāyah wa'l-nihāyah*, vol. VII, p. 36.

5. The Prophet said: "Arbitration has been divided into ten parts. Nine parts are given to Ali and one part is divided among all the people." *al-Bidāyah wa'l-nihāyah*, vol. VII, p. 359. Salmān Farsī has transmitted this saying from the Prophet: "After me the most learned of men is Ali." *Ghāyat al-marām*, p. 528. Ibn 'Abbās has said that the Prophet said: "Ali is the most competent among people in judgment." From the book *Faḍā'il al-ṣaḥābah*, mentioned in *Ghāyat al-marām*, p. 528. Umar used to say: "May God never afflict me with a difficult task where Ali is not present." *al-Bidāyah wa'l-nihāyah*, vol. VII, p. 359.

6. *Editor's note:* According to Shi'ite beliefs, on returning from the last pilgrimage to Mecca on the way to Medina at a site called Ghadīr Khumm the Prophet chose Ali as his successor before the vast crowd that was accompanying him. The Shi'ites celebrate this event to this day as a major religious feast marking the day when the right of Ali to succession was universally acclaimed.

7. The hadith of Ghadir in its different versions is one of the definitely estab-

lished hadiths among Sunnis and Shiʿah. More than a hundred of the companions have recounted it with different chains of transmission and expressions, and it has been recorded in books of Sunnism and Shiʿism alike. Concerning details refer to *Ghāyat al-marām*, p. 79, *ʿAbaqāt* of Mūsawī, India, 1317 (Volume on *Ghadīr*) and *al-Ghadīr* of Amīnī, Najaf, 1372.

8. *Tārīkh-i Yaʿqūbī*, Najaf, 1358, vol. II, pp. 137 and 140; *Tārīkh-i Abi'l-Fidā'*, vol. I, p. 156; *Ṣāḥīḥ* of Bukhārī, Cairo, 1315, vol. IV, p. 207; *Murūj al-dhahab* of Masʿūdī, Cairo, 1367, vol. II, p. 437, vol. III, pp. 21 and 61.

9. *Ṣaḥīḥ* of Muslim, vol. XV, p. 176; *Ṣaḥīḥ* of Bukhārī, vol. IV, p. 207; *Murūj al-dhahab*, vol. III, p. 23 and vol. II, p. 437; *Tārīkh-i Abi'l-Fidā'*, vol. I, pp. 127 and 181.

10. Jābir says: "We were in the presence of the Prophet when Ali appeared from far away. The Prophet said: 'I swear by Him who holds my life in His hands, this person and his partisans (Shiʿah) will have salvation on the Day of Judgment.'" Ibn 'Abbās says: "When the verse: '(And) lo! those who believe and do good works are the best of created beings' (Quran, XCVII, 7) was revealed, the Prophet told Ali: 'This verse pertains to you and your partisans who will possess felicity on the Day of Judgment and God will also be satisfied with you.'" These two hadiths and several others are recorded in the book *al-Durr al-manthūr* of Suyūṭī, Cairo, 1313, vol. VI, p. 379, and *Ghāyat al-marām*, p. 326.

11. While suffering from the illness that led to his death, Muhammad organized an army under the command of Usāmah ibn Zayd and insisted that everyone should participate in this war and go out of Medina. A number of people disobeyed the Prophet including Abu Bakr and Umar and this disturbed the Prophet greatly. (*Sharḥ Ibn Abi'l-Hadīd*, Cairo, 1329, vol. I, p. 53.) At the moment of his death the Holy Prophet said: "Prepare ink and paper so that I will have a letter written for you which will be a cause of guidance for you and prevent you from being misled." Umar, who prevented this action, said: "His illness has run out of hand and he is delirious." (*Tārīkh-i Ṭabarī*, vol. II, p. 436: *Ṣaḥīḥ* of Bukhārī, vol. III and *Ṣaḥīḥ* of Muslim, Cairo, 1349, vol. V; *al-Bidāyah wa'l-nihāyah*, vol. V, p. 227; *Ibn Abi'l-Ḥadīd*, vol. I, p. 133.) A somewhat similar situation occurred again during the illness which led to the death of the first caliph. In his last testament the first caliph chose Umar and even fainted while making the testament but Umar said nothing and did not consider him to be delirious, although he had fainted while the testament was being written. The Prophet had been inerrant and fully conscious when he asked them to write down a letter of guidance. (*Rauḍat al-Ṣafā'* of Mīr Khwānd, Lucknow, 1332, vol. II, p. 260.)

12. *Ibn Abi'l-Ḥadīd*, vol. I, p. 58 and pp. 123–135; *Tārīkh-i Yaʿqūbī*, vol. II, p. 102; *Tārīkh-i Ṭabarī*, vol. II, pp. 445–460.

13. *Tārīkh-i Yaʿqūbī*, vol. II, pp. 103–106; *Tārīkh-i Abi'l-Fidā*, vol. I, pp. 156 and 166; *Murūj al-dhahab*, vol. II, pp. 307 and 352; *Ibn Abi'l-Ḥadīd*, vol. I, pp. 17 and 134. In answer to Ibn Abbas's protest Umar said, "I swear to God Ali was the most deserving of all people to become caliph, but for three reasons we pushed him aside: (1) he was too young, (2) he was attached to the descendants of 'Abd al-Muṭṭalib, (3) people did not like to have prophecy and the caliphate assembled in one household." (*Ibn Abi'l-Ḥadīd*, vol. I, p. 134.) Umar said to Ibn Abbas, "I swear to God that Ali deserved the caliphate, but the Quraysh would not have been able to bear his caliphate, for had he become caliph he would have forced the people to accept the pure truth and follow the right path. Under his caliphate they would not have been able to transgress the boundaries of justice and thus would have sought to engage in war with him." (*Tārīkh-i Yaʿqūbī*, vol. II, p. 137.)

14. Umar ibn Ḥarīth said to Saʿīd ibn Zayd, "Did anyone oppose paying allegiance to Abu Bakr?" He answered, "No one was opposed to him except those who had become apostates or were about to become so." *Tārīkh-i Ṭabarī*, vol. II, p. 447.

15. In the famous hadith of *thaqalayn* the Prophet says, "I leave two things of value amidst you in trust which if you hold on to you will never go astray: the Quran and the members of my household; these will never be separated until the Day of Judgment." This hadith has been transmitted through more than a hundred channels by over thirty-five of the companions of the Holy Prophet. (*ʿAbaqāt*, volume on hadith-i thaqalayn; *Ghāyat al-marām*, p. 211.) The Prophet said, "I am the city of knowledge and Ali is its gate. Therefore whosoever seeks knowledge should enter through its door." (*al-Bidāyah wa'l-nihāyah*, vol. VII, p. 359.)

16 *Yaʿqūbī*, vol. II, pp. 105–150, where this is mentioned often.

17. The Book of God and the sayings of the Holy Prophet and his household are replete with encouragement and exhortation to acquire knowledge, to the extent that the Holy Prophet says: "To seek knowledge is incumbent upon every Muslim." *Biḥār al-anwār* of Majlisī, Tehran, 1301–15, vol. I, p. 55.

18. *al-Bidāyah wa'l-nihāyah*, vol. VII, p. 360.

19. *Editor's note:* The Quraysh was the most aristocratic tribe in pre-Islamic Arabia from which rose the Holy Prophet himself. But the Quraysh, being the guardians of the Kaʿbah, first opposed his prophecy and offered the greatest resistance against him. Only later did they surrender to the new religion in which they have always continued to hold a place of honor, especially the branch directly connected with the family of the Prophet.

20. *Tārīkh-i Yaʿqūbī*, pp. 111, 126 and 129.

21. *Editor's note:* The traditions of the Prophet as contained in his sayings are called hadith, while his actions, deeds, words and all that made up the life which has become an example to all Muslims are called sunnah.

22. God says in His Word: "For lo! it is an unassailable Scripture. Falsehood cannot come at it from before it or behind it." (Quran, XLI, 41–42) And He says, "The decision is for Allah only" (Quran, VI, 57, also XII, 40 and 67), meaning the only shariʿah is the Shariʿah and laws of God which must reach man through prophecy. And He says, "but he [Muhammad] is the messenger of Allah and the Seal of the Prophets." (Quran, XXXIII, 40) And He says, "Whoso judgeth not by that which Allah hath revealed: such are the disbelievers." (Quran, V, 44)

23. *Editor's note:* According to Shiʿite sources after the death of the Prophet people gathered in the "covered porch" (*saqīfah*) of Bani Sāʿidah and swore allegiance to Abu Bakr as caliph. As for the hadith of "ink and paper" it refers to the last moments in the life of the Prophet as related above in Note 11.

24. *Editor's note:* The mujtahid is one who through mastery of the religious sciences and the possession of moral qualities has the right to practice ijtihad or the giving of fresh opinion on matters pertaining to the Shariʿah. The right of exercising one's independent judgment based on the principles of the Law, or ijtihad, has ceased in Sunni Islam since the 3rd/9th century whereas the "gate of ijtihad" has been always open in Shiʿite Islam. The leading authorities in the Divine Law are called in Shiʿism *mujtahids*.

25 *Tārīkh-i Yaʿqūbī*, vol. II, p. 110; *Tārīkh-i Abi'l Fidā'*, vol. I, p. 158.

26. *Editor's note:* A religious tax paid to the family of the Prophet which was discontinued in Sunni Islam after his death but continues in Shiʿite Islam to this day.

27. *al-Durr al-manthūr*, vol. III, p. 186; *Tārīkh-i Yaʿqūbī*, vol. III, p. 48. Besides these, the necessity of the khums has been mentioned in the Holy Quran: "And know that whatever ye take of spoils of war, lo! a fifth (khumus) thereof is for Allah, and for the messenger and for kinsmen . . ." (Quran, VIII, 41).

28. During his caliphate Abu Bakr collected five hundred hadiths. A'ishah recounts: "One night I saw my father disturbed until morning. In the morning he told me: 'Bring the hadiths.' Then he set them all on fire." (*Kanz al-ʿummāl* of ʿAlā' al-Dīn Muttaqī, Hyderabad, 1364–75, vol. V, p. 237.) Umar wrote to all cities

stating that whosoever had a hadith should destroy it. (*Kanz al-ʿummāl*, vol. V, p. 237.) Muhammad ibn Abī Bakr says: "During the time of Umar hadiths increased. When they were brought to him he ordered them to be burned." (*Ṭabaqāt Ibn Saʿd*, Beirut, 1376, vol. V, p. 140.)

29. *Editor's note:* The first four caliphs, Abu Bakr, Umar, Uthman, and Ali, are together called the Khulafa rashidun, the rightly guided caliphs, and their period of caliphate is sharply distinguished from that of the Umayyads which followed because the rule of the first four caliphs was strongly religious in character while the Umayyad caliphate was colored by mundane and worldly considerations.

30. *Tārīkh-i Abi'l-Fidā'*, vol. I, p. 151, and other similar sources.

31. *Editor's note:* For the benefit of non-Muslim readers, all dates will be given in both A.H. (Islamic, lunar calendar dating from the Hijrah) and the corresponding A.D. years (13/634-25/644); when a reference is made to a century, we have given first the Islamic century and then the corresponding Christian century: (4th/10th century).

32. *Tārīkh-i Yaʿqūbī*, vol. II, p. 131; *Tārīkh-i Abi'l-Fidā'*, vol. I, p. 160.

33. *Usd al-ghābah* of Ibn Athīr, Cairo, 1280, vol. IV, p. 386; *al-Iṣābah* of Ibn Ḥajar ʿAsqalānī, Cairo, 1323, vol. III.

34. *Tārīkh-i Yaʿqūbī*, vol. II, p. 150; *Abu'l-Fidā'*, vol. I, p. 168; *Tārīkh-i Tabarī*, vol. III, p. 377, etc.

35. *Tārīkh-i Yaʿqūbī*, vol. II, p. 150; *Tārīkh-i Ṭabarī*, vol. III, p. 397.

36. *Tārīkh- Ṭabarī*, vol. III, pp. 402–409; *Tārīkh-i Yaʿqūbī*, vol. II, pp. 150–151.

37. *Tārīkh-i Ṭabarī*, vol. III, p. 377.

38. *Ṣaḥīḥ* of Bukhārī, vol. VI, p. 98; *Tārīkh-i Yaʿqūbī*, vol. II, p. 113.

39. *Yaʿqūbī*, vol. II, p. 111; *Ṭabarī*, vol. III, pp. 129–132.

40. *Editor's note:* The word *ʿilm* means science in its most universal sense, like the Latin *scientia*, and applies to the religious as well as intellectual, rational and philosophical forms of knowledge. Generally it is distinguished from maʿrifah or irfan which is Divine knowledge and may be compared to the Latin *sapientia*. Certain Muslim masters, however, consider ʿilm in its highest sense to stand above irfan since it is a Divine Quality, one of God's Names being *al-ʿAlīm*, He Who knows.

41. *Tārīkh-i Yaʿqūbī*, vol. II, p. 113; *Ibn Abi'l-Ḥadīd*, vol. I, p. 9.

42. *Editor's note:* The title amīr al-mu'minīn, "commander of the faithful," is used in Shiʿism solely for Ali, whereas in Sunni Islam it is a general title conferred upon all the caliphs.

43. *Yaʿqūbī*, vol. II, p. 154.

44. *Yaʿqūbī*, vol. II, p. 155; *Murūj al-dhahab*, vol. II, p. 364.

45. *Editor's note:* Revolutionary in this context does not of course bear the same meaning that it carries generally today. In a traditional context a revolutionary movement is the reestablishment or reapplication of immutable principles of a transcendent order whereas in an anti-traditional context it means rebellion against either these principles or their application or against any established order in general.

46. *Nahj al-balāghah*, the fifteenth sermon.

47. *Murūj al-dhahab*, vol. II, p. 362; *Nahj al-balāghah*, sermon 122; *Yaʿqūbī*, vol. II, p. 160; *Ibn Abi'l-Ḥadīd*, vol. I, p. 180.

48. *Yaʿqūbī*, vol. II, p. 156; *Abu'l-Fidā'*, vol. I, p. 172; *Murūj al-dhahab*, vol. II, p. 366.

49. *Yaʿqūbī*, vol. II, p. 152.

50. *Editor's note:* The *muhājirūn* refers to the early converts to Islam who immigrated with the Prophet to Medina from Mecca.

51. *Yaʿqūbī*, vol. II, p. 154; *Abu'l-Fidā*, vol. I, p. 171.

52. *Yaʿqūbī*, vol. II, p. 152.

53. When Uthman was surrounded by those who had rebelled he wrote to

Muʿawiyah asking for help. Muʿawiyah prepared an army of twelve thousand men and sent them toward Medina. But he asked them to camp around Damascus and came to Uthman himself to report on the readiness of the army. Uthman said, "You have made your army stop on purpose so that I will be killed. Then you will make the spilling of my blood an excuse to revolt yourself." *Yaʿqūbī*, vol. II, p. 152; *Murūj al-dhahab*, vol. III, p. 25; *Ṭabarī*, vol. III, p. 403.

54. *Murūj al-dhahab*, vol. II, p. 415.

55. For instance, see the traditional commentaries which describe the circumstances at the time of the revelation of these verses: "The chiefs among them go about, exhorting: Go and be staunch to your gods!" (Quran, XXXVIII, 7) and "And if We had not made thee wholly firm thou mightest almost have inclined unto them a little" (Quran, XVII, 74 and "Who would have had thee compromise, that they may compromise." (Quran, LXVIII, 9)

56. *Murūj al-dhahab*, vol. II, p. 431; *Ibn Abi'l-Ḥadīd*, vol. I, p. 181.

57. *Abu'l-Fidā'*, vol. I, p. 182; *Ibn Abi'l-Ḥadīd*, vol. I, p. 181.

58. *Nahj al-balāghah* and hadiths found in books of both Sunnis and Shiʿites.

59. *Kitāb al-ghurar wa'l-durar* of Āmidī, Sidon, 1349.

60. Such works as the *Naḥw* (*Grammar*) of Suyūṭī, Tehran, 1281 etc., vol. II, *Ibn Abi'l-Ḥadīd*, vol. I, p. 6.

61. See *Nahj al-balāghah.*

62. Amidst the fighting of the Battle of Jamal a Bedouin asked Ali: "Oh, Commander of the Faithful! You say God is one?" People attacked him from two sides and said: "Don't you see that Ali is worried and his mind occupied with so many diverse matters? Why do you engage in a discussion with him?" Ali told his companions, "Leave this man alone. My goal in fighting with these people is none other than to clarify true doctrines and the ends of religion." Then he set out to answer the Bedouin. *Bihār al-anwār*, vol. II, p. 65.

63. *Ibn Abi'l-Ḥadīd*, vol. I, pp. 6–9.

64. *Yaʿqūbī*, vol. II, p. 191, and other histories.

65. *Yaʿqūbī*, vol. II, p. 192; *Abu'l-Fidā'*, vol. I, p. 183.

66. *al-Nasā'iḥ al-kāfiyah* of Muḥammad al-ʿAlawī, Baghdad, 1368, vol. II, p. 161 and others.

67. *Yaʿqūbī*, vol. II, p. 193.

68. *Yaʿqūbī*, vol. II, p. 207.

69. Yazid was a lecherous and self-indulgent person. He was always drunk and wore silk and unbecoming dress. His nightly parties were combined with music and wine. He had a dog and a monkey which were always with him as companions with which he amused himself. His monkey was named Abū Qays. He would dress him in beautiful attire and make him be present at his drinking parties. Sometimes he would mount him on horseback and send him to races. *Yaʿqūbī*, vol. II, p. 196; *Murūj al-dhahab*, vol. III, p. 77.

70. *Murūj al-dhahab*, vol. III, p. 5; *Abu'l-Fidā'*, vol. I, p. 183.

71. *al-Naṣā'iḥ al-kāfiyah* p. 72, recounted from *Kitāb al-aḥdāth.*

72. *Yaʿqūbī*, vol. II, pp. 199 and 210; *Abu'l-Fidā*, vol. I, p. 186; *Murūj al-dhahab*, vol. III, pp. 33 and 35.

73. *al-Naṣā'ih al-kāfiyah*, pp. 72–73.

74. *al-Naṣā'ih al-kāfiyah*, pp. 58, 64, 77–78.

75. See Quran, IX, 100.

76. *Yaʿqūbī*, vol. II, p. 216; *Abu'l-Fidā'*, vol. I, p. 190; *Murūj al-dhahab*, vol. III, p. 64, and other histories.

77. *Yaʿqūbī*, vol. II, p. 223; *Abu'l-Fidā'*, vol. I, p. 192; *Murūj al-dhahab*, vol. III, p. 78.

78. *Yaʿqūbī*, vol. II, p. 224; *Abu'l-Fidā'*, vol. I, p. 192; *Murūj al-dhahab*, vol. III, p. 81.

79. Walīd ibn Yazīd; mentioned in *Ya'qūbī*, vol. III, p. 73.
80. Walīd ibn Yazīd; mentioned in *Murūj al-dhahab*, vol. III, p. 228.
81. *Muʿjam al-buldān*, Yāqūt Ḥamawī, Beirut, 1957.
82. *Murūj al-dhahab*, vol. III, pp. 217–219; *Yaʿqūbī*, vol. II, p. 66.
83. *Biḥār al-anwār*, vol. XII, and other Shiʿite sources.
84. *Yaʿqūbī*, vol. III, p. 84.
85. *Yaʿqūbī*, vol. III, p. 79; *Abu'l-Fidā'*, vol. I, p. 208, and other histories.
86. *Yaʿqūbī*, vol. III, p. 86; *Murūj al-dhahab*, vol. III, p. 268.
87. *Yaʿqūbī*, vol. III, p. 86; *Murūj al-dhahab*, vol. III, p. 270.
88. *Yaʿqūbī*, vol. III, pp. 91–96; *Abu'l-Fidā'*, vol. I, p. 212.
89. *Abu'l-Fidā'*, vol. II, p. 6.
90. *Yaʿqūbī*, vol. III, p. 198; *Abu'l-Fidā'*, vol. II, p. 33.
91. *Biḥār al-anwār*, vol. XII, on the life of Imam Jaʿfar al-Ṣādiq.
92. *al-Aghānī* of Abu'l-Faraj Iṣfahānī, Cairo 1345–51, the story of the bridge of Baghdad.
93. *al-Aghānī*, the story of Amīn.
94. *Abu'l-Fidā'* and other histories.
95. *al-Ḥaḍārat al-islāmīyah* of Adam Mez, Cairo, 1366, vol. I, p. 97.
96. *Murūj al-dhahab*, vol. IV, p. 373; *al-Milal wa'l-niḥal* of Shahristānī, Cairo, 1368, vol. I, p. 254.
97. *Abu'l-Fidā'*, vol. II, p. 63 and vol. III, p. 50.
98. See the histories *al-Kāmil* of Ibn Athīr, Cairo, 1348; *Rauḍat al-ṣafā'*; and *Ḥabīb al-siyar* of Khwānd Mīr, Tehran, 1333.
99. *Ibid.*
100. *Ibid.*
101. *Ibid.*
102. *Rayḥānat al-adab* of Muḥammad ʿAlī Tabrīzī, Tehran 1326–32, vol. II, p. 365, and most works on the biography of famous men.
103. *Rayḥānat al-adab*, vol. II, p. 380.
104. *Rauḍat al-ṣafā'*, *Ḥabīb al-siyar* and others.
105. *Tārīkh-i ʿālam ārāy-i ʿabbāsī* of Iskandar Bayk, Tehran, 1334 A.H. solar.

CHAPTER II DIVISIONS WITHIN SHI'ISM

Each religion possesses a certain number of primary principles which form its essential basis and other principles of secondary importance. When the followers of a religion differ as to the nature of the primary principles and their secondary aspects but preserve a common basis, the result is called division (*inshi'āb*) within that religion. Such divisions exist in all traditions and religions, and more particularly in the four "revealed" religions[1] of Judaism, Christianity, Zoroastrianism, and Islam.

Shi'ism did not undergo any divisions during the imamate of the first three Imams: Ali, Hasan, and Husayn. But after the martyrdom of Husayn, the majority of the Shi'ites accepted the imamate of Ali ibn Husayn al-Sajjād, while a minority known as the Kīsānīyah believed that the third son of Ali, Muhammad ibn Ḥanafīyah, was the fourth Imam as well as the promised Mahdi, and that he had gone into occultation in the Raḍwā mountains[2] and one day would reappear. After the death of Imam al-Sajjad the majority of the Shi'ites accepted as Imam his son, Muhammad al-Bāqir, while a minority followed Zayd al-Shahīd, another son of Imam al-Sajjad, and became known as Zaydis. Following Imam Muhammad al-Bāqir, the Shi'ites accepted his son Ja'far al-Sadiq as Imam and after the death of Imam Ja'far the majority followed his son Imam Mūsā al-Kāẓim as the seventh Imam. However, one group followed the older son of the sixth Imam, Isma'il, who had died while his father was still alive, and when this latter group separated from the majority of Shi'ites it became known as Isma'ilis. Others accepted as Imam either 'Abdallāh al-Aftaḥ or Muhammad, both sons of the sixth Imam. Finally, another party stopped with the sixth Imam himself and considered him as the last Imam. In the same way, after the martyrdom of Imam Musa al-Kazim the majority followed his son, Ali al-Riḍā, as the eighth Imam. However, some stopped with the seventh Imam and became known as the Wāqifīyah.[3]

From the eighth Imam to the twelfth, whom the majority of the Shiʿites believe to be the promised Mahdi, no division of any importance took place within Shiʿism. Even if certain events occured in the form of division, they lasted but a few days and dissolved by themselves. For example, Jaʿfar, the son of the tenth Imam, claimed to be Imam after the death of his brother, the eleventh Imam. A group of people followed him but scattered in a few days and Jaʿfar himself did not follow his claim any further. Furthermore, there are differences between Shiʿites in theological and juridical matters which must not be considered as divisions in religious schools. Also the Babi and Bahaʿi sects, which like the Batinis (the Qarāmiṭah) differ in both the principles (uṣūl) and branches (*furūʿ*) of Islam from the Muslims, should not in any sense be considered as branches of Shiʿism.

The sects which separated from the majority of Shiʿites all dissolved within a short period, except two: the Zaydi and the Ismaʿili which continue to exist until now. To this day communities of these branches are active in various parts of the world such as the Yemen, India, and Syria. Therefore, we shall limit our discussion to these two branches along with the majority of Shiʿites who are Twelvers.

Zaydism and Its Branches

The Zaydis are the followers of Zayd al-Shahid, the son of Imam al-Sajjad. Zayd rebelled in 121/737 against the Umayyad caliph Hishām ʿAbd al-Malik and a group paid allegiance to him. A battle ensued in Kufa between Zayd and the army of the caliph in which Zayd was killed.

The followers of Zayd regard him as the fifth Imam of the Household of the Prophet. After him his son, Yaḥyā ibn Zayd, who rebelled against the caliph Walīd ibn Yazīd and was also killed, took his place. After Yahya, Muḥammad ibn ʿAbdallāh and Ibrāhīm ibn ʿAbdallāh, who revolted against the Abbasid caliph Manṣūr al-Dawānīqī and were also killed, were chosen as Imams.

Henceforth for some time there was disorder in Zaydi ranks until Nāṣir al-Uṭrūsh, a descendant of the brother of Zayd, arose in Khurasan. Being pursued by the governmental authorities in that region, he fled to Mazandaran (Tabaristan) whose people had not as yet accepted Islam. After thirteen years of missionary activity in this region he brought a large number of people into the Zaydi branch of Islam. Then in the year 301/913 with their aid he conquered the region of Mazandaran, becoming himself Imam. For some time his descendants continued to rule as Imams in that area.

According to Zaydi belief any descendant of Fatimah (the daughter of the Prophet) who begins an uprising in the name of defending the truth may become Imam if he is learned in the religious sciences, ethically pure, courageous and generous. Yet for some time after Utrush and his descendants there was no Imam who could bring about an insurrection with the sword until recently when, about sixty years ago, Imam Yaḥyā revolted in the Yemen, which had been a part of the Ottoman Empire, made it independent, and began to rule there as Imam. His descendants continued to rule in that region as Imams until very recently.

At the beginning the Zaydis, like Zayd himself, considered the first two caliphs, Abu Bakr and Umar, as their Imams. But after a while some of them began to delete the name of the first two caliphs from the list of Imams and placed Ali as the first Imam.

From what is known of Zaydi beliefs it can be said that in the principles of Islam (usul) they follow a path close to that of the Muʿtazilites, while in the branches or derivative institutions of the law (furuʿ) they apply the jurisprudence of Abu Hanifah, the founder of one of the four Sunni schools of law. They also differ among themselves concerning certain problems.[4]

Ismaʿilism and Its Branches

Imam Jaʿfar al-Sadiq had a son named Ismaʿil who was the oldest of his children. Ismaʿil died during the lifetime of his father who summoned witnesses to his death, including the governor of Medina.[5] Concerning this question, some believed that Ismaʿil did not die but went into occultation, that he would appear again and would be the promised Mahdi. They further believed that the summoning of witnesses on the part of the Imam for Ismaʿil's death was a way of hiding the truth in fear of al-Mansur, the Abbasid caliph. Another group believed that the true Imam was Ismaʿil whose death meant the imamate was transferred to his son Muhammad. A third group also held that although he died during the lifetime of his father he was the Imam and that the imamate passed after him to Muhammad ibn Ismaʿil and his descendants. The first two groups soon became extinct, while the third branch continues to exist to this day and has undergone a certain amount of division.

The Ismaʿilis have a philosophy in many ways similar to that of the Sabaeans (star worshippers)[6] combined with elements of Hindu gnosis. In the sciences and decrees of Islam they believe that each exterior reality (zahir) has an inner aspect (batin) and each element of revelation (*tanzīl*) a hermeneutic and esoteric exegesis (ta'wil).[7]

The Ismaʿilis believe that the earth can never exist without a Proof (*ḥujjah*) of God. The Proof is of two kinds: "speaker" (*nāṭiq*) and "silent one" (*ṣāmit*). The speaker is a prophet and the silent one is an Imam or Guardian (wali) who is the inheritor, or executor of the testament (wasi) of a prophet. In any case the Proof of God is the perfect theophany of the Divinity.

The principle of the Proof of God revolves constantly around the number seven. A prophet (*nabī*), who is sent by God, has the function of prophecy (*nubuwwat*), of bringing a Divine Law or Shariʿah. A prophet, who is the perfect manifestation of God, has the esoteric power of initiating men into the Divine Mysteries (walayat).[8] After him there are seven executors of his testament (wasi) who possess the power of executing his testament (waṣāyat) and the power of esoteric initiation into the Divine Mysteries (walayat). The seventh in the succession possesses those two powers and also the additional power of prophecy (nubuwwat). The cycle of seven executors (wasis) is then repeated with the seventh a prophet.

The Ismaʿilis say that Adam was sent as a prophet with the power of prophecy and of esoteric guidance and he had seven executors of whom the seventh was Noah, who had the three functions of nubuwwat, wasayat, and walayat. Abraham was the seventh executor (wasi) of Noah, Moses the seventh executor of Abraham, Jesus the seventh executor of Moses, Muhammad the seventh executor of Jesus, and Muhammad ibn Ismaʿil the seventh executor of Muhammad.

They consider the wasis of the Prophet to be: Ali, Husayn ibn Ali (they do not consider Imam Hasan among the Imams), Ali ibn Husayn al-Sajjad, Muhammad al-Baqir, Jaʿfar al-Sadiq, Ismaʿil ibn Jaʿfar, and Muhammad ibn Ismaʿil. After this series there are seven descendants of Muhammad ibn Ismaʿil whose names are hidden and secret. After them there are the first seven rulers of the Fatimid caliphate of Egypt the first of whom, ʿUbaydallāh al-Mahdī, was the founder of the Fatimid dynasty. The Ismaʿilis also believe that in addition to the Proof of God there are always present on earth twelve "chiefs" (*naqīb*) who are the companions and elite followers of the Proof. Some of the branches of the Batinis, however, like the Druzes, believe six of the "chiefs" to be from the Imams and six from others.

The Batinis

In the year 278/891, a few years before the appearance of Ubaydallah al-Mahdi in North Africa, there appeared in Kufa an unknown person from Khuzistan (in southern Persia) who never revealed his name and identity. He would fast during the day and worship at night and made a living from his own labor. In addition he invited people to join the Ismaʿili cause and was able to assemble a large number of people about him. From among them he chose twelve "chiefs" (naqib) and then he set out for Damascus. Having left Kufa he was never heard of again.

This unknown man was replaced by Aḥmad, known as the Qaramite, who began to propagate Batini teachings in Iraq. As the historians have recorded, he instituted two daily prayers in place of the five of Islam, removed the necessity of ablution after sexual intercourse, and made the drinking of wine permissible. Contemporary with these events, other Batini leaders rose to invite people to join their cause and assembled a group of followers.

The Batinis had no respect for the lives and possessions of those who were outside their group. For this reason they began uprisings in the cities of Iraq, Bahrain, the Yemen, and Syria, spilling the blood of people and looting their wealth. Many times they stopped the caravans of those who were making the pilgrimage to Mecca, killing tens of thousands of pilgrims and plundering their provisions and camels.

Abū Ṭāhir al-Qarmaṭī, one of the Qaramite leaders who in 311/923 had conquered Basra and did not neglect to kill and plunder, set out with a large number of Batinis for Mecca in 317/929. After overcoming the brief resistance of government troops he entered the city and massacred the population as well as the newly arrived pilgrims. Even within the Masjid al-ḥarām (the mosque containing the Kaʿbah) and within the Holy Kaʿbah itself, there flowed streams of blood. He divided the covering of the Kaʿbah between his disciples. He tore away the door of the Kaʿbah and took the black stone from its place back to the Yemen. For twenty-two years the black stone was in Qaramite hands. As a result of these actions the majority of Muslims turned completely away from the Batinis and considered them outside the pale of Islam. Even ʿUbaydallāh al-Mahdi, the Fatimid ruler, who had risen in those days in North Africa and considered himself the promised Mahdi, abhorred them.

According to the view of historians the distinguishing characteristic of the Batini school is that it interprets the external aspects of Islam in an esoteric manner and considers the externals of the Shariʿah to be only for simple-minded people of little intelligence who are deprived of spiritual perfection. Yet occasionally the Batini Imams did order certain regulations and laws to be practiced and followed.

The Nizaris, Mustaʿlis, Druzes and Muqannaʿah

The Nizaris. Ubaydallah al-Mahdi, who rose in North Africa in 292/904 and as an Ismaʿili declared his imamate and established Fatimid rule, is the founder of the dynasty whose descendants made Cairo the center of their caliphate. For seven generations this sultanate and Ismaʿili imamate continued without any divisions. At the death of the seventh Imam, al-Mustanṣir bi'llah Muʿidd ibn Ali, his sons, Nizār and al-Mustaʿlī, began to dispute over the caliphate and imamate. After long disputes and bloody battles al-Mustaʿli was victorious. He captured his brother Nizar and placed him in prison, where he died.

Following this dispute those who accepted the Fatimids divided into two groups: the Nizaris and the Mustaʿlis. The Nizaris are the followers of Hasan al-Ṣabbāḥ who was one of the close associates of al-Mustansir. After Nizar's death, because of his support of Nizar, Hasan al-Sabbah was expelled from Egypt by al-Mustaʿli. He came to Persia and after a short while appeared in the Fort of Alamut near Qazwin. He conquered Alamut and several surrounding forts. There he established his rule and also began to invite people to the Ismaʿili cause.

After the death of Hasan in 518/1124 Buzurg Umīd Rūdbārī and after him his son, Kiyā Muhammad, continued to rule following the methods and ways of Hasan al-Sabbah. After Kiya Muhammad, his son Hasan ʿAlā Dhikrihu'l-Salām, the fourth ruler of Alamut, changed the ways of Hasan al-Sabbah, who had been Nizari, and became Batini. Henceforth the Ismaʿili forts continued as Batini. Four other rulers, Muhammad ibn Ala Dhikruhu'l-Salām, Jalāl al-Dīn Hasan, ʿAlā' al-Dīn, and Rukn al-Dīn Khurshāh, became Sultan and Imam one after another until Hulāgū, the Mongol conqueror, invaded Persia. He captured the Ismaʿili forts and put all the Ismaʿilis to death, leveling their forts to the ground.

Centuries later, in 1255/1839, the Āqā Khān of Mahalat in Persia, who belonged to the Nizaris, rebelled against Muḥammad

Shāh Qājār in Kerman, but he was defeated and fled to Bombay. There he propagated his Batini-Nizari cause which continues to this day. The Nizaris are today called the Aqa Khanids.

The Mustaʿlis. The Mustaʿlis were the followers of al-Mustaʿli. Their imamate continued during Fatimid rule in Egypt until it was brought to an end in the year 567/1171. Shortly thereafter, the Bohra sect, following the same school, appeared in India and survives to this day.

The Druzes. The Druzes, who live in the Druze mountains in Syria (and also in Lebanon), were originally followers of the Fatimid caliphs. But as a result of the missionary activity of Nashtakīn, the Druzes joined the Batini sect. The Druzes stop with the sixth Fatimid caliph al-Ḥākim bi'llāh, whom others believe to have been killed, and claim that he is in occultation. He has ascended to heaven and will appear once again to the world.

The Muqannaʿah. The Muqannaʿah were at first disciples of ʿAtā' al-Marwī known as Muqannaʿ, who according to historical sources was a follower of Abū Muslim of Khurasan. After the death of Abu Muslim, Muqannaʿ claimed that Abu Muslim's soul had become incarnated in him. Soon he claimed to be a prophet and later a divinity. Finally, in the year 162/777 he was surrounded in the fort of Kabash in Transoxiana. When he became certain that he would be captured and killed, he threw himself into a fire along with some of his disciples and burned to death. His followers soon adopted Ismaʿilism and the ways of the Batinis.

Differences Between Twelve-Imam Shiʿism and Ismaʿilism and Zaydism

The majority of the Shiʿites, from whom the previously mentioned groups have branched out, are Twelve-Imam Shiʿites, also called the Imamites. As has already been mentioned, the Shiʿites came into being because of criticism and protest concerning two basic problems of Islam, without having any objections to the religious ways which through the instructions of the Prophet had become prevalent among their contemporary Muslims. These two problems concerned Islamic government and authority in the religious sciences, both of which the Shi'ites considered to be the particular right of the Household of the Prophet.

The Shi'ites asserted that the Islamic caliphate, of which esoteric guidance and spiritual leadership are inseparable elements, belongs to Ali and his descendants. They also believed that according to the specification of the Prophet the Imams of the Household of the Prophet are twelve in number. Shi'ism held, moreover, that the external teachings of the Quran, which are the injunctions and regulations of the Shari'ah and include the principles of a complete spiritual life, are valid and applicable for everyone at all times, and are not to be abrogated until the Day of Judgment. These injunctions and regulations must be learned through the guidance of the Household of the Prophet.

From a consideration of these points it becomes clear that the difference between Twelve-Imam Shi'ism and Zaydism is that the Zaydis usually do not consider the imamate to belong solely to the Household of the Prophet and do not limit the number of Imams to twelve. Also they do not follow the jurisprudence of the Household of the Prophet as do the Twelve-Imam Shi'ites.

The difference between Twelve-Imam Shi'ism and Isma'ilism lies in that for the latter the imamate revolves around the number seven and prophecy does not terminate with the Holy Prophet Muhammad. Also for them, change and transformation in the injunctions of the Shari'ah are admissible, as is even rejection of the duty of following the Shari'ah, especially among the Batinis. In contrast, the Twelve-Imam Shi'ites consider the Prophet to be the "seal of prophecy" and believe him to have twelve successors and executors of his will. They hold the external aspect of the Shari'ah to be valid and impossible to abrogate. They affirm that the Quran has both an exoteric and an esoteric aspect.

Summary of the History of Twelve-Imam Shi'ism

As has become clear from the previous pages, the majority of Shi'ites are Twelvers. They were originally the same group of friends and supporters of Ali who, after the death of the Prophet, in order to defend the right of the Household of the Prophet in the question of the caliphate and religious authority, began to criticize and protest against prevalent views and separated from the majority of the people.

During the caliphate of the "rightly-guided caliphs" (11/632-35/656) the Shiʿites were under a certain amount of pressure which became much greater during the Umayyad Caliphate (40/661-132/750) when they were no longer protected in any way against destruction of their lives and property. Yet the greater the pressure placed upon them, the firmer they became in their belief. They especially benefited from their being oppressed in spreading their beliefs and teachings.

From the middle of the 2nd/8th century when the Abbasid caliphs established their dynasty, Shiʿism was able to gain a new life as a result of the languid and weak state prevailing at that time. Soon, however, conditions became difficult once again and until the end of the 3rd/9th century became ever more stringent.

At the beginning of the 4th/10th century, with the rise of the influential Buyids, who were Shiʿites, Shiʿism gained power and became more or less free to carry out its activities. It began to carry out scientific and scholarly debates and continued in this manner until the end of the 5th/11th century. At the beginning of the 7th/13th century when the Mongol invasion began, as a result of the general involvement in war and chaos and the continuation of the Crusades, the different Islamic governments did not put too great a pressure upon the Shiʿites. Moreover, the conversion to Shiʿism of some Mongol rulers in Persia and the rule of the Sādāt-i Marʿashī (who were Shiʿites) in Mazandaran were instrumental in the spread of the power and territory of Shiʿism. They made the presence of large concentrations of Shiʿite population in Persia and other Muslim lands felt more than ever before. This situation continued through the 9th/15th century.

At the beginning of the 10th/16th century, as a result of the rise of the Safavids, Shiʿism became the official religion of the vast territories of Persia and continues in this position to the present day. In other regions of the world also there are tens of millions of Shiʿites.

NOTES

CHAPTER II

1. *Editor's note:* From the general theological perspective of Islam the "revealed religions" are those possessing Divine Scriptures and usually numbered as above. This does not, however, prevent Muslims from believing in the universality of revelation, which is particularly accented in Sufism. Whenever the situation arose, Muslims applied this principle outside the Semitic and Iranian monotheistic worlds, as for example when they encountered Hinduism whose divine origin many Muslim religious authorities admitted openly.

2. *Editor's note:* The Radwa mountains are a range located near Medina and well known for the role they played in early Islamic history.

3. *Editor's note:* It must be remembered that most of the branches cited here had very few adherents and are not in any way comparable to Twelve-Imam Shiʿism or Ismaʿilism.

4. The material of this section is based on *al-Milal wa'l-niḥal* and the *Kāmil* of Ibn Athīr.

5. The material of this section is taken from the *Kāmil, Rauḍat al-ṣafā', Ḥabib al-siyar, Abu'l-Fidā', al-Milal wa'l-niḥal*, and some of its details from *Tārīkh-i Āqā Khānīyah* of Maṭbaʿī, Najaf, 1351.

6. *Editor's note:* Here Sabaean refers to the people of Harran who had a religion in which stars played a major role. Moreover, they were the depository of Hermetic and Neopythagorean philosophy and played an important role in the transmission to Islam of the more esoteric schools of Hellenistic philosophy as well as astronomy and mathematics. They became extinct during the first few centuries of Islamic history and must not be confused with the Sabaeans or Mandeans of Southern Iraq and Persia who still survive.

7. *Editor's note:* The term "ta'wīl," which plays a cardinal role in Shiʿism as well as Sufism, means literally to return to the origin of a thing. It means to penetrate the external aspect of any reality, whether it be sacred scripture or phenomena of nature, to its inner essence, to go from the phenomenon to the noumenon.

8. *Editor's note:* The term "wali" in Islam means saint and wilayah as usually employed, particularly in Sufism, means sanctity. But in the context of Shiʿism, wilayah (usually pronounced walayat) means the esoteric power of the Imam whereby he is able to initiate men into the Divine Mysteries and provide for them the key to attaining sanctity. The use of the two terms, therefore, is related, since on the one hand it pertains to the saintly life and on the other to the particular esoteric power of the Imam which leads men to the saintly life. In the case of the Imam it also has other cosmic and social connotations usually not identified with wilayah in the general sense of sanctity.

PART II: SHI'ITE RELIGIOUS THOUGHT

CHAPTER III THREE METHODS OF RELIGIOUS THOUGHT

By "religious thought" we mean that form of thought which is concerned with any of the problems of a religious nature within a particular religion, in the same sense that mathematical thought is the form of thought which deals with mathematical questions and solves mathematical problems.

Needless to say religious thought, like other forms of thought, must have reliable sources from which the raw material of its thought originates and upon which it depends. Similarly, the process of reasoning necessary for the solution of mathematical problems must have a series of established mathematical facts and principles.

The single source upon which the divinely revealed religion of Islam depends and upon which it is based, inasmuch as it is based on a revelation of celestial origin, is none other than the Holy Quran. It is the Quran which is the definitive testament of the universal and ever-living prophethood of the Prophet and it is the content of the Quran that bears the substance of the Islamic call. Of course the fact that the Quran is alone the source of Islamic religious thought does not eliminate other sources and origins of correct thinking, as will be explained later.

There are three methods of religious thought in Islam. The Holy Quran in its teachings points to three paths for Muslims to follow in order to comprehend the purposes of religion and the Islamic sciences: (1) the path of the external and formal aspect of religion (the Shari'ah); (2) the path of intellectual understanding; and (3) the path of spiritual comprehension achieved through sincerity (*ikhlāṣ*) in obeying God.

It can be seen that the Holy Quran in its formal aspect addresses all people without providing any demonstration or proof. Rather, depending on the unique sovereignty of God, it commands people to accept the principles of faith such as divine unity, prophethood, eschatology; it gives them practical injunctions such as the daily prayers, fasting, etc.; and at the same time it prohibits them from committing certain other actions. Yet if the Quran had not provided authority for these commands it would never have expected man to accept and obey them. It must, therefore, be said that such simple utterances of the Quran are a path toward the understanding of ultimate religious ends and the comprehension of the Islamic sciences. We call such verbal expressions as "Believe in God and His Prophet" and "Perform the prayers," the external or formal aspect of religion.

In addition to guidance in the external aspect of religion, we see that the Holy Quran in many verses guides man toward intellectual understanding. It invites man to meditate, contemplate and deliberate upon the signs of God in the macrocosm and the microcosm. It explains many verities through unfettered intellectual reasoning. It must be said in truth that no sacred book praises and recommends science and intellectual knowledge for man as much as does the Quran. In many of its words and utterances the Quran attests to the validity of intellectual proof and rational demonstration, that is, it does not claim that man should first accept the validity of the Islamic sciences and then through intellectual proofs justify these sciences. Rather, with complete confidence in the truth of its own position it proclaims that man should use his intellect to discover the truth of the Islamic sciences, and only then accept this truth. He should seek the affirmation of the words contained in the Islamic message in the world of creation which is itself a truthful witness. And finally man should find the affirmation of his faith in the results of rational demonstration; he should not have to gain faith first and then, in obedience to it, seek proofs. Thus philosophical thought is also a way whose validity and efficacy is confirmed by the Holy Quran.[1]

Also, in addition to guidance in the external and intellectual aspects of religion, we see that the Holy Quran in subtle terms explains that all true religious science originates and comes from

Divine Unity (tawhid) and the knowledge of God and His Attributes. The perfection of the knowledge of God belongs to those whom He has drawn from all places and elevated solely to Himself. It is these men who have forgotten themselves and all things and as a result of sincerity in obedience to God have been able to concentrate all their powers and energies upon the transcendent world. Their eyes have become illuminated through the vision of the light of the Pure Creator. With the eye of discernment they have seen the reality of things in the kingdom of heaven and earth, for through sincerity of obedience they have reached the station of certainty (*yaqīn*). As a result of this certainty the kingdoms of heaven and earth and the immortal life of the eternal world have become revealed to them.

Deliberation upon the following holy verses illuminates fully this claim: "And We sent no messenger before thee but We inspired him (saying): There is no God save Me (Allah), so worship Me" (Quran, XXI, 25);[2] and, "Glorified be Allah from that which they attribute (unto Him), Save single-minded slaves of Allah" (Quran, XXXVII, 159–160);[3] and, "Say, I am only a mortal like you. My Lord inspireth in me that your God is only One God. And whoever hopeth for the meeting with his Lord, let him do righteous work, and make none sharer of the worship due unto his Lord" (Quran, XVIII, 111);[4] and, "And serve the Lord till the inevitable [al-yaqin] cometh unto thee" (Quran, XV, 99);[5] and God says, "Thus did We show Abraham the Kingdom of the heavens and the earth that he might be of those possessing certainty" (Quran, VI, 76);[6] and "Nay, but the record of the righteous is in 'Iliyīn—Ah! what will convey unto thee what 'Iliyīn is! —A written record, attested by those who are brought near (unto their Lord)" (Quran, LXXXIII, 18–21);[7] and, "Nay, would that ye knew (now) with a sure knowledge ['ilm al-yaqin]! For ye will behold hellfire" (Quran, XII, 5–6).[8]

Thus it may be said that one of the paths for the comprehension of religious verities and sciences is the purification of the carnal soul and sincerity in obedience to God.

From what has been said it becomes clear that the Holy Quran proposes three methods for the comprehension of religious truths: the external, or formal aspects of religion; intellectual reasoning;

and sincerity in obedience leading to the intellectual intuition which results in the unveiling of the truth and its inward vision. Yet it must be understood that these three methods differ from each other in several ways. For instance, since the external forms of religion are verbal expressions in the simplest language, they are in the hands of all people, and everyone benefits from them according to his own capacity.[9] On the other hand, the other two paths, which are appropriate to a particular group (the elite—*khawāṣṣ*), are not common to all. The path of the external forms of religion leads to the understanding of the principles and the obligations of Islam and results in knowledge of the substance of the beliefs and practices of Islam, and of the principles of the Islamic sciences, ethics, and jurisprudence. This is in contrast to the other two paths. The intellectual path can discover the problems connected with faith, ethics, and the general principles governing practical questions, but the intellectual method cannot discover the specific religious injunctions given in the Quran and the Sunnah. The path of purification of the carnal soul, since it leads to the discovery of God-given spiritual truths, can have no limits nor measure of its results or of the truths revealed through this divine gift. Men who have reached this knowledge have cut themselves off from everything and forgotten everything but God and are under the direct guidance and dominion of God Himself—May His Name be Glorified. Whatever He wants and not what they want is revealed to them.

We will now take up in detail the three methods of religious thought in Islam.

FIRST METHOD: THE FORMAL ASPECT OF RELIGION

The Different Facets of the Formal Aspect of Religion

It has become clear from what has been said thus far that the Holy Quran, which is the principal source of religious thought in

Islam, has given full authority to the external meanings of its words for those who give ear to its message. The same external meaning of the Quranic verses has made the sayings of the Prophet complementary to the words of the Quran and has declared them to be authoritative like the Quran. For as the Quran says: "And We have revealed unto thee the Remembrance that thou mayst explain to mankind that which hath been revealed for them" (Quran, XVI, 44). And, "He it is who hath sent among the unlettered ones a messenger of their own, to recite unto them His revelations and to make them grow, and to teach them the scripture and Wisdom" (Quran, LXII, 2). And, "And whatsoever the messenger giveth you, take it. And whatsoever he forbiddeth, abstain (from it)" (Quran, LIX, 7). And, "Verily in the messenger of Allah ye have a good example" (Quran, XXXIII, 21).

It is quite evident that such verses would not have any real meaning if the words and deeds of the Prophet and even his silence and approval were not authority for us just as the Quran itself is. Thus the words of the Prophet are authoritative and must be accepted by those who have heard them orally or received them through reliable transmission. Moreover, through such a completely authentic chain of transmission it is known that the Holy Prophet said, "I leave two things of value amidst you in trust which if you hold on to you will never go astray: the Quran and the members of my household. These will never be separated until the Day of Judgment."[10] According to this and other definitely established hadiths the words of the Family and Household of the Prophet form a corpus that is complementary to the Prophetic hadith. The Household of the Prophet in Islam have authority in religious sciences and are inerrant in the explanation of the teachings and injunctions of Islam. Their sayings, received orally or through reliable transmission, are reliable and authoritative.

Therefore, it is clear that the traditional source from which the formal and external aspect of religion is derived, which is an authoritative document and which is also the basic source for the religious thought of Islam, consists of two parts: The Book (the Quran) and the Sunnah. By the Book is meant the external aspect of the verses of the Holy Quran; and by the Sunnah, hadith received from the Prophet and his revered Household.

Traditions of the Companions

In Shi'ism hadiths transmitted through the companions are dealt with according to this principle: if they deal with the words and actions of the Prophet and do not contradict the hadiths of the Household of the Prophet, they are acceptable. If they contain only the views or opinions of the companions themselves and not those of the Prophet, they are not authoritative as sources for religious injunctions. In this respect the ruling of the companions is like the ruling of any other Muslim. In the same way, the companions themselves dealt with other companions in questions of Islamic law as they would with any Muslim, not as someone special.

The Book and Tradition

The Book of God, the Holy Quran, is the principal source of every form of Islamic thought. It is the Quran which gives religious validity and authority to every other religious source in Islam. Therefore, it must be comprehensible to all. Moreover, the Quran describes itself as the light which illuminates all things. Also it challenges men and requests them to ponder over its verses and observe that there are no disparities or contradictions in them. It invites them to compose a similar work, if they can, to replace it. It is clear that if the Holy Quran were not comprehensible to all there would be no place for such assertions.

To say that the Quran is in itself comprehensible to all is not in any way contradictory to the previous assertion that the Prophet and his Household are religious authorities in the Islamic sciences, which sciences in reality are only elaborations of the content of the Quran. For instance, in the part of the Islamic sciences which comprises the injunctions and laws of the Shari'ah, the Quran contains only the general principles. The clarification and elaboration of their details, such as the manner of accomplishing the daily prayers, fasting, exchanging merchandise, and in fact all acts of worship (*'ibādāt*) and transactions (*mu'āmalāt*), can be achieved only by referring to the traditions of the Holy Prophet and his Household.

As for the other part of the Islamic sciences dealing with doctrines and ethical methods and practices, although their content and details can be comprehended by all, the understanding of their full meaning depends on accepting the method of the Household of the Prophet. Also each verse of the Quran must be explained and interpreted by means of other Quranic verses, not by views which have become acceptable and familiar to us only through habit and custom.

Ali has said: "Some parts of the Quran speak with other parts of it revealing to us their meaning and some parts attest to the meaning of others."[11] And the Prophet has said, "Parts of the Quran verify other parts."[12] And also: "Whosoever interprets the Quran according to his own opinion has made a place for himself in the fire."[13]

As a simple example of the commentary of the Quran through the Quran may be cited the story of the torture of the people of Lot about whom in one place God says, "And we rained on them a rain,"[14] and in another place He has changed this phrase to, "Lo! We sent a storm of stones upon them (all)."[15] By relating the second verse to the first it becomes clear that by "rain" is meant "stones" from heaven. Whoever has studied with care the hadiths of the Household of the Prophet, and the outstanding companions who were the followers of the Prophet, will have no doubt that the commentary of the Quran through the Quran is the sole method of Quranic commentary taught by the Household of the Prophet.[16]

The Outward and Inward Aspects of the Quran

It has been explained that the Holy Quran elucidates religious aims through its own words and gives commands to mankind in matters of doctrine and action. But the meaning of the Quran is not limited to this level. Rather, behind these same expressions and within these same meanings there are deeper and wider levels of meaning which only the spiritual elite who possess pure hearts can comprehend.

The Prophet, who is the divinely appointed teacher of the Quran, says:[17] "The Quran has a beautiful exterior and a profound interior." He has also said, "The Quran has an inner dimension, and that inner dimension has an inner dimension up to seven inner dimensions."[18] Also, in the sayings of the Imams there are numerous references to the inner aspect of the Quran.

The main support of these assertions is a symbol which God has mentioned in Chapter XIII, verse 17, of the Quran. In this verse divine gifts are symbolized by rain that falls from heaven and upon which depends the life of the earth and its inhabitants. With the coming of the rain, floods begin to flow and each river bed accepts a certain amount of the flood, depending on its capacity. As it flows, the flood is covered with foam, but beneath the foam there is that same water which is life-giving and beneficial to mankind.

As is indicated by this symbolic story, the capacity for comprehension of divine sciences, which are the source of man's inner life, differs among people. There are those for whom there is no reality beyond physical existence and the material life of this world which lasts but a few days. Such people are attached to material appetites and physical desires alone and fear nothing but the loss of material benefits and sensory enjoyment. Such people, taking into consideration the differences of degree among them, can at best accept the divine sciences on the level of believing in a summary fashion in the doctrines and performing the practical commands of Islam in a purely outward manner without any comprehension. They worship God with the hope of recompense or fear of punishment in the next world.

There are also those who, because of the purity of their nature, do not consider their well-being to lie in attachment to the transient pleasures of the fleeting life of this world. The losses and gains and bitter and sweet experiences of this world are for them no more than an attractive illusion. Memory of those who have passed before them in the caravan of existence, who were pleasure-seekers yesterday and no more than subjects of stories today, is a warning that is continuously present before their eyes. Such men who possess pure hearts are naturally attracted to the world of eternity. They view the different phenomena of this passing world as symbols and portents of the higher world, not as persisting and independent realities.

It is at this point that through earthly and heavenly signs, signs upon the horizons and within the souls of men,[19] they "observe" in a spiritual vision the Infinite Light of the Majesty and Glory of God. Their hearts become completely enamored with the longing to reach an understanding of the secret symbols of creation. Instead of being imprisoned in the dark and narrow well of personal gain and selfishness they begin to fly in the unlimited space of the world of eternity and advance ever onwards toward the zenith of the spiritual world.

When they hear that God has forbidden the worship of idols, which outwardly means bowing down before an idol, they understand this command to mean that they should not obey other than God, for to obey means to bow down before someone and to serve him. Beyond that meaning they understand that they should not have hope or fear of other than God; beyond that, they should not surrender to the demands of their selfish appetites; and beyond that, that they should not concentrate on anything except God, May His Name be Glorified.

Likewise when they hear from the Quran that they should pray, the external meaning of which is to perform the particular rites of prayers, through its inner meaning they comprehend that they must worship and obey God with all their hearts and souls. Beyond that they comprehend that before God they must consider themselves as nothing, must forget themselves and remember only God.[20]

It can be seen that the inner meaning present in these two examples is not due to the outward expression of the command and prohibition in question. Yet the comprehension of this meaning is unavoidable for anyone who has begun to meditate upon a more universal order and has preferred to gain a vision of the universe of reality rather than his own ego, who has preferred objectivity to an egocentric subjectivism.

From this discussion the meaning of the outward and inward aspects of the Quran has become clear. It has also become evident that the inner meaning of the Quran does not eradicate or invalidate its outward meaning. Rather, it is like the soul which gives life to the body. Islam, which is a universal and eternal religion and places the greatest emphasis upon the "reformation" of mankind, can never dispense with its external laws which are for the benefit of society, nor with its simple doctrines which are the guardians and preservers of these laws.

How can a society, on the pretense that religion is only a matter of the heart, that man's heart should be pure and that there is no value to actions, live in disorder and yet attain happiness? How can impure deeds and words cause the cultivation of a pure heart? Or how can impure words emanate from a pure heart? God says in His Book, "Vile women are for vile men, and vile men for vile women. Good women are for good men, and good men for good women." (Quran, XXIV, 26) He also says, "As for the good land, its vegetation cometh forth by permission of its Lord; while as for that which is bad, only evil cometh forth (from it)." (Quran, VII, 58) Thus it becomes evident that the Holy Quran has an outward and an inward aspect and the inward aspect itself has different levels of meaning. The hadith literature, which explains the content of the Quran, also contains these various aspects.

The Principles of Interpretation of the Quran

At the beginning of Islam it was commonly believed by some Sunnis that if there was sufficient reason one could ignore the outward meaning of Quranic verses and ascribe to them a contrary meaning. Usually the meaning which opposed the outward, literal meaning was called ta'wil, and what is called "ta'wil of the Quran" in Sunni Islam is usually understood in this sense.

In the religious works of Sunni scholars, as well as in the controversies that have been recorded as taking place between different schools, one often observes that if a particular point of doctrine (that has been established through the consensus of the ulama of a school or through some other means) is opposed to the outward meaning of a verse of the Quran, that verse is interpreted by ta'wil to have a meaning contrary to its apparent meaning. Sometimes two contending sides support two opposing views and present Quranic verses in proof of their contentions. Each side interprets the verses presented by the other side through ta'wil. This method has also penetrated more or less into Shi'ism and can be seen in some Shi'ite theological works.

Yet, sufficient deliberation upon Quranic verses and the hadith of the Household of the Prophet demonstrates clearly that the Holy Quran with its attractive language and eloquent and lucid expression never uses enigmatic or puzzling methods of exposition and always expounds any subject in a language suitable for that subject. What has been rightly called ta'wil, or hermeneutic interpretation, of the Holy Quran is not concerned simply with the denotation of words. Rather, it is concerned with certain truths and realities that transcend the comprehension of the common run of men; yet it is from these truths and realities that the principles of doctrine and the practical injunctions of the Quran issue forth.

The whole of the Quran possesses the sense of ta'wil, of esoteric meaning, which cannot be comprehended directly through human thought alone. Only the prophets and the pure among the saints of God who are free from the dross of human imperfection can contemplate these meanings while living on the present plane of existence. On the Day of Resurrection the ta'wil of the Quran will be revealed to everyone.

This assertion can be explained by pointing to the fact that what forces man to use speech, create words and make use of expressions is nothing other than his social and material needs. In his social life man is forced to try to make his fellow-men understand his thoughts and intentions and the feelings which exist within his soul. To accomplish this end he makes use of sounds and hearing. Occasionally also he uses to a degree his eyes and gestures. That is why between the mute and the blind there can never be any mutual comprehension, for whatever the blind man says the deaf cannot hear, and whatever the mute makes understood through gestures the blind man cannot see.

The creation of words and the naming of objects have been

accomplished mostly with a material end in view. Expressions have been created for those objects, states, and conditions which are material and available to the senses or near to the sensible world. As can be seen in those cases where the person addressed lacks one of the physical senses, if we wish to speak of matters which can be comprehended through the missing sense we employ a kind of allegory and similitude. For example, if we wish to describe light or color to one who is born blind, or the pleasures of sex to a child that has not reached the age of adolescence, we seek to achieve our purpose through comparison and allegory and through providing appropriate examples.

Therefore, if we accept the hypothesis that in the scale of Universal Existence there are immense levels of reality which are independent of the world of matter (and this is in reality the case), and that in each generation there are among mankind but a handful who have the capability of comprehending and having a vision of these realities, then questions pertaining to these higher worlds cannot be understood through common verbal expressions and modes of thought. They cannot be referred to except by allusion and through symbolism. Since religious realities are of this kind, the expression of the Quran in such matters must of necessity be symbolic.

God says in his book, "Lo! We have appointed it a Lecture in Arabic that haply ye may understand. And Lo! in the Source of Decrees, which We possess, it is indeed sublime, decisive." (Common comprehension cannot understand it or penetrate into it.) (Quran, XLIII, 3–4) He also says, "That (this) is indeed a noble Quran, In a book kept hidden, Which none toucheth save the purified" (Quran, LVI, 77–79). Concerning the Prophet and his Household he says, "Allah's wish is but to remove uncleanness far from you, O Folk of the Household, and cleanse you with a thorough cleansing" (Quran, XXXIII, 33).

As proved by these verses, the Holy Quran emanates from sources beyond the comprehension of common man. No one can have a full comprehension of the Quran save those servants of God whom He has chosen to purify. And the Household of the Prophet are among those pure beings.

In another place God says, "Nay, but they denied that (the (Quran), the knowledge whereof they could not compass, and whereof the interpretation (in events) [ta'wil] hath not yet come into them" (Quran, X, 40) (meaning the day of Resurrection when the truth of things will become known). And again he says, "On the day (the Day of Resurrection) when the fulfillment [ta'wil] thereof (of the whole Quran) cometh, those who were before forgetful thereof will say: The messengers of our Lord did bring the Truth!" (Quran, VII, 53)

Hadith

The principle that the hadith possesses validity, as attested by the Quran, is not at all disputed among Shi'ites or in fact among all Muslims. But because of the failure of some of the early rulers of Islam in preserving and guarding the hadith, and the excesses of a group among the companions and followers of the Prophet in propagating hadith literature, the corpus of hadith came to face a certain number of difficulties.

On the one hand the caliphs of the time prevented the writing down and recording of the hadith and ordered any pages containing texts of hadith to be burned. Sometimes also any increase in activity in the transmission and study of hadith was forbidden.[21] In this way a certain number of hadiths were forgotten or lost and a few were even transmitted with a different or distorted meaning. On the other hand another tendency also prevailed among another group of the companions of the Holy Prophet who had had the honor of seeing his presence and actually hearing his words. This group, which was respected by the caliphs and the Muslim community, began an intense effort to propagate the hadith. This was carried to such an extent that sometimes hadith overruled the Quran and the injunction of a Quranic verse was even considered abrogated by some people through a hadith.[22] Often the transmitters of hadith would travel many miles and bear all the difficulties of traveling in order to hear a single saying.

A group of outsiders who had worn the dress of Islam and also some of the enemies within the ranks of Islam began to change and distort some of the hadith and thus diminished the reliability and validity of the hadith that was then heard and known.[23] For this very reason Islamic scholars began to think of a solution. They created the sciences concerned with the biography of learned men and chains of transmission of hadith in order to be able to discriminate between true and false hadith.[24]

The Method of Shiʿism in Authenticating the Hadith

Shiʿism, in addition to seeking to authenticate the chain of transmission of hadith, considers the correlation of the text of the hadith with the Quran as a necessary condition for its validity. In Shiʿite sources there are many hadiths of the Prophet and the Imams with authentic chains of transmission which themselves assert that a hadith contrary to the Quran has no value. Only that hadith can be considered valid which is in agreement with the Quran.[25]

Basing itself on these hadiths, Shiʿism does not act upon those hadiths which are contrary to the text of the Quran. As for hadiths whose agreement or disagreement cannot be established, according to instructions received from the Imams they are passed by in silence without being accepted or rejected.[26] Needless to say there are also within Shiʿism those who, like a group among the Sunnis, act on any hadith whatsoever which they happen to find in different traditional sources.

The Method of Shiʿism in Following the Hadith

A hadith heard directly from the mouth of the Prophet or one of the Imams is accepted as is the Quran. As for hadiths received through intermediaries, the majority of Shiʿites act upon them if their chain of transmission is established at every step or if there exists definite proof concerning their truth, and, if they are concerned with principles of doctrine which require knowledge and certainty, according to the text of the Quran. Other than these two kinds of hadith, no other hadith has any validity concerning principles of doctrine, the invalid hadith being called "tradition with a single transmitter" (*khabar wāḥid*). However, in establishing the injunctions of the Shari'ah, because of reasons that have been given, Shi'ites act also on a tradition which is generally accepted as reliable. Therefore it can be said that for Shi'ism a certain and definitely established hadith is absolutely binding and must be followed, while a hadith which is not absolutely established but which is generally considered as reliable is utilized only in the elaboration of the injunctions of the Shari'ah.

Learning and Teaching in Islam

To acquire knowledge is a religious duty in Islam. The Prophet has said, "To seek knowledge is incumbent upon every Muslim."[28] According to fully established hadiths which elucidate the meaning of this saying, knowledge here means the three principles of Islam: unity or tawhid; prophecy or nubuwwat; and eschatology or ma'ad. In addition to these principles, Muslims are expected to acquire knowledge of the subsidiary branches and the details of the injunctions and laws of Islam according to their individual circumstances and needs.

It is clear that acquiring knowledge of the principles of religion, even if it be in summary fashion, is possible to a certain extent for everyone. But acquiring detailed knowledge of the injunctions and laws of religion through use of the basic documents of the Book and the Sunnah and technical reasoning based upon them (or what is called demonstrative jurisprudence, *fiqh-i istidlālī*) is not possible for every Muslim. Only a few persons have the capacity for demonstrative jurisprudence, nor is such acquiring of detailed knowledge required of everyone, for there are no injunctions in Islam requiring one to do what lies beyond his abilities.[29]

Therefore, the study of Islamic injunctions and laws through reasoning has been limited through the principle of "sufficient necessity" (*wājib-i kifā'ī*) to those individuals who have the necessary capability and are worthy of such study. The duty of the rest of the people, according to the general principle of the necessity for the ignorant to depend on the one who knows, is to seek guidance from capable and worthy men of learning, who are called mujtahids and *faqīhs*. This act of following mujtahids is called imitation or *taqlīd*. Of course this imitation differs from imitation in the principles of religious knowledge which is forbidden according to the very text of the Quran, "(O man), follow not that whereof thou hast no knowledge." (Quran, XVII, 36).

It must be known that Shi'ism does not permit imitation of a dead mujtahid. That is to say, a person who does not know the answer to a problem through ijtihad and through religious duty must imitate a living mujtahid and cannot depend on the view of a mujtahid who is not living, unless he had received that guidance while the mujtahid was alive. This practice is one of the factors which have kept Islamic Shi'ite jurisprudence alive and fresh throughout the ages. There are individuals who continuously follow the path of independent judgment, ijtihad, and delve into the problems of jurisprudence from one generation to another.

In Sunnism, as a result of a consensus of opinion (ijma') that occurred in the 4th/10th century, it was decided that submission to one of the four schools (of Abu Hanifah, Ibn Mālik, al-Shāfi'ī, and Ahmad ibn Hanbal) was necessary. Free ijtihad or imitation of a school other than these four (or one or two smaller schools that died out later) was not considered permissible. As a result, their jurisprudence has remained in the same condition as it was about 1100 years ago. In recent times certain individuals in the Sunni world have turned away from this consensus and have begun to exercise free ijtihad.

Shi'ism and the Transmitted Sciences

The Islamic sciences, which owe their existence to the ulama of Islam who organized and formulated them, are divided into the two categories of intellectual (*'aqlī*) and transmitted (*naqlī*). The intellectual sciences include such sciences as philosophy and mathematics. The transmitted sciences are those which depend upon transmission from some source, such as the sciences of language, hadith, or history. Without doubt the major cause for the appearance of the transmitted sciences in Islam is the Holy Quran. With the exception of a few disciplines such as history, genealogy, and prosody, the other transmitted sciences have all come into being under the influence of the Holy Book. Guided by religious discussions and research, Muslims began to cultivate these sciences, of which the most important are Arabic literature (grammar, rhetoric, and the science of metaphors) and the sciences pertaining to the external form of religion (recitation of the Quran, Quranic commentary (*tafsīr*), hadith, biography of learned men, the chain of transmission of hadith, and the principles of jurisprudence).

Shi'ites played an essential role in the foundation and establishment of these sciences. In fact, the founders and creators of many of these sciences were Shi'ites. Arabic grammar was put into a systematic form by Abu'l-Aswad al-Du'alī, one of the companions of the Holy Prophet, and by Ali. Ali dictated an outline for the organization of the science of Arabic grammar.[30] One of the founders of the science of eloquence (rhetoric and the science of metaphors) was Sāhib ibn 'Abbād, a Shi'ite, who was a vizier of the Buyids.[31] The first Arabic dictionary is the *Kitāb al-'ayn* composed by the famous scholar, Khalīl ibn Aḥmad al-Baṣrī, the Shi'ite who founded the science of prosody. He was also the teacher of the great master of grammar, Sībuwayh.

The Quranic recitation of 'Āṣim goes back to Ali through one intermediary, and 'Abdallāh ibn 'Abbās, who in hadith was the foremost among the companions, was a student of Ali. The contributions of the Household of the Prophet and their associates in hadith and jurisprudence are well known. The founders of the four Sunni schools of law are known to have associated with the fifth and sixth Shi'ite Imams. In the principles of jurisprudence the remarkable advances accomplished by the Shi'ite scholar Waḥīd Bihbahānī and followed by Shaykh Murtaḍā Anṣārī have never been matched in Sunni jurisprudence according to existing evidence.

SECOND METHOD: THE WAY OF INTELLECTION AND INTELLECTUAL REASONING

Philosophical and Theological Thought in Shi'ism

It has been mentioned before that Islam has legitimized and approved rational thought, which it considers a part of religious thought. Rational thought in its Islamic sense, after confirming the prophecy of the Prophet, provides intellectual demonstrations of the validity of the external aspect of the Quran, which is a divine revelation, as well as of the definitely established sayings of the Prophet and his noble Household.

Intellectual proofs, which aid man in finding solutions for these problems through his God-given nature, are of two kinds: demonstration (burhan) and dialectic (*jadal*). Demonstration is a proof whose premises are true (accord with reality) even if they be not observable or evident. In other words, it is a proposition which man comprehends and confirms by necessity through his God-given intelligence, as for example when he knows that "the number three is less than four." This type of thought is called rational thought; and in case it concerns universal problems of existence, such as the origin and end of the world and of man, it becomes known as philosophical thought.

Dialectic is a proof all or some of whose premises are based on observable and certain data, as for example the case of believers in a religion for whom the common practice is to prove their religious views within that religion by appealing to its certain and evident principles.

The Holy Quran has employed both these methods and there are many verses in the Holy Book attesting to each type of proof. First of all, the Quran commands free investigation and meditation upon the universal principles of the world of existence and the general principles of cosmic order, as well as upon more particular orders such as that of the heavens, the stars, day and night, the earth, the plants, animals, men, etc. It praises in the most eloquent language intellectual investigation of these matters.

Secondly, the Quran has commanded man to apply dialectical thought, which is usually called theological (kalami)[32] discussion, provided it is accomplished in the best manner possible, that is, with the aim of manifesting the truth without contention and by men who possess the necessary moral virtues. It is said in the Quran, "Call unto the way of thy Lord with wisdom and fair exhortation, and reason ["*jādil*," from jadal] with them in the better way" (Quran, XVI, 125).

Shiʿite Initiative in Islamic Philosophy and Kalam

As for theology, kalam, it is clear that from the beginning, when the Shiʿites separated from the Sunni majority they began to debate with their opponents concerning their own particular point of view. It is true that a debate has two sides and that both the opponents share in it. However, the Shiʿites were continuously on the offensive, taking the initiative, while the other side played the defensive role. In the gradual growth of kalam, which reached its height in the 2nd/8th and 3rd/9th centuries with the spread of the Muʿtazilite school, Shiʿite scholars and learned men, who were students of the school of the Household of the Prophet, became among the foremost masters of kalam.[33] Furthermore, the chain of theologians of the Sunni world, whether it be the Ashʿarites, Muʿtazilites or others, goes back to the first Imam of the Shiʿites, Ali.

As for philosophy,[34] those who are acquainted with the sayings and works of the companions of the Prophet (of which the names of 12,000 have been recorded and 120,000 are known to exist) know that there is little in them containing an appreciable discussion of philosophical questions. It is only Ali whose compelling metaphysical utterances contain the deepest philosophical thought.

The companions and the scholars who followed them, and in fact the Arabs of that day in general, were not acquainted with free intellectual discussion. There is no example of philosophical thought in the works of the scholars of the first two centuries. Only the profound sayings of the Shiʿite Imams, particularly the first and eighth, contain an inexhaustible treasury of philosophical meditations in their Islamic context. It is they who acquainted some of their students with this form of thought.

The Arabs were not familiar with philosophical thought until they saw examples of it during the 2nd/8th century in the translation of certain philosophical works into Arabic. Later, during the 3rd/9th century, numerous philosophical writings were translated into Arabic from Greek, Syriac, and other languages and through them the method of philosophical thought became known to the general public. Nevertheless, most jurists and theologians did not look upon philosophy and other intellectual sciences, which were newly arrived guests, with favor. At the beginning, because of the support of the governmental authorities for these sciences, their opposition did not have much effect. But conditions soon changed and through strict orders many philosophical works were destroyed. The *Epistles* of the Brethren of Purity, which is the work of a group of unknown authors, is a reminder of those days and attests to the unfavorable conditions of that epoch.

After this period of difficulty, philosophy was revived at the beginning of the 4th/10th century by the famous philosopher Abū Naṣr al-Fārābī. In the 5th/11th century, as a result of the works of the celebrated philosopher Ibn Sina (Avicenna), Peripatetic philosophy reached its full development. In the 6th/12th century Shaykh al-Ishrāq Shihāb al-Dīn Suhrawardī systematized the philosophy of illumination(*ishrāq*) and because of this was executed by the order of Ṣalaḥ al-Dīn Ayyūbī. Thereafter, philosophy ceased to exist among the Muslim majority in the Sunni world. There was no further outstanding philosopher in that part of the Muslim world except in Andalusia at the edge of the Islamic world where at the end of the 6th/12th century Ibn Rushd (Averroes) sought to revive the study of philosophy.[35]

Shi'ite Contributions to Philosophy and the Intellectual Sciences

In the same way that from the beginning Shi'ism played an effective role in the formation of Islamic philosophical throught, it was also a principal factor in the further development and propagation of philosophy and the Islamic sciences. Although after Ibn Rushd philosophy disappeared in the Sunni world, it continued to live in Shi'ism. After Ibn Rushd there appeared such celebrated philosophers as Khwājah Naṣīr al-Dīn Ṭūsī, Mīr Dāmad, and Ṣadr al-Dīn Shīrāzī, who studied, developed and expounded philosophical thought one after another. In the same manner, in the other intellectual sciences, there appeared many outstanding figures such as Nasir al-Din Tusi (who was both philosopher and mathematician) and Bīrjāndi, who was also an outstanding mathematician.

All the sciences, particularly metaphysics or theosophy (falsafah-i ilahi or hikmat-i ilahi), made major advances thanks to the indefatigable endeavor of Shi'ite scholars. This fact can be seen if one compares the works of Nasir al-Din Tusi, Shams al-Din Turkah, Mir Damad, and Sadr al-Din Shirazi with the writings of those who came before them.[36]

It is known that the element that was instrumental in the appearance of philosophical and metaphysical thought in Shi'ism and through Shi'ism in other Islamic circles was the treasury of knowledge left behind by the Imams. The persistence and continuity of this type of thought in Shi'ism is due to the existence of this same treasury of knowledge, which Shi'ism has continued to regard with a sense of reverence and respect.

In order to clarify this situation it is enough to compare the treasury of knowledge left by the Household of the Prophet with the philosophical works written over the course of the centuries. In this comparison one can see clearly how each day Islamic philosophy approached this source of knowledge ever more closely, until in the 11th/17th century Islamic philosophy and this inspired treasury of wisdom converged more or less completely. They were separated only by certain differences of interpretation of some of the principles of philosophy.

Outstanding Intellectual Figures of Shi'ism

Thiqat al-islām Muḥammad ibn Ya'qūb Kulaynī (d. 329/940) is the first person in Shi'ism to have separated the Shi'ite hadiths from the books called *Principles* (usul) and to have arranged and organized them according to the headings of jurisprudence and articles of faith. (Each one of the Shi'ite scholars of hadith had assembled sayings he had collected from the Imams in a book called *Aṣl*, or *Principle.*) The book of Kulayni known as *Kāfī* is divided into three parts: Principles, Branches, and Miscellaneous Articles, and contains 16,199 hadiths. It is the most trustworthy and celebrated work of hadith known in the Shi'ite world.

Three other works which complement the *Kafi* are the book of the jurist Shaykh-i Ṣadūq Muḥammad ibn Bābūyah Qumī(d. 381/991), and *Kitāb al-tahdhīb* and *Kitāb al-istibṣār*, both by Shaykh Muhammad Tusi (d. 460/1068).

Abu'l-Qāsim Ja'far ibn Hasan ibn Yaḥyā Ḥillī (d. 676/1277), known as Muḥaqqiq, was an outstanding genius in the science of jurisprudence and is considered to be the foremost Shi'ite jurist. Among his masterpieces are *Kitāb-i mukhtaṣar-i nāfi'* and *Kitāb-i sharāyi'*, which have been passed from hand to hand for seven hundred years among Shi'ite jurists and have always been regarded with a sense of awe and wonder.

Following Muhaqqiq, we must cite Shahīd-i Awwal (the First Martyr) Shams al-Dīn Muḥammad ibn Makkī, who was killed in Damascus in 786/1384 on the accusation of being Shi'ite. Among his juridical masterpieces is his *Lum'ah-i dimashqīyah* which he wrote in prison in a period of seven days. Also we must cite Shaykh Ja'far Kāshif al-Ghitā' Najafī (d. 1327/1909) among whose outstanding juridical works is *Kitāb kashf al-ghitā'*.

Khwajah Nasir al-Din Tusi (d. 672/1274) is the first to have made kalam a thorough and complete science. Among his masterpieces in this domain is his *Tajrīd al-kalām* which has preserved its authority among masters of this discipline for more than seven centuries. Numerous commentaries have been written on it by Shi'ites and Sunnis alike. Over and above his genius in the science of kalam, he was one of the outstanding figures of his day in philosophy and mathematics as witnessed by the valuable contributions he made to the intellectual sciences. Moreover, the Maraghah observatory owed its existence to him.

Sadr al-Din Shirazi (d. 1050/1640), known as Mulla Sadra and Ṣadr al-Muta'allihīn, was the philosopher who, after centuries of philosophical development in Islam, brought complete order and harmony into the discussion of philosophical problems for the first time. He organized and systematized them like mathematical problems and at the same time wed philosophy and gnosis, thereby bringing about several important developments. He gave to philosophy new ways to discuss and solve hundreds of problems that could not be solved through Peripatetic philosophy. He made possible the analysis and solution of a series of mystical questions which to that day had been considered as belonging to a domain above that of reason and beyond comprehension through rational thought. He clarified and elucidated the meaning of many treasuries of wisdom, contained in the exoteric sources of religion and in the profound metaphysical utterances of the Imams of the Household of the Prophet, that for centuries had been considered as insoluble riddles and usually believed to be of an allegorical or even unclear nature. In this way gnosis, philosophy and the exoteric aspect of religion were completely harmonized and began to follow a single course.

By following the methods he had developed, Mulla Sadra succeeded in proving "transubstantial motion" (*ḥarakat-i jawharīyah*),[37] and in discovering the intimate relation of time to the three spatial dimensions in a manner that is similar to the meaning given in modern physics to the "fourth dimension" and which resembles the general principles of the theory of relativity (relativity of course in the corporeal world outside the mind, not in the mind), and many other noteworthy principles. He wrote nearly fifty books and treatises. Among his greatest masterpieces is the four-volume *Asfār*.

It should be noted here that before Mulla Sadra certain sages like Suhrawardi, the 6th/12th century philosopher and author of *Ḥikmat al-ishrāq*, and Shams al-Din Turkah, a philosopher of the 8th/14th century, had taken steps toward harmonizing gnosis, philosophy and exoteric religion, but credit for complete success in this undertaking belongs to Mulla Sadra.

Shaykh Murtaḍā Anṣārī Shūshtarī (d. 1281/1864) reorganized the science of the principles of jurisprudence upon a new foundation and formulated the practical principles of this science. For over a century his school has been followed diligently by Shi'ite scholars.

THIRD METHOD: INTELLECTUAL INTUITION OR MYSTICAL UNVEILING

Man and Gnostic Comprehension[38]

Even though most men are occupied with gaining a livelihood and providing for their daily needs and show no concern for spiritual matters, there lies within the nature of man an innate urge to seek the ultimately Real. In certain individuals this force which is dormant and potential becomes awakened and manifests itself openly, thus leading to a series of spiritual perceptions.

Every man believes in a permanent Reality despite the claim of sophists and skeptics, who call every truth and reality illusion and superstition. Occasionally when man views with a clear mind and a pure soul the permanent Reality pervading the universe and the created order, and at the same time sees the impermanence and transient character of the diverse parts and elements of the world, he is able to contemplate the world and its phenomena as mirrors which reflect the beauty of a permanent reality. The joy of comprehending this Reality obliterates every other joy in the eye of the viewer and makes everything else appear as insignificant and unimportant.

This vision is that same gnostic "divine attraction" (*jadhbah*) which draws the attention of the God-centered man toward the transcendent world and awakens the love of God in his heart. Through this attraction he forgets all else. All his manifold desires and wishes are obliterated from his mind. This attraction guides man to the worship and praise of the Invisible Deity who is in reality more evident and manifest than all that is visible and audible. In truth it is this same inner attraction that has brought into being the different religions within the world, religions which are based on the worship of God. The gnostic (*'ārif*) is the one who worships God through knowledge and because of love for Him, not in hope of reward or fear of punishment.[39]

From this exposition it becomes clear that we must not consider gnosis as a religion among others, but as the heart of all religions. Gnosis is one of the paths of worship, a path based on knowledge combined with love, rather than fear. It is the path for realizing the inner truth of religion rather than remaining satisfied only with its external form and rational thought. Every revealed religion and even those that appear in the form of idol-worship have certain followers who march upon the path of gnosis. The polytheistic religions[40] and Judaism, Christianity, Zoroastrianism, and Islam all have believers who are gnostics.

Appearance of Gnosis (Sufism) in Islam

Among the companions of the Prophet, Ali is known particularly for his eloquent exposition of gnostic truths and the stages of the spiritual life. His words in this domain comprise an inexhaustible treasury of wisdom. Among the works of the other companions which have survived there is not a great deal of material that concerns this type of question. Among the associates of Ali, such as Salmān Fārsī, Uways Qaranī, Kumayl ibn Ziyād, Rashīd Ḥajarī, Maytham Tammār, Rabīʿ ibn Khaytham, and Ḥasan Baṣrī, however, there are figures who have been considered by the majority of the Sufis, Sunni and Shiʿite alike, as the heads of their spiritual chain (*silsilah*) after Ali.

After this group there appeared others, such as Ṭāwūs Yamānī, Shaybān Rāʾī, Mālik ibn Dīnār, Ibrāhīm Adham, and Shaqīq Balkhī, who were considered by the people to be saints and men of God. These men, without publicly talking about gnosis and Sufism, appeared externally as ascetics and did not hide the fact that they had been initiated by the earlier group and had undergone spiritual training under them.

After them there appeared at the end of the 2nd/8th century and the beginning of the 3rd/9th century men such as Bāyazīd Basṭāmī, Maʿrūf Karkhī, Junayd Baghdādī and others like them, who followed the Sufi path and openly declared their connection with Sufism and gnosis. They divulged certain esoteric sayings based on spiritual vision which, because of their repellent external form, brought upon them the condemnation of some of the jurists and theologians. Some of them were imprisoned, flogged, and even occasionally killed.[41] Even so, this group persisted and continued its activities despite its opponents. In this manner gnosis and the "Way" (*Ṭarīqah*, or Sufism) continued to grow until in the 7th/13th and 8th/14th centuries it reached the height of its expansion and power. Since then, sometimes stronger and at other times less so, it has continued its existence to this very day within the Islamic world.

Gnosis or Sufism as we observe it today first appeared in the Sunni world and later among the Shiʿites. The first men who openly declared themselves to be Sufis and gnostics, and were recognized as spiritual masters of Sufi orders, apparently followed Sunnism in the branches (furuʿ) of Islamic law. Many of the masters who followed them and who expanded the Sufi orders were also Sunnis in their following of the law.

Even so, these masters traced their spiritual chain, which in the spiritual life is like the genealogical chain of a person, through their previous masters to Ali. Also the results of their visions and intuitions as transmitted to us convey mostly truths concerning divine unity and the stations of the spiritual life which are found in the sayings of Ali and other Shiʿite Imams. This can be seen provided we are not affected by some of the striking and even sometimes shocking expressions used by these Sufi masters and consider the total content of their teachings with deliberation and patience. Sanctity[42] resulting from initiation into the spiritual path, which Sufis consider as the perfection of man, is a state which according to Shiʿite belief is possessed in its fullness by the Imam and through the radiance of his being can be attained by his true followers. And the Spiritual Pole (*quṭb*), [43] whose existence at all times is considered necessary by all the Sufis—as well as the attributes associated with him—correlates with the Shiʿite conception of the Imam. According to the saying of the Household of the Prophet, the Imam is, to use the Sufi expression, Universal Man, the manifestation of the Divine Names and the spiritual guide of the lives and actions of men. Therefore, one could say, considering the Shiʿite concept of walayat, that Sufi masters are

"Shi'ite" from the point of view of the spiritual life and in connection with the source of walayat although, from the point of view of the external form of religion they follow the Sunni schools of law.

It is necessary to mention that even in classical Sunni treatises it has sometimes been said that the spiritual method of the "Path,"[44] or the "techniques" whereby one comes to know and realize himself, cannot be explained through the external forms and teachings of the Shari'ah. Rather, these sources claim that individual Muslims themselves have discovered many of these methods and practices, which then have become accepted by God, much as is the case with monasticism in Christianity.[45] Therefore each master has devised certain actions and practices which he has deemed necessary in the spiritual method, such as the particular type of ceremony of being accepted by the master, the details of the way in which the invocation is given to the new adept along with a robe, and the use of music, chanting and other methods of inducing ecstasy during the invocation of the Divine Name. In some cases the practices of the Tariqah have outwardly become separated from those of the Shari'ah and it may seem difficult for an outsider to see the intimate and inward relation between them. But by taking into consideration the theoretical principles of Shi'ism and then studying in depth the basic sources of Islam, namely the Quran and the Sunnah, he will soon realize that it is impossible to say that this spiritual guidance has not been provided by Islam itself or that Islam has remained negligent in clarifying the nature of the spiritual program to be followed.

Guidance Provided by the Quran and Sunnah for Gnostic Knowledge

God—exalted be His Name—has commanded man in several places in the Quran to deliberate upon the Holy Book and be persistent in this effort and not to be satisfied with a merely superficial and elementary understanding of it. In many verses the world of creation and all that is in it without exception are called portents (*āyāt*), signs and symbols of the Divine.[46] A degree of deliberation upon the meaning of portents and signs and penetration into their real significance will reveal the fact that things are called by these names because they manifest and make known not so much themselves but a reality other than themselves. For example, a red light placed as a sign of danger, once seen, reminds one completely of the idea of danger so that one no longer pays attention to the red light itself. If one begins to think about the form or quiddity of the light or its color, there will be in his mind only the form of the lamp or its glass or color rather than the conception of danger. In the same manner, if the world and its phenomena are all and in every aspect signs and portents of God, the Creator of the Universe, they have no ontological independence of their own. No matter how we view them they display nothing but God.

He who through guidance of the Holy Quran is able to view the world and the people of the world with such an eye will apprehend nothing but God. Instead of seeing only this borrowed beauty which others see in the attractive appearance of the world, he will see an Infinite Beauty, a Beloved who manifests Himself through the narrow confines of this world. Of course, as in the example of the red light, what is contemplated and seen in "signs" and "portents" is God the Creator of the world and not the world itself. The relation of God to the world is from a certain point of view like (1 + 0) not (1 + 1) nor (1 × 1) (that is, the world is nothing before God and adds nothing to him). It is at the moment of realization of this truth that the harvest of man's separative existence is plundered and in one stroke man entrusts his heart to the hands of Divine love. This realization obviously does not take place through the instrument of the eye or the ear or the other outward senses, nor through the power of imagination or reason, for all these instruments are themselves signs and portents and of little significance to the spiritual guidance sought here.[47]

He who has attained the vision of God and who has no intention but to remember God and forget all else, when he hears that in another place in the Quran God says, "O ye who believe! Ye have charge of your own souls. He who erreth cannot injure you if ye are rightly guided" (Quran, V, 105), then he understands that the sole royal path which will guide him fully and completely is the path of "self-realization." His true guide who is God Himself obliges him to know himself, to leave behind all other ways and to seek the path of self-knowledge, to see God through the window of his soul, gaining in this way the real object of his search. That is why the Prophet has said, "He who knows himself verily knows the Lord."[48] And also he has said, "Those among you know God better who know themselves better."[49]

As for the method of following this path, there are many verses of the Quran which command man to remember God, as for example where He says, "Therefore remember Me, I will remember you" (Quran, II, 152) and similar sayings. Man is also commanded to perform right actions which are described fully in the Quran and hadith. At the end of this discussion of right actions God says, "Verily in the Messenger of Allah ye have a good example" (Quran, XXXIII, 21).

How can anyone imagine that Islam could discover that a particular path is the path which leads to God without recommending this path to all the people? Or how could it make such a path known and yet neglect to explain the method of following it? For God says in the Quran, "And We reveal the Scripture unto thee as an exposition of all things" (Quran, XVI, 89).

NOTES

CHAPTER III

1. *Editor's note:* As indicated in the introduction there has been in the Shiʿite world a continuous tradition of theosophy or wisdom (hikmah), which is also called *falsafah*, or philosophy, to which the author refers often in this book. This school is, however, a traditional school of philosophy wedded to metaphysics and to means of spiritual realization. It should not be identified with profane or purely rationalistic modes of thought and is therefore not the same as philosophy as currently understood in the West, although it does use rational demonstrations and the laws of logic.

2. We can deduce from this verse that worship in the religion of God is subservient to Unity (tawhid) and is based upon it.

3. To be able to attribute and describe depends on knowledge of that which is to be described. From this verse it can be concluded that except for those who are devoted in sincerity to God and those who have become purified, no others can come to know God in the manner in which He should be known. He therefore cannot be properly known or described by others and is beyond whatever attributes they give Him.

4. We can deduce from this verse that there is no other way to meet the Lord except through Unity and right action.

5. From this verse it can be concluded that the true worship of God results in certainty (yaqin).

6. We can conclude from this verse that one of the necessary conditions for reaching certainty is to gain a vision of the "angelic" or "archetypal" heavens and earth.

7. From these verses it becomes known that the destiny of the righteous (*abrār*) is contained in a book called ʿIlliyīn (the very elevated), known by those close to God through spiritual vision. The verb "attested by" (*yashhaduhu* in Arabic) shows that by "a written record" is not meant a written book in the ordinary sense; rather it refers to the world of "divine proximity and elevation."

8. From this verse it can be understood that the science of certainty (ʿilm al-yaqīn) results in the vision of the final end of those who are in a state of wretchedness, this end being called *jaḥīm* or hell.

9. It is with reference to this truth that the Holy Prophet in a hadith accepted by Sunnis and Shiʿites alike says, "We prophets speak to mankind according to the degree of their understanding." *Biḥār al-anwār*, vol. I, p. 37; *Uṣūl al-kāfī*, Kulaynī, Tehran, 1357, vol. I, p. 203.

10. The source for this hadith has been mentioned in Part I of this work.

11. *Nahj al-balāghah*, sermon 231. This question has been discussed in our work on the Quran which is also to appear shortly in English.

12. *Al-Durr al-manthūr*, vol. II, p. 6.
13. *Tafsīr al-ṣāfī*, Mullā Muḥsin Fayḍ Kāshānī, Tehran, 1269, p. 8; *Biḥār al-anwār*, vol. XIX, p. 28.
14. Quran, XXVI, 173.
15. Quran, LIV, 34.
16. *Editor's note:* It may be added that this is the method employed by the author in his monumental Quranic commentary, *al-Mīzān*, of which seventeen volumes have already appeared.
17. *Tafsīr al-ṣāfī*, p. 4.
18. This has been recounted of the Prophet in the *Tafsīr al-ṣāfī*, p. 15 *Safīnat al-biḥār* of Abbās Qumī, Najaf, 1352-55, and other well-known commentaries.
19. *Editor's note:* This is in reference to the Quranic verse, "We shall show them our portents upon the horizons and within themselves, until it be manifest unto them that it is the Truth" (XLI, 53).
20. *Editor's note:* This is a direct reference to the practice of *dhikr* or invocation which also means remembrance and is the fundamental technique of spiritual realization in Sufism.
21. *Bihār al-anwār*, vol. I, p. 117.
22. The question of the abrogation or substitution of certain verses of the Quran is one of the difficult problems of the science of the principles of jurisprudence and at least some of the 'ulama in Sunnism seem to have accepted abrogation. The incident of Fadak seems also to involve the question of different kinds of interpretations given to Quranic verses through the use of hadith.
23. The proof of this question lies in the large number of works written by traditional religious scholars on fabricated hadith. Also in books dealing with the biography of learned men, some transmitters of hadith have been described as unreliable and others as weak.
24. *Editor's note:* The traditional Islamic criticism of hadith literature and the creation of criteria for distinguishing between true and false hadith must not be in any way confused with the criticism of European orientalists made against the whole corpus of hadith. From the Islamic view this is one of the most diabolical attacks made against the whole structure of Islam.
25. *Biḥār al-anwār*, vol. I, p. 139.
26. *Biḥar al-anwār*, vol. I. p. 117.
27. See the discussion concerning "a single tradition" in works on the science of the principles of jurisprudence (usul).
28. *Biḥār al-anwār*, vol. I. p. 55.
29. In these matters one should refer to the discussions concerning ijtihad and taqlid in works on the science of the principles of jurisprudence.
30. *Wafayāt al-a'yān* of Ibn Khallikān, Tehran, 1284 p. 78; *A'yān al-shī'ah* of Muḥsin 'Amilī, Damascus, 1935 onward, vol. XI, p. 231.
31. *Wafayāt al-a'yān*, p. 190; *A'yān al-shī'ah*, and other works on the biography of learned men.
32. *Editor's note:* Kalam is a special discipline in Islam; the word is usually rendered into European languages as theology, although the role and scope of kalam and theology are not the same. Henceforth, the word kalam itself, which is now gradually coming into use in English, will be employed in its original Arabic form and will not be translated.
33. *Ibn Abi'l-Ḥadīd*, beginning of vol. I.
34. *Editor's note:* As pointed out before, philosophy in this context means traditional philosophy, which is based on certainty, and not the specifically modern philosophy that begins with doubt and limits the intellect to reason.
35. These matters are amply treated in *Akhbār al-ḥukamā'* of Ibn al-Qifṭī, Leipzig, 1903, *Wafayāt al-a'yān*, and other biographies of learned men.

36. *Editor's note:* These are all outstanding philosophers of the later period (from the 7th/13th to the 11th/17th centuries) and are nearly unknown in the West, except for Tusi who is, however, known more for his mathematical works than for his philosophical contributions.

37. *Editor's note:* Earlier Muslim philosophers believed, like Aristotle, that motion is possible only in the accidents of things, not in their substance. Mulla Sadra asserted, on the contrary, that whenever something partakes of motion (in the sense of medieval philosophy) its substance undergoes motion and not just its accidents. There is thus a becoming within things through which they ascend to the higher orders of universal existence. This view, however, should not be confused with the modern theory of evolution.

38. *Editor's note:* Islamic esotericism is called Sufism (*taṣawwuf*) or gnosis (ʿirfān); the first word concerns more the practical and the second the theoretical aspect of the same reality. It has been common among Shiʿite religious scholars since the Safavid period to refer to Islamic esotericism more often as irfan than as tasawwuf. This is due to historical reasons connected with the fact that the Safavids were at first a Sufi order and later gained political power, with the result that many worldly men sought to put on the garb of Sufism in order to gain political or social power, therefore discrediting Sufism in the eyes of the devout.

39. The sixth Imam has said, "There are three kinds of worship: a group worship God in fear and that is the worship of slaves; a group worship God in order to receive rewards and that is the worship of mercenaries; and a group worship God because of their love and devotion to Him and that is the worship of free men. That is the best form of worship." *Biḥār al-anwār*, vol. XV, p. 208.

40. *Editor's note:* The author has here in mind the religions of India and the Far East in which different aspects of the Divinity are symbolized by mythical and symbolic forms and deities and which therefore appear in the eye of Muslims in general as "polytheism".

41. See the works on the biographies of learned men and also *Tadhkirat al-awliyā'* of ʿAṭṭār, Tehran, 1321 (A.H. solar), and *Ṭarā'iq al-ḥaqā'iq* of Maʿṣūm ʿAlī Shāh, Tehran, 1318.

42. In the language of the gnostics, when the gnostic forgets himself, he becomes annihilated in God and surrenders to His guidance or walayat.

43. The gnostics say that through the Divine Names the world has gained an apparent existence and thus runs its course. All the Divine Names are derived from the "Complete and Supreme Name." The Supreme Name is the station (*maqām*) of the Universal Man who is also called the spiritual pole (qutb) of the Universe. In no time can the world of man be without a qutb.

44. *Editor's note:* The spiritual path in Islam is called *sayr wa sulūk* (meaning "traveling and wayfaring") to indicate the way or journey which symbolizes the movement from man to God.

45. God—Exalted be His Name—says, "But monasticism they [the Christians] invented—We ordained it not for them—only seeking Allah's pleasure, and they observed it not with right observance." (Quran, LVII, 27)

46. *Editor's note:* There is a difference between a sign which signifies a meaning through agreement and a symbol which reveals the meaning symbolized through an essential and ontological bond between the symbol and the symbolized. Here the author is using the concept of signs and portents (ayat) in the world in the sense of true symbols.

47. Ali has said, "God is not that which can enter under one of the categories of knowledge. God is That which guides reasoning toward Himself." *Biḥār al-anwār*, vol. II, p. 186.

48. A famous hadith repeated especially in works of well-known Sufis and gnostics, Shiʿite and Sunni alike.

49. This hadith is also found in many gnostic works, both Shiʿite and Sunni.

PART III: ISLAMIC BELIEFS FROM THE SHI'ITE POINT OF VIEW

CHAPTER IV ON THE KNOWLEDGE OF GOD

The World Seen from the Point of View of Being and Reality; The Necessity of God

Consciousness and perception, which are intertwined with man's very being, make evident by their very nature the existence of God as well as the world. For, contrary to those who express doubt about their own existence and everything else and consider the world as illusion and fantasy, we know that a human being at the moment of his coming into existence, when he is already conscious and possesses perception, discovers himself and the world. That is to say, he has no doubt that "He exists and things other than he exist." As long as man is man this comprehension and knowledge exist in him and cannot be doubted, nor do they undergo any change.

The perception of this reality and existence which man affirms through his intelligence, in opposition to the views of the sophist and skeptic, is immutable and can never be proven false. That is to say, the claim of the sophist and the skeptic which negates reality can never be true, because of man's very existence. There is within the immense world of existence a permanent and abiding reality which pervades it and which reveals itself to the intelligence.

Yet each of the phenomena of this world which possesses the reality that we discover as conscious and perceiving human beings loses its reality sooner or later and becomes nonexistent. From this fact itself it is evident that the visible world and its parts are not the essence of reality (which can never be obliterated or destroyed). Rather, they rely upon a permanent Reality through which they gain reality and by means of which they enter into existence. As long as they are connected and attached to it they possess existence and as soon as they are cut off from it they become nonexistent.[1] We call this Immutable Reality, which is imperishable (that is, the Necessary Being), God.

Another Point of View Concerning the Relation Between Man and the Universe

The path chosen in the previous section to prove the existence of God is a very simple and evident one which man treads with his God-given nature and intelligence without any complication. Yet, for the majority of people, because of their continuous preoccupation with material things and their being drowned in the pleasures of the senses, it has become very difficult to return to their God-given, simple, primordial, and untainted nature. That is why Islam, which describes itself as universal, and which believes all people to be equal in religion, has made it possible for such people to find another way to prove the existence of God. It seeks to speak to them and to make God known to them by means of the very path through which they have turned away from their simple, primordial nature.

The Holy Quran instructs the multitude of men in the knowledge of God through different ways. Most of all, it draws their attention to the creation of the world and the order which reigns over it. It invites men to contemplate the "horizons" and "their own souls,"[2] for man in his few days of earthly life, no matter what path he chooses or what state he loses himself in, will never step outside the world of creation and the order which reigns over it. His intelligence and power of comprehension cannot overlook the marvelous scenes of heaven and earth which he observes.

This vast world of existence which stretches before our eyes is, as we know, in its parts and as a whole continuously in the process of change and transformation. At each moment it manifests itself in a new and unprecedented form. It becomes actualized under the influences of laws which know no exception. From the farthest galaxies to the smallest particles which form the parts of this world, each part of creation possesses an inward order and runs its course in a most amazing manner under laws which do not admit any exceptions. The world extends its domain of activity from the lowest to the most perfect state and reaches its own goal of perfection.

Above these particular orders stand more universal orders and finally the total cosmic order which brings together the countless parts of the universe and relates the more particular orders with each other, and which in its continuous course accepts no exceptions and permits no breaches.

The order of creation is such that if, for example, it places a man upon the earth, it constitutes him in such a way that he can live in harmony with his environment. It arranges the environment in such a way that it raises him like a loving nurse. The sun, the moon, the stars, water and earth, the night and the day, the seasons of the year, the clouds, wind and rain, the treasures beneath the earth and on its surface, in other words all the forces of nature, use their energy and resources in providing well-being and peace of mind for him. Such a relation and harmony can be discovered among all phenomena and also between man and his neighbors near and far, as well as within man's own habitat.

Such a continuity and harmony can also be observed within the internal structure of every phenomenon in the world. If creation has given man bread, it has also given him feet to seek it, hands to grasp it, a mouth to eat it, and teeth to chew it. It has related man through a series of means, which are connected with each other like the links of a chain, to the final goal envisaged for this creature, which is subsistence and perfection.

Many men of science have no doubt that the countless relations among things which they have discovered as a result of several thousand years of effort are but humble samples and a foretaste of the secrets of creation and their myriad ramifications. Each new discovery declares to man the existence of an endless number of unknown elements. Could anyone say that this vast world of existence, all of the parts of which either separately or in unity and interconnection bear witness to an infinite knowledge and power, need not have a creator and could have come into being without reason and cause? Or could it be said of these particular and universal domains of order and equilibrium, and finally of this total cosmic order which through innumerable interrelations has made the world a single unit running its course according to laws which know no exceptions, that all this has occurred without plan and only through accident and chance? Or could anyone say that each of the phenomena and domains in the cosmos has chosen for itself, before coming into being, an order and law which it puts into effect after coming into being? Or could anyone claim that this world, which is a single unit and which possesses complete unity, harmony and the interconnection of parts, could be the result of multiple and different commands issuing from different sources?

Obviously, an intelligent man, who relates every event and phenomenon to a cause, and who sometimes spends long periods in investigation and efforts to gain knowledge of a cause that is unknown to him, will never accept the possibility of a world existing without a Being as its cause. Such a person, who by observing a few bricks placed upon one another in an orderly manner considers them to be the effect of an agent possessing knowledge and power and who denies the possibility of chance and accident in the putting of the bricks together and therefore concludes that a plan and purpose must have existed beforehand, will not regard the cosmic order as being the result of an accident or the play of chance.

A deeper awareness of the order reigning in the world is enough to show that the world, along with the order reigning over it, is the creation of an omnipotent Creator who has brought it into being through His limitless knowledge and power and who directs it toward an end. All the partial causes which bring about individual events in the world ultimately end in Him. They are in every way under His dominance and are guided by His wisdom. Everything that exists is in need of Him, while He has need of nothing and does not depend on any causes or conditions.

God, the Exalted, says, "Lo! in the heavens and the earth are portents for believers. And in your creation, and all the beasts that

He scattereth in the earth, are portents for a folk whose faith is sure. And the difference of night and day and the provision that Allah sendeth down from the sky and thereby quickeneth the earth after her death, and the ordering of the winds, are portents for a people who have sense. These are the portents of Allah which we recite unto thee (Muhammad) with truth. Then in what fact, after Allah and His portents, will they believe?" (Quran, XLV, 3–6).

Every reality in this world which we can possibly imagine is a limited reality, that is, one whose actualization depends upon certain necessary causes and conditions. If these do not exist that reality cannot exist in the world. Every reality has a boundary beyond which it cannot extend its existence. Only God is such that He has no limit or boundary, for His reality is absolute and He exists in His Infinity no matter how we try to conceive of Him. His Being does not depend upon and is not in need of any causes or conditions. It is clear that in the case of something limitless we cannot conceive of multiplicity, for any supposedly second reality will be other than the first, as a result of which each would be limited and bound and would set a boundary to the reality of the other. For example, if we consider a limitless volume we cannot conceive another limitless volume alongside it. And if we do suppose another, it will be the same as the first. Therefore, God is one and has no partner.

We have already mentioned the Bedouin who approached Ali in the middle of the fighting during the Battle of the Camel and asked if he asserted that God was one. In answer Ali said, "To say that God is one has four meanings: Two of those meanings are false and two correct. As for the two incorrect meanings, one is that one should say 'God is one' and be thinking of number and counting. This meaning is false because that which has no second cannot enter into the category of number. Do you not see that those who said that God is the third of a trinity [i.e., the Christians] fell into infidelity? Another meaning is to say that so and so is one of this people, namely a species of this genus or a member of this species. This meaning also is not correct when applied to God, for it implies likening something to God and God is above all likeness.

"As for the two meanings which are correct when applied to God, one is that it should be said that God is one in the sense that there is no likeness unto Him among things. God possesses such uniqueness. And one is to say that God is one in the sense that there is no multiplicity or division conceivable in Him, neither outwardly nor in the mind nor in the imagination. God possesses such a unity." (*Biḥār al-anwār*, vol. II, p. 65)

Ali has also said, "To know God is to know His Oneness." (*Biḥār al-anwār*, vol. II, p. 186) This means that to prove that the Being of God is unlimited and infinite suffices to prove His Oneness, for to conceive a second for the Infinite is impossible. There is therefore no need of any other proofs, although there exist many others.

The Divine Essence and Qualities

If we analyze the nature of a human being, we see that he has an essence which is his individual humanity and also qualities through which his essence is known, such as the quality of being born in such a land, or being the son of such a person, or being learned and capable, or tall and handsome; or he possesses the contrary of these qualities. Some of these qualities, like the first and second, can never be separated from the essence, and others, like being learned or capable, have the possibility of separation and alternation. Yet all are different from the essence and at the same time different from each other.

This point, namely the difference between the essence and qualities and between the qualities themselves, is the best proof that an essence that has qualities, and a quality that makes known an essence, are both limited and finite. For if the essence were limitless and infinite it would encompass the qualities as well, and also the qualities would include each other, and as a result all would become one. For example, the essence of man would be the same as capability and also capability the same as knowledge; height and beauty would be the same; and all of these would possess the same meaning.

From this example it is clear that the Divine Essence cannot be conceived to have qualities in the sense that human beings have qualities. A quality can come about only through setting limits and the Divine Essence transcends all limitations (even the limitation of this transcendence which in reality is a quality).

The Meaning of the Divine Qualities

In the world of creation we are aware of many perfections which appear in the form of qualities. These are positive qualities which, wherever they appear, make the object of which they are the quality more perfect and increase its ontological value, as can be seen clearly in the comparison between the live being such as man and a lifeless one such as a stone. Doubtless God has created and bestowed these perfections upon creatures; if He had not possessed them in their fullness Himself He could not have bestowed them upon others and perfected others through them. Therefore, if we follow the judgment of sound reasoning we must conclude that God, the Creator, has knowledge, power, and every other real perfection. Furthermore, as has already been mentioned, the marks of His knowledge and power and, as a result, the marks of life are seen in the order of the cosmos.

But because the Divine Essence is limitless and infinite these perfections which are shown to be His Qualities are in reality the same as His Essence and one with each other. The difference observed between the Essence and the Qualities and at the same time between the Qualities themselves is only on the plane of concepts. Essentially there is but one Reality involved which is one and indivisible.[3]

In order to avoid the inadmissible error of limiting the Essence through attributing qualities to it or denying the principle of perfection in it, Islam has commanded its followers to preserve a just balance between affirmation and negation. It has ordered them to believe that God has knowledge but not like the knowledge of others. He has power but not like the power of others. He hears but not with ears. He sees but not with eyes like those of men, and so on.[4]

Further Explanations Concerning the Qualities

Qualities in general are of two types: qualities of perfection, and qualities of imperfection. Qualities of perfection, as mentioned above, are of a positive nature and give higher ontological value and greater ontological effect to the object that they qualify. This is clear from the comparison between a live, knowing and capable being and a dead being which lacks knowledge and capability. Qualities of imperfection are the reverse of such qualities. When we analyze these imperfect qualities we see that they are negative and show a lack of perfection, such as ignorance, impatience, ugliness, illness, and the like. Therefore, it can be said that the negation of the quality of imperfection is the quality of perfection. For example, the negation of ignorance is knowledge and the negation of impotence is power and capability.

For this reason the Holy Quran has related each positive quality directly to God and negated every quality of imperfection from Him, attributing the negation of such imperfections to Him, as He says: "He is the knower, the Omnipotent," or He says, "He is the Alive" or "Neither slumber nor sleep overtaketh Him," or "Know that ye cannot frustrate Allah."

The point that must never be forgotten is that God, the Most Exalted, is Absolute Reality without any limit or boundary. Therefore, a positive quality attributed to Him will not possess any limitation. He is not material and corporeal or limited to space and time. While possessing all positive qualities He is beyond every quality and state which belongs to creatures. Every quality which in reality belongs to Him is purified from the notion of limitedness, as He says, "Nought is as His likeness." (Quran, XLII, 11)[5]

Qualities of Action

In addition, qualities are also divided into qualities of essence and qualities of action. A quality sometimes depends only on the qualified itself, such as life, knowledge and power, which depend on the person of a living, knowing and capable human being. We can conceive of man in himself possessing these qualities without taking into consideration any other factor.

At other times a quality does not depend only on the qualified in itself, but, in order to qualify, it also requires the existence of something external as in the case of writing, conversation, desire, and the like. A person can be a writer if he possesses ink, pen, and paper, and he can converse when there is someone with whom to speak. In the same way he can desire when there is an object of desire. The sole existence of man is not sufficient to bring these qualities into existence.

From this analysis it becomes clear that the Divine Qualities which are the same as God's Essence, as already pointed out, are only of the first kind. As for the second kind, whose actualization depends upon an external factor, they cannot be considered as Qualities of the Essence and the same as the Essence, for all that is other than God is created by Him and so, being situated in the created order, comes after Him.

Qualities that pertain to God after the act of creation such as creator, omnipotent, giver of life, giver of death, sustainer, etc., are not the same as His Essence but are additional to it; they are Qualities of Action. By Quality of Action is meant that after the actualization of an act the meaning of a quality is understood from that act, not from the Essence (that performs the act), such as "Creator", which is conceived after the act of creation has taken place. From the creation is understood the quality of God as Creator. That quality depends upon creation, not upon the sacred Essence of God, the Most Exalted, Himself, so that the Essence does not change from one state to another with the appearance of that quality. Shi'ism considers the two qualities of will (iradah) and speech (kalam) in their literal meaning as Qualities of Action (will meaning wanting something and speech meaning conveying a meaning through an expression). Most of the Sunni theologians consider them as implying knowledge and thereby take them to be Qualities of Essence.[6]

Destiny and Providence

The law of causality reigns throughout the world of existence without any breach or exception.[7] According to this law each phenomenon in this world depends for its coming into being upon causes and conditions which make its actualization possible. If all of these causes, which are called the complete cause (the sufficient and necessary cause), are actualized, the coming into being of that phenomenon, or the assumed effect, becomes determined and necessary. And assuming the lack of all or some of these causes, the actualization of the phenomenon is impossible. Investigation and analysis of this thesis will clarify this point for us.

(1) If we compare a phenomenon (or effect) with the whole, complete (or sufficient) cause, and also with the parts of the complete cause, its relation to the complete cause is based on necessity and on a completely determined relationship. At the same time its relation to each of the parts of the complete cause (which are called incomplete or partial causes) is one of possiblity and lack of complete determinism. These causes provide the effect only with the possibility of existence, not with its necessity.

The world of existence, in its totality, therefore, is governed throughout by necessity because each of its parts has a necessary connection with its complete cause by the very fact of coming into being. Its structure is composed of a series of necessary and certain events. Yet, the character of possibility is preserved in its parts if we consider each part separately and in itself in the phenomena which are related and connected to partial causes which are other than their complete cause.

The Holy Quran in its teachings has called this reign of necessity Divine Destiny (*qaḍā'*), for this necessity issues from that Source that gives existence to the world and is therefore a command (*ḥukm*) and "Divine Decree" that is certain and is impossible to breach or disobey. It is based on justice and accepts no exception or discrimination. God Almighty says, "His verily is all creation and commandment" (Quran, VII, 54), and "When He decreeth [qada] a thing, He saith unto it only: Be! and it is"

(Quran, II, 117), and also "(When) Allah doometh there is none that can postpone His doom [hukm]" (Quran, XIII, 41).

(2) Each part of the cause provides the appropriate measure and "model" for the effect, and the coming into being of the effect is in accordance with the totality of the measures determined for it by the complete cause. For example, the causes that make respiration possible for man do not cause respiration in the absolute and unconditioned sense; rather they send a determined amount of the air around the mouth and nose through the respiratory channel to the area of the lungs in a determined time and with a determined shape. Likewise, the causes of man's vision (including man himself) do not bring into being vision as such without limits or conditions, but rather a vision which, through the means and organs provided, is limited and measured for men in every respect. This truth is to be found without exception in all the phenomena of the world and all the events that occur in it.

The Holy Quran has called this aspect of the truth "Providence" (*qadar*) and has related it to God Almighty who is the origin of creation, as has been said, "And there is not a thing but with Us are the stores thereof. And we send it not down save in appointed measure [qadar]" (Quran, XV, 21).[8]

In the same way that according to Divine Destiny the existence of each phenomenon and event which occurs in the cosmic order is necessary and cannot be avoided, so also according to Providence each phenomenon and event that occurs will never trespass or disobey in the least degree the measure which God has provided for it.

Man and Free Will

The action which man performs is one of the phenomena of the world of creation and its appearance depends, completely, like other phenomena in the world, upon its cause. And since man is a part of the world of creation and has an ontological relation with other parts of the cosmos, we cannot accept the premise that other parts should not have an effect upon his actions.

For example, when a man takes a bite of bread he needs not only the instruments of his hands, feet, mouth as well as knowledge, power and will, but also the existence of the bread in the external world, its availability, the lack of obstacles and other temporal and spatial conditions. If any of these causes were not actualized, the action would not be possible. Conversely, with the actualization of all of them (the complete cause) the occurrence of the action becomes completely necessary. The necessity of the action in relation to all of the parts of the complete cause is not contradictory to the possibility of the relation of the action with respect to man, who is one of the parts of the complete cause. Man has the possibility or free will (*ikhtiyār*) to perform the act. The necessity existing in the relation between the action and all of the parts of the cause does not mean that the relation of the action to some of the parts of the cause, of which man is one, should also be that of necessity and determinism.

Man's simple and untainted comprehension also confirms this point of view, for we see that people through their God-given nature and intelligence distinguish between such things as eating, drinking, coming and going on the one hand, and on the other, such things as health and illness, age and youth or the height of the body. The first group, which is directly related to man's will, is considered to be performed according to the free choice of the individual so that people command and prohibit them and blame or condemn them. But concerning the second group man has no duty and is not under any Divine command because he cannot exercise a free choice over them.

At the beginning of Islam among the Sunnis there were two schools that were concerned with the theological aspects of human action. One group, holding the view that human action is the result of the unbreakable will of God, considered man to be determined in his actions and held human free will to be devoid of any value and sense. The other group believed man to be independent in his actions, which did not depend upon the Divine will and were outside of the command of Providence (qadar).

But according to the instruction of the Household of the Prophet, which is also in conformity with the literal instructions of the Quran, man is free (*mukhtār*) in his actions but not independent (*mustaqill*). Rather, God the Almighty through free will has willed the act. According to our previous analysis, God the Exalted has willed and made necessary the act through all of the parts of the complete cause, of which one is the will and free choice of man. As a result of this kind of Divine will, the action is necessary but in it man has also free will, that is, the action is necessary with respect to all the parts of its cause, and possible and free in choice with respect to one of those parts which is man.[9] The sixth Imam—upon whom be peace—has said, "It is neither determination nor free will but something between the two."

The fifth and sixth Imams said that "God loves His creation so much that He will not force it to commit sin and then punish it. And God is so powerful that whatever He commands comes to be." Also the sixth Imam has said, "God is so generous that He does not make it a duty for men to do what is not in their power. He is so powerful that nothing comes into being in His kingdom which He does not will." (This is an allusion to the two schools of predestination and free will.) (*Biḥār al-anwār*, vol. III, pp. 5, 6, 15)

NOTES

CHAPTER IV

1. In the Book of God reference is made to this reasoning in the verse: "Can there be doubt concerning Allah, the Creator of the heavens and the earth?" (Quran, XIV, 10)

2. *Editor's note:* This is again in reference to the Quranic verse, "We shall show them our portents . . ." referred to above. Both the phenomena of nature and the realities within the human soul are "signs" of God. See S. H. Nasr, *An Introduction to Islamic Cosmological Doctrines*, Cambridge (U.S.A.), 1964, introduction.

3. The sixth Imam has said, "God has an immutable Being. His knowledge was Himself when there was nothing to be known. His hearing was Himself when there was nothing audible. His vision was Himself when there was nothing visible. His power was Himself when there was nothing over which to exercise power." *Biḥār al-anwār*, vol. II, p. 125.

There are innumerable traditions of the Household of the Prophet on this question. See *Nahj al-balāghah*, *Tawḥīd* of Ṣadūq, Tehran, 1375; *'Uyūn al-akhbār* of Ibn Qutaybah, Cairo, 1925–35; and *Biḥār al-anwār*, vol. II.

4. The fifth and sixth Imams have said, "God is a light that is not mixed with darkness, a knowledge into which ignorance cannot penetrate, a life in which there is no death." (*Biḥār al-anwār*, vol. II, p. 129) The eighth Imam has said, "Considering the question of Divine Attributes, people have followed three paths. A first group considers God to have Attributes similar to those of others. A second group negates the Attributes. The correct path is that of the third group who affirm the existence of the Attributes without their resemblance to the attributes of creatures." *Biḥār al-anwār*, vol. II, p. 94.

5. The sixth Imam has said, "God cannot be described by time, space, motion, translation or rest; rather, He is the creator of time, space, motion, translation and rest." *Biḥār al-anwār*, vol. II, p. 96.

6. The sixth Imam has said, "God was forever knowing in his Essence when there was nothing to be known and was powerful when there was nothing over which He could exercise power." The transmitter of the tradition recounts, "I said, 'and He had speech.' He replied, 'The Word (kalam) is created. God was, and He had no speech. Then He created and brought into being the Word (kalam).'" *Biḥār al-anwār*, vol. II, p. 147. And the eighth Imam has said, "Will comes from the inner being of people and following it action appears. In the case of God there is only His act of bringing into being, for unlike us God does not possess intention, purpose and discursive thought." *Biḥār al-anwār*, vol. II, p. 144.

7. *Editor's note:* Needless to say this assertion holds true whether there is strict causality on the microphysical level or not, because on the macrophysical plane strict causality is observed and is of the greatest importance for the understanding of the nature of this plane of existence. Causality also dominates over higher levels of existence than the corporeal.

8. The sixth Imam has said, "When God, the Exalted, wills a thing, He makes it predestined, and when He has made it predestined, He decrees it, and when He decrees it, He executes it and puts it into effect." *Biḥār al-anwār*, vol. III, p. 34.

9. *Editor's note:* The question of free will and determinism is one of the most difficult to solve theologically because it comprises a reality that transcends the dichotomy of discursive reason. With respect to Absolute Reality there is no free will because there is no partial reality independent of the Absolute. But to the extent that man is real in the relative sense, he possesses free will. From the point of view of causality there is determination in relation to the total cause but freedom with respect to man's action which is part of that total cause.

CHAPTER V ON THE KNOWLEDGE OF THE PROPHET

Toward the Goal: General Guidance

A grain of wheat that is placed within the bosom of the earth under appropriate conditions begins to grow and enters upon a path of development in which at every moment it takes on a new form and state. Following a particular order and sequence it treads this path until it becomes a grown plant with spikes of wheat; if once again one of the seeds were to fall upon the ground it would begin the previous cycle all over again until it reached the final goal. Likewise if the seed is that of a fruit placed within the bosom of the soil it begins its transformation, breaking its shell, from which a green stem shoots out. It follows an orderly and distinct path of transformation until finally it becomes a fully grown tree, green and full of fruit. Or if it is the sperm of an animal it begins to develop within the egg or in the womb of the mother, following the line of development peculiar to that animal until it becomes a perfected individual of that animal species.

This distinct path and orderly development is to be observed in each species of creatures in this world and is determined by the inner nature of that species. The green wheat plant which has sprung up from the grain will never bear oats or become a sheep, a goat, or an elephant, and an animal that has become pregnant from its male will never bear spikes of wheat or a plane tree. Even if an imperfection were to occur in the organs or the natural functions of the newly born, or if a lamb were to be born without an eye, or a wheat plant develop without spikes of wheat, we would have no doubt that such an occurrence was due to some pest or plague or to unnatural causes. Continuous order and regularity in the development and generation of things, and the belonging of each species of creatures in its generation and development to a particular order and rule, is an undeniable fact.

From this evident thesis two conclusions can be drawn. (1) Between the various stages that each species of creatures traverses from the beginning to the end of its existence there is continuity and interconnection, as if that species in each stage of its development were pushed from behind and attracted by what is to come. (2) Due to the above-mentioned continuity and interconnection, the last stage in the development of each species is from the beginning of its generation the goal and point of "existential attention" of that species. For example, the "attention" of the walnut that sends out a green shoot from below the earth is centered from that very moment on a fully grown walnut tree. And a sperm in the egg or the womb is from the moment of its generation moving toward the state of the perfected animal.

The Holy Quran, which teaches that the creation and the preservation of things belong absolutely to God, considers this movement and attraction, which each species in creation possesses in treading its path of development, to be derived from Divine guidance. As He says, "Our Lord is He Who gave unto everything its nature, then guided it aright" (Quran, XX, 50).[1] And also, "Who createth, then disposeth; who measureth then guideth" (Quran, LXXXVII, 2–3). And He refers to the result of these sayings in these words: "And each one hath a goal toward which he turneth" (Quran, II, 148).[2] And also: "And We created not the heavens and the earth, and all that is between them in play. We created them not save with truth, but most of them know not" (Quran, XLIV, 38–39).[3]

Special Guidance

Obviously the human species is not an exception to this general rule. The same guidance which rules over all species of creatures governs man as well. In the same way that each species through its particular nature follows its path of perfection and is guided to it, so must man with the help of this guidance be guided toward that which is his real perfection.

Although man shares many elements with other species of animals and with plants, the one special characteristic which distinguishes him is intellect.[4] It is with the help of his intellect and reason that man is able to think and to make use of every means possible for his own benefit, to fly into the endless spaces of the sky or swim in the depth of the sea, or to bring under his service and command all kinds of created things, whether they be minerals, plants or animals on the surface of the earth, and to benefit even from members of his own species to the greatest extent possible.

Owing to his primordial nature, man sees his happiness and perfection in gaining complete freedom. Yet, he must of necessity sacrifice some of his freedom because he is created as a social being and has endless demands which by himself he can never satisfy, and also because he is in cooperation and social intercourse with other members of his species who themselves have the same instinct of self-centeredness and love of freedom that he has. For the sake of the benefit he gains from others he must in turn be of benefit to them. Equivalent to what he reaps from the toil of others he must give of his own work. Or, in summary, he must of necessity accept a society based upon mutual cooperation.

This point is clear in the case of newborn babies and children. At the beginning, when desiring anything, they make use of no other means but force and crying and refuse to accept any constraint or discipline. But gradually, as a result of mental development, they realize that one cannot succeed in the problems of life only through rebellion and force; therefore, slowly they approach the condition of social beings. Finally they reach the age when they become social individuals with developed mental powers and are ready to obey the social regulations of their environment.

When man comes to accept the necessity for mutual cooperation among members of society he also recognizes the necessity for laws which rule over society, clarifying the duty of each individual and specifying the punishment for each offender. He accepts laws through whose application each individual in society can realize real happiness and find felicity in proportion to the social value of his efforts. These laws are the same universal and applicable laws which man, from the first day of his existence until today, has been continuously seeking and to which he has always been attracted as the foremost among all his desires. If the attainment of such a thing were not possible and were not written upon the tablet of human destiny, it would not have been the perennial yearning of man.[5]

God, the Exalted, has referred to this reality of human society, saying, "We have apportioned among them their livelihood in the life of the world, and raised some of them above others in rank that some of them may take labor from others" (Quran, LXIII, 32).[6] Concerning man's selfishness and desire to monopolize things to himself He says, "Lo! man was created anxious, fretful when evil befalleth him, and, when good befalleth him, grudging" (Quran, LXX, 19–21).[7]

Reason and Law

If we delve into the matter carefully we will discover that man seeks continuously those laws which can bring him happiness in the world; that people as individuals and in groups recognize, in accordance with their God-given nature, the necessity for laws which provide felicity for them without discrimination or exception, laws which establish a general norm of perfection among mankind. Obviously, up to now, during the different periods of human history, there have not come into being any such laws which were devised by human reason. If the laws of existence had placed the burden of creating such human laws upon the shoulders of human reason, then during the long period of history such laws would have been established. In that case, each individual who possesses the power of reasoning would comprehend this human law in detail in the same way that everyone realizes the necessity for such laws in society.

In other words, if it had been in the very nature of things that it be the duty of human reason to create a perfect common law which must provide happiness for human society, and that man should be guided to that perfect law through the process of creation and the generation of the world itself, then such laws would have been apprehended by each human being through his reason in the same way that man knows what is of benefit or detriment to him throughout the determined course of daily life. There is, however, as yet no sign of the presence of such laws. Laws which have come about by themselves, or have been devised by a single ruler, or individuals, or nations, and have become prevalent in different societies are considered by some as certain, and by others as doubtful. Some are aware of these laws and others are ignorant of them. Never has it come to pass that all people, who in their basic structure are the same in that they are endowed by God with reason, should have a common awareness of the details of the laws which can bring about happiness in the world of man.

That Mysterious Wisdom and Consciousness Called Revelation

Thus, in the light of the discussion above, it becomes clear that the laws which can guarantee the happiness of human society cannot be perceived by reason. Since according to the thesis of general guidance running throughout creation the existence of an awareness of these laws in the human species is necessary, there must be another power of apprehension within the human species which enables man to understand the real duties of life and which places this knowledge within the reach of everyone. This consciousness and power of perception, which is other than reason and sense, is called the prophetic consciousness, or the consciousness of revelation.

Of course the presence of such a power in mankind does not mean that it should necessarily appear in all individuals, in the same way that although the power of procreation has been placed in all human beings, the awareness of the enjoyment of marriage and being prepared for this enjoyment is possible only for those whose have reached the age of puberty. In the same way that the consciousness of revelation is a mysterious and unknown form of consciousness for those who do not possess it, the apprehension of the joy of sexual union is a mysterious and unknown feeling for those who have not reached the age of puberty.

God, the Exalted, makes reference in His Word to the revelation of His Divine Law (Shari'ah) and the inability of human reason to comprehend this matter in the verses: "Lo! We inspire thee as We inspired Noah and the prophets after him, as We inspired Abraham and Ishmael and Isaac and Jacob and the tribes, and Jesus and Job and Jonah and Aaron and Solomon, and We imparted unto David the Psalms; and messengers We have mentioned unto thee before and messengers We have not mentioned unto thee; and Allah spoke directly unto Moses; Messengers of good cheer and of warning, in order that mankind might have no argument against Allah after the messengers" (Quran, IV, 163–165).[8]

The Prophets—Inerrancy of Prophecy

The appearance of prophets affirms the conception of revelation outlined above. The prophets of God were men who propagated the call of revelation and prophecy and brought definitive proofs for their call. They propagated among people the elements of the religion of God (which is the same divine law that guarantees happiness) and made it available to all men.

Since in all periods of history the number of people endowed with the power of prophecy and revelation has been limited to a few individuals, God—the Most Exalted—has completed and perfected the guidance of the rest of mankind by placing the mission of the propagation of religion upon the shoulders of His prophets. That is why a prophet of God must possess the quality of inerrancy (*'iṣmah*). In receiving the revelation from God, in guarding it and in making possible its reaching the people, he must be free from error. He must not commit sin (*ma'ṣiyah*). The reception of revelation, its preservation and its propagation are three principles of ontological guidance; and error in existence itself is meaningless. Furthermore, sin and opposition to the claims of the religious call and its propagation are impossible in a prophet for they would be a call against the original religious mission; they would destroy the confidence of the people, their reliance upon the truth and the validity of the call. As a result they would destroy the purpose of the religious call itself.

God, the Exalted, refers in His word to the inerrancy of the prophets, saying, "And We chose them and guided them unto a straight path" (Quran, VI, 88).[9] And also, "(He is) the Knower of the Unseen, and He revealeth unto none His secret, save unto every messenger whom He hath chosen, and then He maketh a guard to go before him and a guard behind him, that He may know that they have indeed conveyed the messages of their Lord" (Quran, LXXII, 26–28).[10]

The Prophets and Revealed Religion

What the prophets of God received through revelation and as a message from God and conveyed to mankind was religion (din),[11] that is, a way of life and human duties which guarantee the real happiness of man.

Revealed religion in general consists of two parts: doctrine and practice or method. The doctrinal part of revealed religion consists of a series of fundamental principles and views concerning the real nature of things upon which man must establish the foundations of his life. It is comprised of the three universal principles of unity (tawhid), prophecy (nubuwwat), and eschatology (ma'ad). If there is any confusion or disorder in one of these principles the religion will not be able to gain any following.

The practical part of revealed religion consists of a series of moral and practical injunctions covering the duties man has before God and human society. That is why the secondary duties which have been ordered for man in different Divine laws are of two kinds: morals (*akhlāq*), and actions (*a'māl*). The morals and actions related to the Divine are of two kinds, such as: first, the quality of faith, sincerity, surrender to God, contentment and humility; and second, the daily prayers, fasting, and sacrifice (called acts of worship and symbolizing the humility and servitude of man before the Divine Throne). The morals and actions related to human society are also of two kinds, such as: first, the quality of love for other men, wishing well for others, justice and generosity; and second, the duty to carry out social intercourse, trade and exchange, etc. (called transactions).

Another point that must be considered is that since the human species is directed toward the gradual attainment of perfection, and human society through the passage of time becomes more complete, the appearance of a parallel development must also be seen in revealed laws.[12] The Holy Quran affirms this gradual development, which reason has also discovered. It can be concluded from its verses that each Divine Law (Shariʿah) is in reality more complete than the Shariʿah before; for instance, in this verse where He says, "And unto thee have We revealed the Scripture with the truth, confirming whatever Scripture was before it, and a watcher over it." (Quran, V, 48)[13]

Of course, as scientific knowledge also confirms and the Quran states, the life of human society in this world is not eternal and the development of man is not endless. As a result, the general principles governing the duties of man from the point of view of doctrine and practice must of necessity stop at a particular stage. Therefore, prophecy and the Shariʿah will also one day come to an end when in the perfection of doctrine and expansion of practical regulations they have reached the final stage of their development. That is why the Holy Quran, in order to make clear that Islam (the religion of Muhammad) is the last and most complete of the revealed religions, introduces itself as a sacred book that cannot be abrogated (*naskh*), calls the Prophet the "Seal of the Prophets" (*khātam al-anbiyā'*), and sees the Islamic religion as embracing all religious duties. As He says, "For lo! it is an unassailable Scripture. Falsehood cannot come at it from before it or behind it" (Quran, XLI, 41–42).[14] And also, "Muhammad is not the father of any man among you but he is the messenger of Allah and the Seal of the prophets" (Quran, XXXIII, 40).[15] And, "We reveal the scripture unto thee as an exposition of all things" (Quran, XVI, 89).[16]

The Prophets and Proof of Revelation and Prophecy

Many modern scholars who have investigated the problem of revelation and prophecy have tried to explain revelation, prophecy and questions connected with them by using the principles of social psychology. They say that the prophets of God were men of a pure nature and strong will who had great love for humanity. In order to enable mankind to advance spiritually and materially and in order to reform decadent societies, they devised laws and regulations and invited mankind to accept them. Since people in those days would not accept the logic of human reason, in order to make them obey their teachings the prophets, according to such modern scholars, claimed that they and their thoughts came from the transcendent world. Each prophet called his own pure soul the Holy Spirit; the teachings which he claimed came from the transcendent world were called "revelation and prophecy"; the duties which resulted from the teachings were called "revealed Shari'ah"; and the written record of these teachings and duties were called a "revealed book."

Anyone who views with depth and impartiality the revealed books and especially the Holy Quran, and also the lives of the prophets, will have no doubt that this view is not correct. The prophets of God were not political men. Rather they were "men of God," full of truthfulness and purity. What they perceived they proclaimed without addition or diminution. And what they uttered they acted upon. What they claimed to possess was a mysterious consciousness which the invisible world had bestowed upon them. In this way they came to know from God Himself what the welfare of men was in this world and the next, and propagated this knowledge among mankind.

It is quite clear that in order to confirm and ascertain the call of prophecy there is need of proof and demonstration. The sole fact that the Shari'ah brought by a prophet conforms to reason is not sufficient in determining the truthfulness of the prophetic call. A man who claims to be a prophet, in addition to the claim of the truth of his Shari'ah, claims a connection through revelation and prophecy with the transcendent world, and therefore claims that he has been given by God the mission to propagate the faith. This claim in itself is in need of proof. That is why (as the Holy Quran informs us) the common people with their simple mentality always sought miracles from the prophets of God in order that the truthfulness of their call might be confirmed.

The meaning of this simple and correct logic is that the revelation which the prophet claims is his cannot be found among others who are human beings like him. It is of necessity an invisible power which God miraculously bestows upon His prophets, through which they hear His word and are given the mission to convey this word to mankind. If this be true, then the prophet should ask God for another miracle so that people would believe the truth of his prophetic call.

It is thus clear that the request for miracles from prophets is according to correct logic and it is incumbent upon the prophet of God to provide a miracle at the beginning of his call, or according to the demand of the people, in order to prove his prophecy. The Holy Quran has affirmed this logic, relating miracles about many prophets at the beginning of their mission or after their followers requested them.

Of course many modern investigators and scientists have denied miracles, but their opinions are not based upon any satisfactory reasons. There is no reason to believe that the causes which until now have been discovered for events through investigation and experiment are permanent and unchanging, or that no event ever occurs for reasons other than those which usually bring it about. The miracles related about the prophets of God are not impossible or against reason (as is, for example, the claim that the number three is even). Rather they are a "break in what is habitual" (*kharq-i 'ādat*),[17] an occurrence which, incidentally, has often been observed in a lower degree among people following ascetic practices.

The Number of the Prophets of God

It is known through tradition that in the past many prophets appeared, and the Holy Quran affirms their multitude. It has mentioned some of them by name or by their characteristics, but has not given their exact number. Through definitive traditions also it has not been possible to determine their number except in the well-known saying which Abū Dharr Ghifārī has recited from the Holy Prophet, according to which their number has been set at 124,000.

The Prophets Who are Bringers of Divine Law

From what can be deduced from the Quran, it can be concluded that all the prophets of God did not bring a Shariʿah. Rather, five of them—Noah, Abraham, Moses, Jesus, and the Prophet Muhammad—are "possessors of determination" (*ūlu'l-ʿazm*), those who have brought a Shariʿah. Other prophets follow the Shariʿah of those who "possess determination." God has said in the Quran, "He hath ordained for you that religion which He commended unto Noah, and that which We inspire in thee (Muhammad), and that which We commended unto Abraham and Moses and Jesus" (Quran, XLII, 13).[18] He has also said, "And when We exacted a covenant from the Prophets, and from thee (O Muhammad) and from Noah and Abraham and Moses and Jesus son of Mary, We took from them a solemn covenant" (Quran, XXXIII, 7).[19]

The Prophecy of Muhammad

The last prophet of God is Ḥaḍrat-i Muhammad[20]—upon whom be blessings and peace—who possesses a book and a Shariʿah and in whom Muslims have placed their faith. The Prophet was born fifty-three years before the beginning of the hegira calendar[21] in Mecca in the Hijaz amidst the family of Banū Hāshim of the Tribe of Quraysh, who were considered the most honored of the Arab families.

His father was called ʿAbdallāh and his mother, Āminah. He lost both parents at the beginning of childhood and was placed under the care of his paternal grandfather, ʿAbd al-Muṭṭalib, who also soon passed away. At this time the Prophet's uncle, Abū Ṭālib, took charge of him and became his guardian, taking him into his own house. The Prophet grew up in his uncle's house and even before reaching the age of adolescence used to accompany his uncle on journeys by caravan.

The Prophet had not received any schooling and therefore did not know how to read and write. Yet, after reaching the age of maturity he became famous for his wisdom, courtesy, and trustworthiness. As a result of his sagacity and trustworthiness, one of the women of the tribe of Quraysh, well-known for her wealth, appointed him as the custodian of her possessions and left in his hands the task of conducting her commercial affairs.

The Prophet once journeyed to Damascus with her merchandise and as a result of the ability he displayed was able to make an outstanding profit. Before long she asked to become his wife and the Prophet accepted her proposal. After the marriage, which occurred when he was twenty-five years old, the Prophet began the life of a manager of his wife's fortunes, until the age of forty, gaining meanwhile a widespread reputation for wisdom and trustworthiness. He refused, however, to worship idols, as was the common religious practice of the Arabs of the Hijaz. And occasionally he would make spiritual retreats (*khalwah*) in which he prayed and discoursed secretly with God.

At the age of forty, in the cave of Ḥirā', in the mountains of the Tihāmah region near Mecca, when he was in spiritual retreat, he was chosen by God to become a prophet and was given the mission of propagating the new religion. At that moment the first chapter of the Quran ("The Blood-Clot" [*Sūrah-i ʿalaq*]) was revealed to him. That very day he returned to his house and on the way met his cousin, Ali ibn Abī Ṭālib, who after hearing the account of what had occurred declared his acceptance of the faith. After the Prophet entered the house and told his wife of the revelation, she likewise accepted Islam.

The first time the Prophet invited people to accept his message he was faced with a distressing and painful reaction. Of necessity he was forced henceforth to propagate his message in secret for some time until he was ordered again by God to invite his very close relatives to accept his message. But this call was also fruitless and no one heeded it except Ali ibn Abi Talib, who in any case had already accepted the faith. (But in accordance with documents transmitted from the Household of the Prophet and extant poems composed by Abu Talib, Shi'ites believe that Abu Talib had also embraced Islam; however, because he was the sole protector of the Prophet, he hid his faith from the people in order to preserve the outward power he had with the Quraysh.)

After this period, according to Divine instruction, the Prophet began to propagate his mission openly. With the beginning of open propagation the people of Mecca reacted most severely and inflicted the most painful afflictions and tortures upon the Prophet and the people who had become newly converted to Islam. The severe treatment dealt out by the Quraysh reached such a degree that a group of Muslims left their homes and belongings and migrated to Abyssinia. The Prophet and his uncle, Abu Talib, along with their relatives from the Banu Hashim, took refuge for three years in the "mountain pass of Abu Talib," a fort in one of the valleys of Mecca. No one had any dealings or transactions with them and they did not dare to leave their place of refuge.

The idol-worshipers of Mecca, although at the beginning they considered inflicting all kinds of pressures and tortures such as striking and beating, insult, ridicule and defamation on the Prophet, occasionally would also show kindness and courtesy toward him in order to have him turn away from his mission. They would promise him great sums of money or leadership and the rule of the tribe. But for the Prophet their promises and their threats only resulted in the intensification of his will and determination to carry out his mission. Once, when they came to the Prophet promising him wealth and power, the Prophet told them, using metaphorical language, that if they were to put the sun in the palm of his right hand and the moon in the palm of his left hand he would not turn away from obeying the unique God or refrain from performing his mission.

About the tenth year of his prophecy, when the Prophet left the "mountain pass of Abu Talib," his uncle Abu Talib, who was also his sole protector, died, as did also his devoted wife. Henceforth there was no protection for his life nor any place of refuge. Finally the idol-worshipers of Mecca devised a secret plan to kill him. At night they surrounded his house from all sides with the aim of forcing themselves in at the end of the night and cutting him to pieces while he was in bed. But God, the Exalted, informed him of the plan and commanded him to leave for Yathrib. The Prophet placed Ali in place of himself in his bed and at night left the house under Divine protection, passing amidst his enemies, and taking refuge in a cave near Mecca. After three days when his enemies, having looked everywhere, gave up hope of capturing him and returned to Mecca, he left the cave and set out for Yathrib.

The people of Yathrib, whose leaders had already accepted the message of the Prophet and sworn allegiance to him, accepted him with open arms and placed their lives and property at his disposal. In Yathrib for the first time the Prophet formed a small Islamic community and signed treaties with the Jewish tribes in and around the city as well as with the powerful Arab tribes of the region. He undertook the task of propagating the Islamic message and Yathrib became famous as "Madīnat al-rasūl" (the city of the Prophet).

Islam began to grow and expand from day to day. The Muslims, who in Mecca were caught in the mesh of the injustice and inequity of the Quraysh, gradually left their homes and property and migrated to Medina, revolving around the Prophet like moths around a candle. This group became known as the "immigrants" (muhajirun) in the same way that those who aided the Prophet in Yathrib gained the name of "helpers" (*anṣār*).

Islam was advancing rapidly but at the same time the idol-worshipers of Quraysh, as well as the Jewish tribes of the Hejaz, were unrestrained in their harassment of the Muslims. With the help of the "hypocrites" (*munāfiqūn*) of Mecca, who were amidst the community of Muslims and who were not known for their holding any particular positions, they created new misfortunes for the Muslims every day until finally the matter led to war.

Many battles took place between the Muslims and the Arab polytheists and Jews, in most of which the Muslims were victorious. There were altogether over eighty major and minor battles. In all the major conflicts such as the battles of Badr, Uhud, Khandaq, Khaybar, Hunayn, etc., the Prophet was personally present on the battle scene. Also in all the major battles and many minor ones, victory was gained especially through the efforts of Ali. He was the only person who never turned away from any of these battles. In all the wars that occurred during the ten years after the migration from Mecca to Medina less than two hundred Muslims and less than a thousand infidels were killed.

As a result of the activity of the Prophet and the selfless effort of the muhajirun and ansar during this ten-year period, Islam spread through the Arabian peninsula. There were also letters written to kings of other countries such as Persia, Byzantinum and Abyssinia inviting them to accept Islam. During this time the Prophet lived in poverty and was proud of it.[22] He never spent a moment of his time in vain. Rather, his time was divided into three parts: one spent for God, in worshiping and remembering Him; a part for himself and his household and domestic needs; and a part for the people. During this part of his time he was engaged in spreading and teaching Islam and its sciences, administrating to the needs of Islamic society and removing whatever evils existed, providing for the needs of the Muslims, strengthening domestic and foreign bonds, and similar matters.

After ten years of stay in Medina the Prophet fell ill and died after a few days of illness. According to existing traditions the last words on his lips were advice concerning slaves and women.

The Prophet and the Quran

It was demanded of the Prophet, as it had been of other prophets, that he produce a miracle. The Prophet himself also confirmed the power of prophets to produce miracles as has been asserted clearly by the Quran. Many miracles by the Prophet have been recounted, the transmission of some of which is certain and can be accepted with confidence. But the enduring miracle of the Prophet, which is still alive, is the sacred book of Islam, the Holy Quran. The Holy Quran is a sacred text consisting of six thousand and several hundred verses (*āyah*) divided into one hundred and fourteen large and small chapters (*sūrah*). The verses of the Holy Quran were revealed gradually during the twenty-three year period of prophecy and mission of the Prophet. From less than one verse to a whole and complete chapter were revealed under different circumstances, both at day and night, on journeys or at home, in war or peace, during days of hardship or moments of rest.

The Holy Quran in many of its verses introduces itself in unambiguous language as a miracle. It invited the Arabs of that day to rivalry and competition in composing writings of comparable truth and beauty. The Arabs, according to the testimony of history, had reached the highest stages of eloquence and elegance of language, and in the sweetness of language and flow of speech they ranked foremost among all people. The Holy Quran claims that if it be thought of as human speech, created by the Prophet himself or learned through instruction from someone else, then the Arabs should be able to produce its like[23] or ten chapters like it,[24] or a single one of its verses,[25] making use of whatever means were at their disposal to achieve this end. The celebrated Arab men of eloquence claimed in answer to this request that the Quran was magic and it was thus impossible for them to produce its like.[26]

Not only does the Quran challenge and invite people to compete with its eloquence and elegant language, but also it occasionally invites rivalry from the point of view of its meaning and thus challenges all the mental powers of men and *jinn*,[27] for the Quran is a book containing the total program for human life.[28] If we investigate the matter carefully we will discover that God has made this vast and extensive program which embraces every aspect of the countless beliefs, ethical forms and actions of mankind and takes into account all of their details and particularities, to be the "Truth" (haqq) and to be called the religion of the truth (din-i haqq). Islam is a religion whose injunctions are based on the truth and the real welfare of mankind, not the desires and inclinations of the majority of men or the whims of a single, powerful ruler.

At the foundation of this vast program is placed the most cherished word of God which is belief in His Unity. All the principles of the sciences are deduced from the principle of Unity (tawhid). After that, the most praiseworthy human ethical and moral virtues are deduced from the principles of the religious sciences and included in the program. Then, the countless principles and details of human action and individual and social conditions of man are investigated, and the duties pertaining to them which originate from the worship of the One are elaborated and organized. In Islam the relation and continuity between the principles (usul) and their applications (furuʿ) are such that each particular application in whatever subject it may be, if it is brought back to its source, returns to the principle of Unity or tawhid, and Unity if applied and analyzed becomes the basis for the particular injunction and rule in question.

Of course, the final elaboration of such an extensive religion with such unity and interconnection, or even the preparation of an elementary index for it, is beyond the normal powers of the best authorities on law in the world. But here we speak of a man who in a short span of time was placed amidst a thousand difficulties concerning his life and property, caught in bloody battles and faced with internal and external obstacles and furthermore placed alone before the whole world. Moreover, the Prophet had never received instruction nor learned how to read and write.[29] He had spent two-thirds of his life before becoming a prophet among a people who possessed no learning and had had no taste of civilization. He passed his life in a land without water or vegetation and with burning air, among a people who lived in the lowest social conditions and were dominated by neighboring political powers.

Besides the above, the Holy Quran challenges men in another way.[30] This book was revealed gradually, during a period of twenty-three years, under totally different conditions in periods of difficulty or comfort, war or peace, power or weakness, and the like. If it had not come from God but had been composed and expounded by man, many contradictions and contrasts would be observed in it. Its ending would of necessity be more perfect than its beginning, as is necessary in the gradual perfection of the human individual. Instead, the first Meccan verses are of the same quality as the Medinan verses and there is no difference between the beginning and end of the Quran. The Quran is a book whose parts resemble each other and whose awe-inspiring power of expression is of the same style and quality throughout.

NOTES

CHAPTER V

1. By this is meant guidance toward the goal of life and of creation.
2. For each person there exists a goal which he pursues.
3. Creation with truth means that there is a goal and purpose to creation.
4. *Editor's note:* The author uses the Persian word *khirad*, which like ʿaql means both intellect and reason depending on how it is used. But it certainly does not mean just reason or the modern understanding of intellect as being synonymous with reason. The traditional meaning of intellect as a faculty of immediate perception transcending reason, yet not irrational, is inherent in it.
5. Even the simplest and most thoughtless of men wish by their nature as human beings that human society should be such that all can live in comfort, peace, and tranquillity. From the philosophical point of view, want, love, attraction, appetite and the like are relative qualities connecting two sides, such as that which wishes with that which is wished, or the lover and the beloved. It is clear that if there were to be no one to love, love would have no meaning. Ultimately all this returns to the understanding of the meaning of imperfection. If there were to be no perfection, imperfection would have no meaning.
6. This means that each individual is responsible for a part of life and receives an appointed portion of livelihood. Men are of different ranks in the sense that the manager dominates over the worker, the director over his subordinates, the owner over the tenant or the buyer over the seller.
7. The anxiety mentioned here is related to man's being covetous.
8. This verse clarifies the insufficiency of human reason without prophecy and revelation. If reason were sufficient to provide argument for the existence of God, there would be no need of prophets.
9. To have guided the prophets unto a straight path means that they are directed wholly toward God and obey only Him.
10. A guard before and a guard behind refers to conditions before and after the revelation or the event of the life of the prophet himself.
11. *Editor's note:* As we have already indicated, din is a most universal term in Arabic and Persian and should be translated as religion only if we understand the latter term in the widest sense possible, not as one thing among others, but as a total way of life based upon transcendent principles, or a tradition in the true sense of the word.
12. *Editor's note:* Islam bases its argument upon the gradual development of man and therefore "perfection" of successive revelations although from another

point of view it considers all prophets as equal. In any case this argument should not be confused with modern evolutionism and belief in indefinite historical progress which are the very antithesis of the Islamic conception of time and history.

13. The Scripture at the beginning of the verse refers to the Holy Quran, while the second Scripture refers to such sacred books as the Torah and the Gospels.

14. The "Unassailable Scripture" is the Holy Quran.

15. The idea of the finality of the Quran as a sacred book which cannot be abrogated and the aspect of the Prophet as the "seal of prophecy" are essentially aspects of the same truth.

16. The Quran, according to the Islamic view, contains the principle of all knowledge, and through it every domain can be clarified and elucidated.

17. *Editor's note:* Miracle in Persian as in Arabic is in fact called *khāriq al-ʿādah,* that is, that which breaks the habitual relation between causes and effects in this world which because of its recurrence and persistence appears to us as a closed and unbreakable net of causality. The miracle represents the intrusion into this habitual world of a cause from another world or state of being with naturally different effects from what we have become accustomed to in our everyday experience. It is therefore the "break of habit" or of what has become habitual.

18. This verse is in the form of an obligation. It is clear that in this case if there were prophets other than the five mentioned in this verse who had brought a new Shariʿah, they would have been mentioned.

19. There is again reference to the same prophets who brought new Shariʿahs into the world.

20. *Editor's note:* In Persian and other Muslim languages the name of the Prophet is usually preceded by the honorific title *Ḥaḍrat* and followed by the formula, "Upon whom be blessings and peace" (*ṣall Allāhu ʿalaihi wa sallam*). Hadrat is also used for other prophets, for Shiʿite Imams and even for some very eminent religious authorities.

21. *Editor's note:* The Islamic calendar begins with the migration of the Prophet from Mecca to Medina and is thus called the hegira calendar, from the Arabic word hijrah, meaning emigration.

22. In a famous hadith the Prophet has said, "Poverty (*faqr*) is my glory." concerning the material of this section see the *Sīrah* of Ibn Hishām, Cairo, 1355–56; the *Sīrah* of Ḥalabī, Cairo, 1320; *Biḥār an-anwār*, vol. VI, and other traditional sources on the life of the Holy Prophet.

23. As He says, "Then let them produce speech the like thereof, if they are truthful" (Quran, LII, 34).

24. As He says, "Or they say: He [Muhammad] has invented it. Say: Then bring ten surahs, the like thereof, invented, and call on everyone ye can beside Allah, if ye are truthful!" (Quran, XI, 13).

25. As He says, "Or they say: He hath invented it? Say: then bring a surah like unto it . . ." (Quran, X, 39).

26. As He recounts from the saying of one of the Arab men of letters, "And said: This is naught else than magic from of old; This is naught else than speech of mortal man" (Quran, LXXIV, 24–25).

27. *Editor's note:* The jinn referred to in the Quran are interpreted traditionally as conscious, psychic forces that inhabited this world before the Fall of Adam and who still exist on the subtle plane. The terms jinn and *ins* (mankind) are thus often used together in Islamic sources to refer to the totality of conscious beings possessing mental faculties in this world. See Appendix IV.

28. As He says, "Say: Verily, though mankind and the Jinn should assemble to produce the like of this Quran, they could not produce the like thereof though they were helpers one of another" (Quran, XVII, 88).

29. As He recounts from the tongue of the Holy Prophet, "I dwelt among you a whole lifetime before it (came to me). Have ye then no sense?" (Quran, X, 17). And He says, "And thou (O Muhammad) wast not a reader of any scripture before it, nor didst thou write it with thy right hand . . ." (Quran, XXIX, 48). He also says, "And if ye are in doubt concerning that which We reveal unto Our slave (Muhammad), then produce a surah of the like thereof, and call your witnesses besides Allah if ye are truthful" (Quran, II, 23).

30. As He says, "Will they not then ponder on the Quran? If it had been from other than Allah they would have found herein much incongruity" (Quran, IV, 82).

CHAPTER VI ESCHATOLOGY

Man is Composed of Spirit and Body

Those who are acquainted to a certain extent with the Islamic sciences know that within the teachings of the Holy Book and the traditions of the Prophet there are many references to spirit and corpus, or soul and body. Although it is relatively easy to conceive of the body and what is corporeal, or that which can be known through the senses, to conceive of spirit and soul is difficult and complicated.

People given to intellectual discussions, such as the theologians and philosophers, Shi'ite and Sunni alike, have presented different views concerning the reality of the spirit (*rūḥ*). Yet, what is to some extent certain is that Islam considers spirit and body to be two realities opposed to each other. The body through death loses the characteristics of life and gradually disintegrates, but it is not so with the spirit. Rather, life in its origin and principle belongs to the spirit. When the spirit is joined to the body, the body also derives life from it, and when the spirit separates from the body and cuts its bond to the body—the event that is called death—the body ceases to function while the spirit continues to live.

From what can be learned through deliberation upon the verses of the Holy Quran and the sayings of the Imams of the Household of the Prophet, the spirit of man is something immaterial which has some kind of relation and connection with the material body. God the Almighty in His Book says, "Verily We created man from a product of wet earth; Then placed him as a drop (of seed) in a safe lodging; Then fashioned We the drop a clot, then fashioned

We the clot a little lump, then fashioned We the little lump bones, Then clothed the bones with flesh, and then produced it as another creation" (Quran, XXIII, 12–14). From the order of these verses it is clear that at the beginning the gradual creation of matter is described and then, when reference is made to the appearance of the spirit, consciousness, and will, another kind of creation is mentioned which is different from the previous form of creation.

In another place it is said, in answer to skeptics who ask how it is possible for the body of man, which after death becomes disintegrated and whose elements become dispersed and lost, to have a new creation and become the original man, "Say: The angel of death, who hath charge concerning you, will gather you, and afterwards unto your Lord ye will be returned" (Quran, XXXII, 11). This means that your bodies disintegrate after death and are lost amidst the particles of the earth, but you yourselves, namely, your spirits, have been taken from your bodies by the angel of death and remain protected with Us.

Besides such verses the Holy Quran in a comprehensive explanation expresses the immateriality of the spirit in itself when it asserts, "They will ask thee concerning the Spirit. Say: The Spirit is by command of my Lord" (Quran, XVII, 85).

In another place in explaining His command (*amr*) He says, "But His command, when He intendeth a thing, is only that He saith unto it: Be! and it is. Therefore glory be to Him in Whose hand is the dominion over all things!" (Quran, XXXVI, 81–82). The meaning of these verses is that the command of God in the creation of things is not gradual nor is it bound to the conditions of time and space. Therefore, the spirit which has no reality other than the command of God is not material and in its being does not have material characteristics; that is, it does not have the characteristics of divisibility, change, and situation in time and space.

A Discussion of Spirit from Another Perspective

Intellectual investigation confirms the view of the Holy Quran about the spirit. Each of us is aware of a reality within himself which he interprets as "I" and this awareness exists continuously within man. Sometimes man even forgets his head, hands, feet and other members or the whole of the body. But as long as his self exists, the consciousness of "I" does not leave his awareness. This perception cannot be divided or analyzed. Although the body of man is continuously undergoing change and transformation and chooses different locations in space for itself and passes through different moments of time, the reality of "I" remains fixed. It does not undergo any change or transformation. It is clear that if the "I" were material it would accept the characteristics of matter which are divisibility, change, and situation in time and space.

The body accepts all the characteristics of matter and, because of the relation of the spirit and the body, these characteristics are also considered to belong to the spirit. But if we pay the least attention, it becomes evident to man that this moment in time and the next, this point in space or another, this shape or another shape, this direction of motion or any other, are all characteristics of the body. The spirit is free from them; rather each of these determinations reaches the spirit through the body. This same reasoning can be applied in reverse to the power of consciousness and apprehension or knowledge which is one of the characteristics of the spirit. Obviously if knowledge were a material quality, according to the conditions of matter it would accept divisibility and analysis, and be determined by time and space.

Needless to say, this intellectual discussion could go on at length and there are many questions and answers related to it which cannot be considered in the present context. The brief discussion presented here is only an indication of the Islamic belief concerning body and spirit. A complete discussion will be found in works on Islamic philosophy.[1]

Death from the Islamic Point of View

Although a superficial view would regard death as the annihilation of man and see human life as consisting of only the few days that stand between birth and death, Islam interprets death as the transfer of man from one stage of life to another. According to Islam man possesses eternal life which knows no end. Death, which is the separation of the spirit from the body, introduces man to another stage of life in which felicity or disappointment depends upon good or evil deeds in the stage of life before death. The Holy Prophet has said: "You have been created for subsistence, not annihilation. What happens is that you will be transferred from one house to another."[2]

Purgatory

From what can be deduced from the Holy Book and prophetic traditions, it can be concluded that between death and general resurrection man possesses a limited and temporary life which is the intermediate stage (barzakh) and link between the life of this world and eternal life. After death man is interrogated concerning the beliefs he has held and the good and evil deeds he has performed in this life. After a summary account and judgement he is subjected to either a pleasant and felicitous life, or an unpleasant and wretched one, depending on the results of the account and judgment. With this newly acquired life he continues in expectation until the day of general resurrection. The condition of man in the life of the intermediate state (purgatory) is very similar to the condition of a person who has been called before a judicial organization in order to have the acts he has committed investigated. He is questioned and investigated until his file is completed. Then he awaits trial.

The soul of man in the intermediate state possesses the same form as in his life in this world.[3] If he be a man of virtue, he lives in happiness and bounty in the proximity of those who are pure and close to the Divine Presence. If he be a man of evil, he lives in affliction and pain and in the company of daemonic forces and "leaders of those who have gone astray."[4]

God, the Most Exalted, has said concerning the condition of a group of those in the state of felicity, "Think not of those, who are slain in the way of Allah, as dead. Nay, they are living. With their Lord they have provision. Jubilant (are they) because of that which Allah hath bestowed upon them of His bounty, rejoicing for the sake of those who have not joined them but are left behind:

that there shall no fear come upon them neither shall they grieve. They rejoice because of favor from Allah and kindness, and that Allah wasteth not the wage of the believers" (Quran, III, 169–171). And in describing the condition of another group who in the life of this world do not make legitimate use of their wealth and possessions, He says, "Until, when death cometh unto one of them, he saith: My Lord! Send me back, that I may do right in that which I have left behind! But nay! It is but a word that he speaketh; and behind them is a barrier [barzakh] until the day when they are raised" (Quran, XXIII, 99–100).

The Day of Judgment—Resurrection

Among sacred texts the Quran is the only one to have spoken in detail about the Day of Judgment. Although the Torah has not mentioned this Day and the Gospels have only alluded to it, the Quran has mentioned the Day of Judgment in hundreds of places, using different names. It has described the fate awaiting mankind on this Day sometimes briefly and on other occasions in detail. It has reminded mankind many times that faith in the Day of Recompense (Day of Judgment) is on the same scale in its importance as faith in God and is one of the three principles of Islam. It has mentioned that he who lacks this faith, that is, who denies resurrection, is outside the pale of Islam and has no destiny other than eternal perdition.

And this is the truth of the matter because if there were to be no reckoning in God's actions and no reward or punishment, the religious message, which consists of an assemblage of God's decrees and what He has commanded and forbidden, would not have the least effect. Thus the existence or nonexistence of prophecy and the religious mission would be the same. In fact, its nonexistence would be preferable to its existence, for to accept a religion and follow the regulations of a Divine Law is not possible without the acceptance of restrictions and loss of what appears as "freedom." If to submit to it were to have no effect, people would never accept it and would not give up their natural freedom of action for it. From this argument it becomes clear that the importance of mentioning and recalling the Day of Judgment is equivalent to that of the principle of the religious call itself.

From this conclusion it also becomes evident that faith in the Day of Recompense is the most effective factor which induces man to accept the necessity of virtue and abstention from unbecoming qualities and great sins, in the same way that to forget or lack faith in the Day of Judgment is the essential root of every evil act and sin. God the Almighty has said in His Book, "Lo! those who wander from the way of Allah have an awful doom, forasmuch as they forgot the Day of Reckoning" (Quran, XXXVIII, 27). As can be seen in this sacred verse, the forgetting of the Day of Judgment is considered to be the root of every deviation. Meditation on the purpose of the creation of man and the Universe, or on the purpose and end of Divine Laws, makes it evident that there will be a Day of Judgment.

When we meditate on creation, we see that there is no action (which of necessity is also a kind of motion) without an immutable end and purpose. Never is the action, considered independently and in itself, the end. Rather, action is always the prelude to an end and exists by virtue of that end. Even in actions which superficially appear to be without purpose such as instinctive actions or the play of children and the like, if we study them carefully, we will discover purposes in conformity with the kind of action in question. In instinctive actions, which are usually a form of motion, the end toward which the motion takes place is the purpose and aim of the action. And in the play of children there is an imaginary end, the attainment of which is the purpose of playing. The creation of man and the world is the action of God and God is above the possibility of performing a senseless and purposeless act such as creating, nourishing, taking away life and then again creating, nourishing and taking away life, that is, of making and destroying, without there being an immutable end and a permanent purpose which He pursues in these acts. There must of necessity be a permanent aim and purpose in the creation of the world and of man. Of course, its benefit does not accrue to God, who is above every need, but rather to the creatures themselves. Thus it must be said that the world and man are directed toward a permanent reality and a more perfect state of being which knows no annihilation and corruption.

Also, when we study with care the condition of men from the point of view of religious education and training, we see that as a result of Divine guidance and religious training people become divided into the two categories of the virtuous and the evil. Yet in this life there is no distinction made between them. Rather, on the contrary, success usually belongs to those who are evil and unjust. To do good is combined with difficulty and hardship and every kind of privation and endurance of oppression. Since this is so, Divine Justice requires the existence of another world in which each individual receives the just reward his actions deserve, and lives a life in conformity with his merits.

Thus it is seen that careful consideration of the purpose of creation and of the Divine Laws leads to the conclusion that the Day of Judgment will come for every person. God, the Exalted, makes this clear in His Book, saying, "And We created not the heavens and the earth, and all that is between them, in play. We created them not save with truth; but most of them know not" (Quran, XLIV, 38–39). Also, "And We created not the heavens and the earth and all that is between them in vain. That is the opinion of those who disbelieve. And woe unto those who disbelieve, from the fire! Shall We treat those who believe and do good works as those who spread corruption in the earth; or shall We treat the pious as the wicked?" (Quran, XXXVIII, 28–29). In another place He says, "Or do those who commit ill-deeds suppose that We shall make them as those who believe and do good works, the same in life and death? Bad is their judgment! And Allah hath created the heavens and the earth with truth, and that every soul may be repaid what it hath earned. And they will not be wronged" (Quran, XLV, 21–22).

Another Explanation

In discussing the outward and inward meaning of the Quran we pointed out that the Islamic sciences are explained in the Quran through different means and that these are in general divided into the two dimensions of the exoteric and the esoteric. The exoteric explanation is the one that conforms to the level of the simple thought patterns and understanding of the majority, in contrast to the esoteric, which belongs to the elite alone and which can be comprehended only with the aid of the vision which comes through the practice of the spiritual life.

The explanation that emanates from the exoteric view presents God as the absolute ruler of the world of creation, all of which is His dominion. God has created many angels, whose number is legion, to carry out and execute the commands He issues for every aspect of creation. Each part of creation and its order is connected to a special group of angels who are the protectors of that domain. The human species is His creation and human beings are His servants who must obey His commands and prohibitions; and the prophets are the bearers of His messages, the conveyors of the laws and regulations which He has sent to mankind and has demanded that mankind obey. God has promised reward and recompense for faith and obedience, and punishment and painful retribution for infidelity and sin, and will not break His promise. Also since He is just, His justice demands that in another state of being the two groups of virtuous and evil men, who in this world do not have a mode of life in accordance with their good and evil nature, become separated, the virtuous to possess a good and happy life and the evil a bad and wretched existence.

Thus God, according to His Justice and the promises He has made, will resurrect all men who live in this world after their death, without exception, and will investigate in detail their beliefs and works. He will judge them according to the truth and give everyone who has a right his due. He will carry out justice on behalf of all who have been oppressed. He will render to each person the reward for his own actions. One group will be assigned to eternal heaven and the other group to eternal hell.

This is the exoteric explanation of the Holy Quran. Of course it is true and correct. But its language is composed of terms and images born of man's social life and thought in order that its benefit might be more general and the radius of its action more widespread.

Those who have penetrated into the spiritual meaning of things and are to a certain extent familiar with the esoteric language of the Holy Quran, however, understand from these sayings meanings which lie above the level of simple and popular comprehension. The Holy Quran, amidst its simple and uncomplicated expositions, occasionally alludes to the esoteric aim and purpose of its message. Through many allusions the Holy Quran affirms that the world of creation with all its parts, of which man is one, is moving in its "existential becoming" which is always in the direction of perfection toward God.[5] A day will come when this movement will come to an end and will lose completely its separate and independent existence before the Divine Majesty and Grandeur.

Man, who is a part of the world and whose special perfection is through consciousness and knowledge, is also moving with haste toward God. When he reaches the end of this becoming, he will observe plainly the Truth and Oneness of the Unique God. He will see that power, dominion and every other quality of perfection belong exclusively to the sacred Divine Essence; the reality of each thing *as it is* will be revealed to him. This is the first stage in the world of eternity. If, through his faith and good works in this world, man is able to have communication, relation, familiarity, and friendship with God and the beings in His proximity, then with a felicity and joy that can never be described in human language he will live near God and in the company of the pure beings of the world above. But if, because of desire and attachment to the life of this world and its transient and baseless pleasures, he is cut off from the world above and has no familiarity with or love for God and the pure beings of His Presence, then he becomes afflicted with painful torment and eternal adversity. It is true that a man's good and evil acts in this world are transient and disappear, but the forms of these good and evil acts become established in the soul of man and accompany him everywhere. They are the capital of his future life, be it sweet or bitter.

These affirmations can be drawn from the following verses: God says, "Lo! unto thy Lord is the (absolute) return" (Quran, XCVI, 8). And He says, "Do not all things reach Allah at last?" (Quran, XLII, 53); and "The (absolute) command on that day is

Allah's" (Quran, LXXXII, 19). Also in the account of the address made to certain members of the human race on the Day of Judgment He says, "(And unto the evildoer it is said): Thou wast in heedlessness of this. Now We have removed from thee thy covering, and piercing is thy sight this day" (Quran, L, 22).

Concerning the hermeneutic interpretation (ta'wil) of the Holy Quran (the truth from which the Holy Quran originates) God says, "Await they aught save the fulfillment [ta'wil] thereof? On the day when the fulfillment thereof cometh, those who were before forgetful thereof will say: The messengers of our Lord did bring the Truth! Have we any intercessors, that they may intercede for us? Or can we be returned (to life on earth), that we may act otherwise than we used to act? They have lost their souls, and that which they devised hath failed them" (Quran, VII, 53). He says, "On that day Allah will pay them their just due, and they will know that Allah, He is the Manifest Truth" (Quran, XXIV, 25). And, "Thou verily, O man, art working toward thy Lord a work which thou wilt meet (in His presence)" (Quran, LXXXIV, 6). Also, "Whoso looketh forward to the meeting with Allah (let him know that) Allah's reckoning is surely nigh . . ." (Quran, XXIX, 5). And, "And whoever hopeth for the meeting with his Lord, let him do righteous work, and make none sharer of the worship due unto his Lord" (Quran, XVIII, 111). And, "But ah! thou soul at peace! Return unto thy Lord, content in His good pleasure! Enter thou among My bondmen! Enter thou My Garden!" (Quran, LXXXIX, 27–30). Also He says, "But when the great disaster cometh, The Day when man will call to mind his (whole) endeavor, And hell will stand forth visible to him who seeth, Then, as for him who rebelled, And chose the life of the world, Lo! hell will be his home. But as for him who feared to stand before his Lord and restrained his soul from lust, Lo! the Garden will be his home" (Quran, LXXIX, 34–41).

Concerning the identity of the reward of actions God says, "(Then it will be said): O ye who disbelieve! Make no excuses for yourselves this day. Ye are only being paid for what ye used to do" (Quran, LXVI, 7).

The Continuity and Succession of Creation

This world of creation which we observe does not possess an endless and perpetual life. A day will come when the life of this world and its inhabitants will come to an end as confirmed by the Holy Quran. God says, "We created not the heavens and the earth and all that is between them save with truth, and for a term appointed." (Quran, XLVI, 3)

One could ask if before the creation of this world and the present race of humanity there had been another world and another human race; or, if after the life of this world and its inhabitants terminates, as the Holy Quran declares that it will, another world and humanity will be created. The direct response to these questions cannot be found in the Holy Quran. There, one can only discover allusions to the continuity and succession of creation. But in the traditions (*rawāyāt*) of the Imams of the Household of the Prophet transmitted to us it is asserted that creation is not limited to this visible world. Many worlds have existed in the past and will exist in the future. The sixth Imam has said, "Perhaps you think God has not created a humanity other than you. No! I swear to God that He has created thousands upon thousands of mankinds and you are the last among them."[6]

And the fifth Imam has said, "God, the Exalted, since creating the world has created seven kinds none of whom were of the race of Adam. He created them from the surface of the earth and set each being one after another with its kind upon the earth. Then He created Adam, the father of mankind, and brought his children into being from him."[7] And also the sixth Imam has said, "Do not think that after the passing away of the affair of this world and the Day of Judgment and the placing of the virtuous in heaven and the evil in hell there will no longer be anyone to worship God. No, never! Rather, again God will create servants without the marriage of the male and the female to know His Oneness and to worship Him."[8]

NOTES

CHAPTER VI

1. *Editor's note:* By this reference the author means especially the writings of Sadr al-Din Shirazi (Mulla Sadra) and the later Islamic philosophers of Persia, who have discussed the question of the soul and its becoming much more thoroughly than the earlier philosophers. Yet, in the question of the immateriality of the spirit, substantial intellectual proofs are also offered in the writings of Ibn Sina (Avicenna).
2. *Biḥār al-anwār*, vol. III, p. 161, from the *I'tiqādāt* of Ṣadūq.
3. *Biḥār al-anwār*, vol. IV, *Bāb al-barzakh.*
4. *Ibid.*
5. *Editor's note:* As it has been mentioned before this metaphysical principle should not in any way be confused with the modern theories of evolution or progress as these terms are usually understood.
6. *Biḥār al-anwār*, vol. XIV, p. 79.
7. *Ibid.*
8. *Ibid.*

CHAPTER VII ON THE KNOWLEDGE OF THE IMAM (IMAMOLOGY)

The Meaning of Imam

Imam or leader is the title given to a person who takes the lead in a community in a particular social movement or political ideology or scientific or religious form of thought. Naturally, because of his relation to the people he leads, he must conform his actions to their capabilities in both important and secondary matters.

As is clear from the preceding chapters, the sacred religion of Islam takes into consideration and gives directives concerning all aspects of the life of all men. It investigates human life from the spiritual point of view and guides man accordingly, and it intervenes on the plane of formal and material existence from the point of view of the life of the individual. In the same way it intervenes on the plane of social life and its regulation (i.e., on the plane of government).

Thus the imamate and religious leadership in Islam may be studied from three different perspectives: from the perspective of Islamic government, of Islamic sciences and injunctions, and of leadership and innovative guidance in the spiritual life. Shi'ism believes that since Islamic society is in dire need of guidance in each of these three aspects, the person who occupies the function of giving that guidance and is the leader of the community in these areas of religious concern must be appointed by God and the Prophet. Naturally, the Prophet himself was also appointed by Divine Command.

The Imamate and Succession

Man through his God-given nature realizes without any doubt that no organized society, such as a country or city or village or tribe or even a household consisting of a few human beings, can continue to subsist without a leader and ruler who puts the wheel of the society in motion and whose will governs each individual's will and induces the members of that society to perform their social duty. Without such a ruler the parts of this society become dispersed in a short time and disorder and confusion reign. Therefore, he who is the ruler and governor of a society, whether it be great or small, if he is interested in his own position and the continued existence of his society, will appoint a successor for himself if he is to be absent from his function temporarily or permanently. He will never abandon the domain of his rule and be oblivious to its existence or annihilation. The head of a household who bids farewell to his house and household for a journey of a few days or months will appoint one of the members of the household or someone else as his successor and will leave the affairs of the house in his hands. The head of an institution, or the principal of a school, or the owner of a shop, if he is to be absent even for a few hours will select someone to represent him.

In the same way Islam is a religion which according to the text of the Holy Book and the Sunnah is established upon the basis of the primordial nature of things. It is a religion concerned with social life, as has been seen by every observer near and far. The special attention God and the Prophet have given to the social nature of this religion can never be denied or neglected. It is an incomparable feature of Islam. The Holy Prophet was never oblivious to the problem of the formation of social groupings wherever the influence of Islam penetrated. Whenever a city or village fell into Muslim hands he would, in the shortest time possible, appoint a governor or ruler in whose hands he would leave the affairs of the Muslims.[1] In very important military expeditions ordered for the Holy War (jihad), he would appoint more than one leader and commander, in order of succession. In the war of Mu'tah he even appointed four leaders, so that if the first were to be killled the second would be recognized as the head and his command accepted and if the second were to be killed, then the third, and so on.[2]

The Prophet also displayed great interest in the problem of succession and never failed to appoint a successor when necessary. Whenever he left Medina he would appoint a governor in his own place.[3] Even when he migrated from Mecca to Medina and there was as yet no idea as to what would occur, in order to have his personal affairs managed in Mecca for those few days and to give back to people what had been entrusted to him, he appointed Ali—may peace be upon him—as his successor.[4] In the same way, after his death Ali was his successor in matters concerning his debts and personal affairs.[5] The Shiʿites claim that for this very reason it is not conceivable that the Prophet should have died without appointing someone as his successor, without having selected a guide and leader to direct the affairs of Muslims and to turn the wheels of Islamic society.

Man's primordial nature does not doubt the importance and value of the fact that the creation of a society depends on a set of common regulations and customs which are accepted in practice by the majority of the groups in that society, and that the existence and continuation of that society depend upon a just government which agrees to carry out these regulations completely. Anyone who possesses intelligence does not neglect or forget this fact. At the same time one can doubt neither the breadth and detailed nature of the Islamic Shariʿah, nor the importance and value the Prophet considered it to possess, so that he made many sacrifices for its application and preservation. Nor can one debate about the mental genius, perfection of intelligence, perspicacity of vision or power of deliberation of the Prophet (beside the fact that this is affirmed through revelation and prophecy).

According to established traditions in both Sunni and Shiʿite collections of hadith (in the chapter on temptations and seditions and others) transmitted from the Prophet, the Prophet foretold seditions and tribulations which would entangle Islamic society after his death, and the forms of corruption which would penetrate the body of Islam, and later worldly rulers who would sacrifice this pure religion for their own impure, unscrupulous ends. How is it possible that the Prophet should not neglect to speak of the details of events and trials of years or even thousands of years after him, and yet would neglect the condition that had to be brought into being most urgently after his death? Or that he should be negligent and consider as unimportant a duty that is on the one hand simple and evident and on the other significant to such a degree? How could he concern himself with the most natural and common acts such as eating, drinking and sleeping and give hundreds of commands concerning them, yet remain completely silent about this important problem and not appoint someone in his own place?

Even if we accepted the hypothesis (which Shi'ism does not accept) that the appointment of the ruler of Islamic society is given by the Shari'ah to the people themselves, still it would be necessary for the Prophet to give an explanation concerning this matter. He would have had to give the necessary instructions to the community so that they would be aware of the problem upon which the existence and growth of Islamic society and the life of religious symbols and observances depended and relied. Yet there is no trace of such a prophetic explanation or religious instruction. If there had been such a thing, those who succeeded the Prophet and held the reins of power in their hands would not have opposed it. Actually, the first caliph transferred the caliphate to the second caliph by bequest. The second caliph chose the third caliph through a six-man council of which he was himself a member and whose order of procedure he had himself determined and ordered. Mu'awiyah forced Imam Hasan to make peace and in this way carried away the caliphate. After this event the caliphate was converted into an hereditary monarchy. Gradually many religious observances identified with the early years of Islamic rule (such as holy war, commanding what is lawful and prohibiting what is forbidden, the establishment of boundaries for human action) were weakened or even disappeared from the political life of the community, nullifying in this domain the efforts of the Prophet of Islam.

Shi'ism has studied and investigated the primordial nature of man and the continuous tradition of wisdom that has survived among men. It has penetrated into the principal purpose of Islam, which is to revivify man's primordial nature, and has investigated such things as the methods used by the Prophet in guiding the community; the troubles which entangled Islam and the Muslims and which led to division and separation; and the short life of the Muslim governments of the early centuries, which were characterized by negligence and lack of strict religious principles. As a result of these studies Shi'ism has reached the conclusion that there are sufficient traditional texts left by the Prophet to indicate the procedure for determining the Imam and successor of the Prophet. This conclusion is supported by Quranic verses and hadiths which Shi'ism considers as sound, such as the verse on walayat and the hadiths of Ghadir, Safīnah, Thaqalayn, Haqq, Manzilah, Da'wat-i 'ashīrah-i aqrabīn and others.[6] But of course these hadiths, most of which are also accepted by Sunnism, have not been understood in the same way by Shi'ism and Sunnism. Otherwise the whole question of succession would not have arisen. Whereas these hadiths appear to Shi'ites as a clear indication of the Prophet's intention in the question of succession, they have been interpreted by Sunnis in quite another way so as to leave this question open and unanswered.

To prove the caliphate of Ali ibn Abi Talib, Shi'ites have had recourse to Quranic verses, including the following: "Your friend [wali] can be only Allah; and His messenger and those who believe, who establish worship and pay the poor-due, and bow down (in prayer) [or, and this reading is accepted by 'Allāmah Ṭabāṭabā'ī: "... pay the poor-due while bowing down (in prayer)"]" (Quran, V, 55). Shi'ite and Sunni commentators alike agree that this verse was revealed concerning Ali ibn Abi Talib, and many Shi'ite and Sunni traditions exist supporting this view. Abu Dharr Ghifari has said: "One day we prayed the noontime prayers with the Prophet. A person in need asked people to help but no one gave him anything. The person raised his hands to the sky saying, 'Oh God! Be witness that in the mosque of the Prophet no one gave me anything.' Ali ibn Abi Talib was in the position of genuflection in the prayers. He pointed with his finger to the person, who took his ring and left. The Prophet, who was observing the scene raised his head toward heaven and said: 'Oh God! My brother Moses said to Thee, "Expand my breast and make easy my tasks and make my tongue eloquent so that they will comprehend my words, and make my brother, Harun, my help and vizier" [cf. Quran, XXVIII, 35]. Oh God! I am also Thy prophet; expand my breast and make easy my tasks and make Ali my vizier and helper.' " Abu Dharr says, "The words of the Prophet had not as yet finished when the verse [cited above] was revealed."[7]

Another verse which the Shi'ites consider as proof of the caliphate of Ali is this: "This day are those who disbelieve in despair of (ever harming) your religion; so fear them not, fear Me! This day have I perfected your religion for you and completed My favour unto you, and have chosen for you as religion AL-ISLAM" (Quran, V, 3). The obvious meaning of this verse is that before that particular day the infidels had hopes that a day would come when Islam would die out, but God through the actualization of a particular event made them lose forever the hope that Islam would be destroyed. This very event was the cause of the strength and perfection of Islam and of necessity could not be a minor occasion such as the promulgation of one of the injunctions of religion. Rather, it was a matter of such importance that the continuation of Islam depended upon it.

This verse seems to be related to another verse which comes toward the end of the same chapter: "O Messenger! Make known that which hath been revealed unto thee from thy Lord, for if thou do it not, thou will not have conveyed His message. Allah will protect thee from mankind." (Quran, V, 67). This verse indicates that God commanded a mission of great concern and importance to the Prophet which if not accomplished would endanger the basis of Islam and prophecy. But the matter was so important that the Prophet feared opposition and interference and in awaiting suitable circumstances delayed it, until there came a definite and urgent order from God to execute this command without delay and not to fear anyone. This matter also was not just a particular religious injunction in the ordinary sense, for to preach one or several religious injunctions is not so vital that if a single one of them were not preached it would cause the destruction of Islam. Nor did the Prophet of Islam fear anyone in preaching the injunctions and laws of religion.

These indications and witnesses add weight to the Shiʿite traditions which assert that these verses were revealed at Ghadir Khumm and concern the spiritual investiture (walayat) of Ali ibn Abi Talib. Moreover, many Shiʿite and Sunni commentators have confirmed this point.

Abū Saʿīd Khudarī says: "The Prophet in Ghadir Khumm invited people toward Ali and took his arm and lifted it so high that the white spot in the armpit of the Prophet of God could be seen. Then this verse was revealed: 'This day have I perfected your religion for you and completed My favor unto you, and have chosen for you as religion AL-ISLAM.' Then the Prophet said, 'God is great (*Allāhu akbar*) that religion has become perfected and that God's bounty has been completed, His satisfaction attained and the walayat of Ali achieved.' Then he added, 'For whomever I am the authority and guide Ali is also his guide and authority. Oh God! Be friendly with the friends of Ali and the enemy of his enemies. Whoever helps him, help him, and whoever leaves him, leave him.'"[8]

In summary we can say that the enemies of Islam who did everything possible to destroy it, when they lost all hope of achieving this end, were left with only one hope. They thought that since the protector of Islam was the Prophet, after his death Islam would be left without a guide and leader and would thus definitely perish. But in Ghadir Khumm their wishes were brought to nought and the Prophet presented Ali as the guide and leader of Islam to the people. After Ali this heavy and necessary duty of guide and leader was left upon the shoulders of his family.[9]

Some of the hadiths pertaining to Ghadir Khumm, the investiture of Ali, and the significance of the Household of the Prophet are cited here:

Hadith-i ghadīr: The Prophet of Islam upon returning from the farewell pilgrimage stopped in Ghadir Khumm, assembled the

Muslims and, after delivering a sermon, chose Ali as the leader and guide of Muslims.

Barā' says: "I was in the company of the Prophet during the farewell pilgrimage. When we reached Ghadir Khumm he ordered that place to be cleaned. Then he took Ali's hand and placed him on his right side. Then he said, 'Am I the authority whom you obey?' They answered, 'We obey your directions.' Then he said, 'For whomever I am his master (*maulā*) and the authority whom he obeys, Ali will be his master. Oh God! Be friendly with the friends of Ali and enemy of the enemies of Ali.' Then Umar ibn al-Khaṭṭāb said to Ali, 'May this position be pleasing to you, for now you are my master and the master of all the believers.' "[10]

Hadith-i safīnah: Ibn 'Abbās says, "The Prophet said, 'My household is like the ship of Noah; whoever embarks upon it will be saved and whoever turns away from it will be drowned.' "[11]

Hadith-i thaqalayn: Zayd ibn Arqam has recounted that the Prophet said, "It seems that God has called me unto Himself and I must obey His call. But I leave two great and precious things among you: the Book of God and My Household. Be careful as to how you behave toward them. These two will never be separated from each other until they encounter me at Kawthar (in paradise)."[12] Hadith-i thaqalayn is one of the most strongly established hadiths, and has been transmitted through many chains of transmission and in different versions. Shi'ites and Sunnis agree concerning its authenticity. Several important points can be deduced from this hadith and its like: (1) In the same way that the Holy Quran will remain until the Day of Judgment, the progeny of the Holy Prophet will also remain. No period of time will be without the existence of the figure which Shi'ism calls the Imam, the real leader and guide of men. (2) Through these two great trusts (*amānat*), the Prophet has provided for all the religious and intellectual needs of the Muslims. He has introduced his Household to Muslims as authorities in knowledge and has pronounced their words and deeds to be worthy and authoritative. (3) One must not separate the Holy Quran from the Household of the Prophet. No Muslim has a right to reject the "sciences" of the members of the Household of the Prophet and remove himself from under their direction and guidance. (4) If people obey the members of the Household and follow their words they will never be led astray. God will always be with them. (5) The answers to the intellectual and religious needs of men are to be found in the hands of the members of the Household of the Prophet. Whoever follows them will not fall into error and will reach true felicity; that is, the members of the Household are free from error and sin and are inerrant. From this it can be concluded that by "Members of the Household" and "progeny" is not meant all the descendants and relatives of the Prophet. Rather, specific individuals are meant who are perfect in the religious sciences and are protected against error and sin so that they are qualified to guide and lead men. For Shi'ism these individuals consist of Ali ibn Abi Talib and his eleven descendants who were chosen to the imamate one after another. This interpretation is also confirmed by the Shi'ite traditions. For example, Ibn 'Abbās has said, "I said to the Prophet, 'Who are your descendants whose love is obligatory [upon Muslims]?' He said, 'Ali, Fatimah, Hasan and Husayn.' "[13] Jabir has transmitted that the Prophet has said, "God placed the children of all prophets in their 'backbone' but placed my children in the backbone of Ali."[14]

Hadith-i haqq: Umm Salmah has said, "I heard from the Prophet of God who said, 'Ali is with the Truth (haqq) and the Quran, and the Truth and the Quran are also with Ali, and they will be inseparable until they come upon me at Kawthar.' "[15]

Hadith-i manzilah: Sa'd ibn Waqqāṣ has said, "The Prophet of God said to Ali, 'Are you not satisfied to be to me what Harun was to Moses except that after me there will not be another prophet?' "[16]

Hadith-i da'wat-i 'ashīrah: The Prophet invited his relatives for luncheon and after the meal told them, "I know of no one who has brought to his people better things than I have brought to you. God has commanded me to invite you to draw toward Him. Who is there who will assist me in this matter and be my brother and inheritor (wasi) and vicegerent (khalifah) among you?" All remained silent, but Ali, who was the youngest of all, exclaimed, "I shall be your deputy and aide." Then the Prophet put his arms around him and said, "He is my brother, inheritor and vicegerent. You must obey him." Then the group began to depart laughing and telling Abu Talib, "Muhammad has ordered you to obey your son."[17]

Ḥudhayfah has said, "The Prophet of God said, 'If you make Ali my vicegerent and successor—which I do not think you will do—you will find him a perspicacious guide who will direct you toward the straight path!'"[18]

Ibn Mardūyah has said that the Prophet said, "Whoever wishes that his life and death be like mine and that he enter paradise should after me love Ali and follow my household, for they are my descendants and have been created from my clay. My knowledge and understanding have been bestowed upon them. Therefore woe unto those who deny their virtues. My intercession [on the Day of Judgement] will never include them."[19]

Affirmation of the Previous Section

Much of the argument of Shi'ism concerning the succession to the Prophet rests on the belief that during the last days of his illness the Prophet in the presence of some of his companions asked for some paper and ink[20] so that something could be written which, if obeyed by the Muslims, would prevent them from going astray. Some of those present considered the Prophet to be too ill to be able to dictate anything and said, "The Book of God is sufficient for us." There was so much clamor raised over this matter that the Holy Prophet told those present to leave, for in the presence of a prophet there should not be any noise or clamor.

Considering what has been said above about hadiths concerning succession and the events that followed upon the death of the Prophet, especially the fact that Ali was not consulted in the question of selecting the Prophet's successor, Shi'ites conclude that the Holy Prophet had wanted to dictate his definitive views about the person who was to succeed him but was not able to do so.

The purpose of the utterances of some of those present seems to have been to cause confusion and prevent this final decision from being clearly announced. Their interruption of the Holy Prophet's discourse does not seem to be what it appears outwardly, that is concern with the possibility that the Prophet might utter incongruous words due to the intensity of his illness. For, first of all, throughout his illness the Holy Prophet was not heard to have uttered any meaningless or incongruous words and no such thing has been transmitted concerning him. Moreover, according to the principles of Islam the Prophet is protected by God from uttering delirious or senseless words and is inerrant.

Secondly, if the words mentioned by some of those present on that occasion before the Prophet were meant to be of a serious nature there would have been no place for the next phrase, "The Book of God is sufficient for us." In order to prove that the Prophet might utter incongruous words under unusual circumstances the reason of his serious illness would have been used rather than the claim that with the Quran there was no need of the Prophet's words. For it could not be hidden from any Muslim that the very text of the Book of God considers the obedience to the Holy Prophet to be obligatory and his words to be in a sense like the Word of God. According to the text of the Holy Quran, Muslims must obey the injunctions of both God and the Prophet.

Thirdly, an incident involving illness occurred during the last days of the life of the first caliph, who in his last will and testament chose the second caliph as his successor. When Uthman was writing the will according to the order of the caliph, the caliph fainted. Yet the second caliph did not repeat the words that had been uttered in the case of the Prophet according to the hadith of "Pen and Paper."[21] This fact has been confirmed in a hadith related by Ibn Abbas.[22] And it has been accounted of the second caliph that he said, "Ali deserved the caliphate but the Quraysh would not have been able to bear his caliphate, for had he become caliph he would have forced the people to accept the pure truth and follow the right path. Under his caliphate they would not have been able to transgress the boundaries of justice and thus would have sought to engage in war with him."[23]

Obviously according to religious principles one must force him who has deviated from the truth to follow the truth; one must not abandon the truth for the sake of one who has abandoned it. When the first caliph was informed[24] that some of the Muslim tribes had refused to pay religious tax, he ordered war and said, "If they do not give me the tithes which they gave to the Prophet, I shall fight against them." Evidently by this saying he meant most of all that truth and justice must be revived at all costs. Surely the problem of the legitimate caliphate was more important and significant than tithes, and Shi'ism believes that the same principle applied by the first caliph to this matter should have been applied by the whole early community to the problem of succession to the Holy Prophet.

The Imamate and Its Role in the Exposition of the Divine Sciences

In the discussion of prophecy it was mentioned that, according to the immutable and necessary law of general guidance, each created species is guided through the path of genesis and generation toward the perfection and felicity of its own kind. The human species is not an exception to this general law. Man must be guided through the very "instinct" of seeking reality and through thought concerning his life in society in such a way that his well-being in this world and the next is guaranteed. In other words, to attain human happiness and perfection, man must accept a series of doctrines and practical duties and base his life upon them.

It has, moreover, already been said that the way to understand that total program for life called religion is not through reason but through revelation and prophecy, which manifests itself in certain pure beings among mankind who are called prophets. It is the prophets who receive from God, through revelation, the knowledge of men's duties and obligations as human beings and who make these known to men, so that by fulfilling them men may attain felicity.

It is evident that in the same way that this reasoning proves the necessity for knowledge to guide men to the attainment of happiness and perfection, it also proves the necessity for the existence of individuals who preserve intact the total body of that knowledge and who instruct the people when necessary. Just as the Divine Compassion necessitates the existence of persons who come to know the duties of mankind through revelation, so also it makes it necessary that these human duties and actions of celestial origin remain forever preserved in the world and as the need arises be presented and explained to mankind. In other words, there must always be individuals who preserve God's religion and expound it when necessary.

The person who bears the duty of guarding and preserving the Divine message after it is revealed and is chosen by God for this function is called the Imam, in the same way that the person who bears the prophetic spirit and has the function of receiving Divine injunctions and laws from God is called the Prophet. It is possible for the imamate[25] and prophecy (nubuwwat) either to be joined in one person or to be separate.

The proof given previously to demonstrate the inerrancy of prophets, also demonstrates the inerrancy of the Imams, for God must preserve His true religion intact and in such a state that it can be propagated among mankind at all times. And this is not possible without inerrancy, without Divine protection against error.

The Difference Between Prophet and Imam

The previous argument about the reception of Divine injunctions and laws by the prophets only proves the basis of prophecy, namely the receiving of Divine injunctions. The argument does not prove the persistence and continuity of prophecy, even though the very fact that these prophetic injunctions have been preserved naturally raises the idea of persistence and continuity. That is why it is not necessary for a prophet (nabi) always to be present among mankind, but the existence of the Imam, who is the guardian of Divine religion, is on the contrary a continuous necessity for human society. Human society can never be without the figure whom Shiʿism calls the Imam whether or not he is recognized and known. God, the Most Exalted, has said in His Book: "So if these disbelieve in it, We have already entrusted it to a people [i.e., the Imams] who do not disbelieve in it" (Quran, VI, 90).[26]

As mentioned above, the functions of prophecy and imamate may be joined in one person who is then appointed to the functions of both prophet and Imam, or to both the reception of the Divine law and its preservation and explanation. And sometimes they can be separated, such as in periods during which there is no prophet living but when there is a true Imam living among men. It is obvious that the number of God's prophets is limited and the prophets have not been present in every period and age.

It is also of significance to note that in God's Book some of the prophets have been introduced as Imams such as the Prophet Abraham, about whom is said, "And (remember) when his Lord tried Abraham with (His) commands, and he fulfilled them, He said: Lo! I have appointed thee a leader [imam] for mankind. (Abraham) said: And of my offspring (will there be leaders)? He said: My covenant includeth not wrongdoers" (Quran, II, 124). And God has also said, "And We made them chiefs [imams] who guide by Our command . . ." (Quran, XXI, 73).

The Imamate and Its Role in the Esoteric Dimension of Religion

In the same way that the Imam is the guide and leader of men in their external actions so does he possess the function of inward and esoteric leadership and guidance. He is the guide of the caravan of humanity which is moving inwardly and esoterically toward God. In order to elucidate this truth it is necessary to turn to the following two introductory comments. First of all, without any doubt, according to Islam as well as other Divine religions the sole means of attaining real and eternal happiness or misery, felicity or wretchedness, is by means of good or evil actions which man comes to recognize through the instruction of Divine religion as well as through his own primordial and God-given nature and intelligence. Second, through the means of revelation and prophecy God has praised or condemned man's actions according to the language of human beings and the society in which they live. He has promised those who do good and obey and accept the teachings of revelation a happy eternal life in which are fulfilled all desires that accord with human perfection. And to the evildoers and the iniquitous He has given warning of a bitter perpetual life in which is experienced every form of misery and disappointment.

Without any doubt God, who stands in every way above all that we can imagine, does not, as we do, possess "thought" moulded by a particular social structure. The relations of master and servant, ruler and ruled, command and prohibition, reward and punishment, do not exist outside our social life. The Divine Order is the system of creation itself, in which the existence and appearance of everything is related solely to its creation by God according to *real* relations and to that alone. Furthermore, as has been mentioned in the Holy Quran[27] and prophetic hadith, religion contains truths and verities above the common comprehension of man, which God has revealed to us in a language we can comprehend on the level of our understanding.

It can thus be concluded that there is a real relationship between good and evil actions and the kind of life that is prepared for man in eternity, a relation that determines the happiness or misery of the future life according to the Divine Will. Or in simpler words it can be said that each good or evil action brings into being a real effect within the soul of man which determines the character of his future life. Whether he understands it or not, man is like a child who is being trained. From the instructions of the teacher, the child hears nothing but do's and don'ts but does not understand the meaning of the actions he performs. Yet, when he grows up, as a result of virtuous mental and spiritual habits attained inwardly during the period of training, he is able to have a happy social life. If, however, he refuses to submit to the instructions of the teacher he will undergo nothing but misery and unhappiness. Or he is like a sick person who, when in the care of a physician, takes medicine, food and special exercises as directed by the physician and who has no other duty than to obey the instructions of his doctor. The result of this submission to his orders is the creation of harmony in his constitution which is the source of health as well as every form of physical enjoyment and pleasure. To summarize, we can say that within his outward life man possesses an inner life, a spiritual life, which is related to his deeds and actions and develops in relation to them, and that his happiness or misery in the hereafter is completely dependent upon this inner life.

The Holy Quran also confirms this explanation.[28] In many verses it affirms the existence of another life and another spirit for the virtuous and the faithful, a life higher than this life and a spirit more illuminated than the spirit of man as we know it here and now. It asserts that man's acts have inner effects upon his soul that remain always with him. In prophetic sayings there are also many references to this point. For example, in the Hadith-i miʿrāj (hadith of the nocturnal ascension) God addresses the Prophet in these words: "He who wishes to act according to My satisfaction must possess three qualities: he must exhibit a thankfulness that is not mixed with ignorance, a remembrance upon which the dust of forgetfulness will not settle, and a love in which he does not prefer the love of creatures rather than My love. If he loves Me, I love him; I will open the eye of his heart with the sight of My majesty and will not hide from him the qualities of My creatures. I will confide in him in the darkness of the night and the light of the day until conversation and intercourse with creatures terminates. I will make him hear My word and the word of My angels. I will reveal to him the secret which I have veiled from My creatures. I will dress him with the robe of modesty until the creatures feel ashamed before him. He will walk upon the earth having been forgiven. I will make his heart possess consciousness and vision and I will not hide from him anything in Paradise or in the Fire. I will make known to him whatever people experience on the Day of Judgement in the way of terror and calamity."[29]

Abū ʿAbdallāh—may peace be upon him—has recounted that the Prophet of God—may peace and blessing be upon him—received Ḥārithah ibn Mālik ibn al-Nuʿmān and asked him, "How art thou, Oh Harithah?" He said, "Oh Prophet of God, I live as a true believer." The Prophet of God said to him, "Each thing possesses its own truth. What is the truth of thy word?" He said,

"Oh Prophet of God! My soul has turned away from the world. My nights are spent in a state of awakedness and my days in a state of thirst. It seems as if I am gazing at the Throne of my Lord and the account has been settled, and as if I am gazing at the people of paradise who are visiting each other in heaven, and as if I hear the cry of the people of hell in the fire." Then the Prophet of God said, "This is a servant whose heart God has illuminated."[30]

It must also be remembered that often one of us guides another in a good or evil matter without himself carrying out his own words. In the case of the prophets and Imams, however, whose guidance and leadership is through Divine Command, such a situation never occurs. They themselves practice the religion whose leadership they have undertaken. The spiritual life toward which they guide mankind is their own spiritual life,[31] for God will not place the guidance of others in someone's hand unless He has guided him Himself. Special Divine guidance can never be violated or infringed upon.

The following conclusions can be reached from this discussion:

(1) In each religious community the prophets and Imams are the foremost in the perfection and realization of the spiritual and religious life they preach, for they must and do practice their own teachings and participate in the spiritual life they profess.

(2) Since they are first among men and the leaders and guides of the community, they are the most virtuous and perfect of men.

(3) The person upon whose shoulders lies the responsibility for the guidance of a community through Divine Command, in the same way that he is the guide of man's external life and acts, is also the guide for the spiritual life, and the inner dimension of human life and religious practice depends upon his guidance.[32]

The Imams and Leaders of Islam

The previous discussions lead us to the conclusion that in Islam, after the death of the Holy Prophet, there has continuously existed and will continue to exist within the Islamic community (ummah), an Imam (a leader chosen by God). Numerous prophetic hadiths[33] have been transmitted in Shiʿism concerning the description of the Imams, their number, the fact that they are all of the Quraysh and of the Household of the Prophet, and the fact that the promised Mahdi is among them and the last of them. Also, there are definitive words of the Prophet concerning the imamate of Ali and his being the first Imam and also definitive utterances of the Prophet and Ali concerning the imamate of the Second Imam. In the same way the Imams before have left definitive statements concerning the imamate of those who were to come after them.[34] According to these utterances contained in Twelve-Imam Shiʿite sources the Imams are twelve in number and their holy names are as follows: (1) ʿAlī ibn Abī Ṭālib; (2) Ḥasan ibn ʿAlī; (3) Ḥusayn ibn ʿAlī; (4) ʿAlī ibn Ḥusayn; (5) Muḥammad ibn ʿAlī; (6) Jaʿfar ibn Muḥammad; (7) Mūsā ibn Jaʿfar; (8) ʿAlī ibn Mūsā; (9) Muḥammad ibn ʿAlī; (10) ʿAlī ibn Muḥammad; (11) Ḥasan ibn ʿAlī; and (12) the Mahdī.

A BRIEF HISTORY OF THE LIVES OF THE TWELVE IMAMS

The First Imam

Amīr al-mu'minīn Ali[35]—upon whom be peace—was the son of Abu Talib, the Shaykh of the Banū Hāshim. Abu Talib was the uncle and guardian of the Holy Prophet and the person who had brought the Prophet to his house and raised him like his own son. After the Prophet was chosen for his prophetic mission, Abu Talib continued to support him and repelled from him the evil that came from the infidels among the Arabs and especially the Quraysh.

According to well-known traditional accounts Ali was born ten years before the commencement of the prophetic mission of the

Prophet. When six years old, as a result of famine in and around Mecca, he was requested by the Prophet to leave his father's house and come to the house of his cousin, the Prophet. There he was placed directly under the guardianship and custody of the Holy Prophet.[36]

A few years later, when the Prophet was endowed with the Divine gift of prophecy and for the first time received the Divine revelation in the cave of Ḥirā', as he left the cave to return to town and his own house he met Ali on the way. He told him what had happened and Ali accepted the new faith.[37] Again in a gathering when the Holy Prophet had brought his relatives together and invited them to accept his religion, he said the first person to accept his call would be his vicegerent and inheritor and deputy. The only person to rise from his place and accept the faith was Ali and the Prophet accepted his declaration of faith.[38] Therefore Ali was the first man in Islam to accept the faith and is the first among the followers of the Prophet to have never worshiped other than the One God.

Ali was always in the company of the Prophet until the Prophet migrated from Mecca to Medina. On the night of the migration to Medina (hijrah) when the infidels had surrounded the house of the Prophet and were determined to invade the house at the end of the night and cut him to pieces while he was in bed, Ali slept in place of the Prophet while the Prophet left the house and set out for Medina.[39] After the departure of the Prophet, according to his wish Ali gave back to the people the trusts and charges that they had left with the Prophet. Then he went to Medina with his mother, the daughter of the Prophet, and two other women.[40] In Medina also Ali was constantly in the company of the Prophet in private and in public. The Prophet gave Fāṭimah, his sole, beloved daughter from Khadijah, to Ali as his wife and when the Prophet was creating bonds of brotherhood among his companions he selected Ali as his brother.[41]

Ali was present in all the wars in which the Prophet participated, except the battle of Tabūk when he was ordered to stay in Medina in place of the Prophet.[42] He did not retreat in any battle nor did he turn his face away from any enemy. He never disobeyed the Prophet, so that the Prophet said, "Ali is never separated from the Truth nor the Truth from Ali."[43]

On the day of the death of the Prophet, Ali was thirty-three years old. Although he was foremost in religious virtues and the most outstanding among the companions of the Prophet, he was pushed aside from the caliphate on the claim that he was too young and that he had many enemies among the people because of the blood of the polytheists he had spilled in the wars fought alongside the Prophet. Therefore Ali was almost completely cut off from public affairs. He retreated to his house where he began to train competent individuals in the Divine sciences and in this way he passed the twenty-five years of the caliphate of the first three caliphs who succeeded the Prophet. When the third caliph was killed, people gave their allegiance to him and he was chosen as caliph.

During his caliphate of nearly four years and nine months, Ali followed the way of the Prophet and gave his caliphate the form of a spiritual movement and renewal and began many different types of reforms. Naturally, these reforms were against the interests of certain parties that sought their own benefit. As a result, a group of the companions (foremost among whom were Ṭalḥah and Zubayr, who also gained the support of A'ishah, and especially Muʿawiyah) made a pretext of the death of the third caliph to raise their heads in opposition and began to revolt and rebel against Ali.

In order to quell the civil strife and sedition, Ali fought a war near Basra, known as the "Battle of the Camel," against Talhah and Zubayr in which A'ishah, "the Mother of the Faithful," was also involved. He fought another war against Muʿawiyah on the border of Iraq and Syria which lasted for a year and a half and is famous as the "Battle of Ṣiffīn." He also fought against the Khawarij[44] at Nahrawān, in a battle known as the "Battle of Nahrawan." Therefore, most of the days of Ali's caliphate were spent in overcoming internal opposition. Finally, in the morning of the 19th of Ramaḍan in the year 40 A.H., while praying in the mosque of Kufa, he was wounded by one of the Khawarij and died as a martyr during the night of the 21st.[45]

According to the testimony of friend and foe alike, Ali had no shortcomings from the point of view of human perfection. And in the Islamic virtues he was a perfect example of the upbringing and training given by the Prophet. The discussions that have taken place concerning his personality and the books written on this subject by Shiʿites, Sunnis and members of other religions, as well as the simply curious outside any distinct religious bodies, are hardly equaled in the case of any other personality in history. In science and knowledge Ali was the most learned of the companions of the Prophet, and of Muslims in general. In his learned discourses he was the first in Islam to open the door for logical demonstration and proof and to discuss the "divine sciences" or metaphysics (*maʿārif-i ilāhīyah*). He spoke concerning the esoteric aspect of the Quran and devised Arabic grammar in order to preserve the Quran's form of expression. He was the most eloquent Arab in speech (as has been mentioned in the first part of this book).

The courage of Ali was proverbial. In all the wars in which he participated during the lifetime of the Prophet, and also afterward, he never displayed fear or anxiety. Although in many battles such as those of Uḥud, Ḥunayn, Khaybar and Khandaq the aides to the Prophet and the Muslim army trembled in fear or dispersed and fled, he never turned his back to the enemy. Never did a warrior or soldier engage Ali in battle and come out of it alive. Yet, with full chivalry he would never slay a weak enemy nor pursue those who fled. He would not engage in surprise attacks or in turning streams of water upon the enemy. It has been definitively established historically that in the Battle of Khaybar in the attack against the fort he reached the ring of the door and with sudden motion tore off the door and cast it away.[46] Also on the day when Mecca was conquered the Prophet ordered the idols to be broken. The idol "Hubal" was the largest idol in Mecca, a giant stone statue placed on the top of the Kaʿbah. Following the command of the Prophet, Ali placed his feet on the Prophet's shoulders, climbed to the top of the Kaʿbah, pulled "Hubal" from its place and cast it down.[47]

Ali was also without equal in religious asceticism and the

worship of God. In answer to some who had complained of Ali's anger toward them, the Prophet said, "Do not reproach Ali for he is in a state of Divine ecstasy and bewilderment."[48] Abū Dardā', one of the companions, one day saw the body of Ali in one of the palm plantations of Medina lying on the ground as stiff as wood. He went to Ali's house to inform his noble wife, the daughter of the Prophet, and to express his condolences. The daughter of the Prophet said, "My cousin (Ali) has not died. Rather, in fear of God he has fainted. This condition overcomes him often."

There are many stories told of Ali's kindness to the lowly, compassion for the needy and the poor, and generosity and munificence toward those in misery and poverty. Ali spent all that he earned to help the poor and the needy, and himself lived in the strictest and simplest manner. Ali loved agriculture and spent much of his time digging wells, planting trees and cultivating fields. But all the fields that he cultivated or wells that he built he gave in endowment (*waqf*) to the poor. His endowments, known as the "alms of Ali," had the noteworthy income of twenty-four thousand gold dinars toward the end of his life.[49]

The Second Imam

Imam Hasan Mujtabā—upon whom be peace—was the second Imam. He and his brother Imam Husayn were the two sons of Amir al-mu'minin Ali and Ḥaḍrat Fatimah, the daughter of the Prophet. Many times the Prophet had said, "Hasan and Husayn are my children." Because of these same words Ali would say to his other children, "You are my children and Hasan and Husayn are the children of the Prophet."[50]

Imam Hasan was born in the year 3 A.H. in Medina[51] and shared in the life of the Prophet for somewhat over seven years, growing up during that time under his loving care. After the death of the Prophet which was no more than three, or according to some, six months earlier than the death of Hadrat Fatimah, Hasan was placed directly under the care of his noble father. After the death of his father, through Divine Command and according to the will of his father, Imam Hasan became Imam; he also occupied the outward function of caliph for about six months, during which time he administered the affairs of the Muslims. During that time Muʿawiyah, who was a bitter enemy of Ali and his family and had fought for years with the ambition of capturing the caliphate, first on the pretext of avenging the death of the third caliph and finally with an open claim to the caliphate, marched his army into Iraq, the seat of Imam Hasan's caliphate. War ensued during which Muʿawiyah gradually subverted the generals and commanders of Imam Hasan's army with large sums of money and deceiving promises until the army rebelled against Imam Hasan.[52] Finally, the Imam was forced to make peace and to yield the caliphate to Muʿawiyah, provided it would again return to Imam Hasan after Muʿawiyah's death and the Imam's household and partisans would be protected in every way.[53]

In this way Muʿawiyah captured the Islamic caliphate and entered Iraq. In a public speech he officially made null and void all the peace conditions[54] and in every way possible placed the severest pressure upon the members of the Household of the Prophet and the Shiʿah. During all the ten years of his imamate, Imam Hasan lived in conditions of extreme hardship and under persecution, with no security even in his own house. In the year 50 A.H. he was poisoned and martyred by one of his own household who, as has been accounted by historians, had been motivated by Muʿawiyah.[55]

In human perfection Imam Hasan was reminiscent of his father and a perfect example of his noble grandfather. In fact, as long as the Prophet was alive, he and his brother were always in the company of the Prophet who even sometimes would carry them on his shoulders. Both Sunni and Shiʿite sources have transmitted this saying of the Holy Prophet concerning Hasan and Husayn: "These two children of mine are Imams whether they stand up or sit down" (allusion to whether they occupy the external function of caliphate or not).[56] Also there are many traditions of the Holy Prophet and Ali concerning the fact that Imam Hasan would gain the function of imamate after his noble father.

The Third Imam

Imam Husayn (Sayyid al-Shuhadā', "the lord among martyrs"), the second child of Ali and Fatimah, was born in the year 4 A.H. and after the martyrdom of his brother, Imam Hasan Mujtaba, became Imam through Divine Command and his brother's will.[57] Imam Husayn was Imam for a period of ten years, all but the last six months coinciding with the caliphate of Muʿawiyah. Imam Husayn lived under the most difficult outward conditions of suppression and persecution. This was due to the fact that, first of all, religious laws and regulations had lost much of their weight and credit, and the edicts of the Umayyad government had gained complete authority and power. Secondly, Muʿawiyah and his aides made use of every possible means to put aside and move out of the way the Household of the Prophet and the Shiʿah, and thus obliterate the name of Ali and his family. And above all, Muʿawiyah wanted to strengthen the basis of the caliphate of his son, Yazid, who because of his lack of principles and scruples was opposed by a large group of Muslims. Therefore, in order to quell all opposition, Muʿawiyah had undertaken newer and more severe measures. By force and necessity Imam Husayn had to endure these days and to tolerate every kind of mental and spiritual agony and affliction from Muʿawiyah and his aides—until in the middle of the year 60 A.H. Muʿawiyah died and his son Yazid took his place.[58]

Paying allegiance (bayʿah) was an old Arab practice which was carried out in important matters such as that of kingship and governorship. Those who were ruled, and especially the well-known among them, would give their hand in allegiance, agreement and obedience to their king or prince and in this way would show their support for his actions. Disagreement after allegiance was considered as disgrace and dishonor for a people and, like breaking an agreement after having signed it officially, it was considered as a definite crime. Following the example of the Holy Prophet, people believed that allegiance, when given by free will and not through force, carried authority and weight.

Muʿawiyah had asked the well-known among the people to give

their allegiance to Yazid, but had not imposed this request upon Imam Husayn.[59] He had especially told Yazid in his last will that if Husayn refused to pay allegiance he should pass over it in silence and overlook the matter, for he had understood correctly the disastrous consequences which would follow if the issue were to be pressed. But because of his egoism and recklessness, Yazid neglected his father's advice and immediately after the death of his father ordered the governor of Medina either to force a pledge of allegiance from Imam Husayn or send his head to Damascus.[60]

After the governor of Medina informed Imam Husayn of this demand, the Imam, in order to think over the question, asked for a delay and overnight started with his family toward Mecca. He sought refuge in the sanctuary of God which in Islam is the official place of refuge and security. This event occurred toward the end of the month of Rajab and the beginning of Shaʿbān of 60 A.H. For nearly four months Imam Husayn stayed in Mecca in refuge. This news spread throughout the Islamic world. On the one hand many people who were tired of the iniquities of Muʿawiyah's rule and were even more dissatisfied when Yazid became caliph, corresponded with Imam Husayn and expressed their sympathy for him. On the other hand a flood of letters began to flow, especially from Iraq and particularly the city of Kufa, inviting the Imam to go to Iraq and accept the leadership of the populace there with the aim of beginning an uprising to overcome injustice and iniquity. Naturally such a situation was dangerous for Yazid.

The stay of Imam Husayn in Mecca continued until the season for pilgrimage when Muslims from all over the world poured in groups into Mecca in order to perform the rites of the hajj. The Imam discovered that some of the followers of Yazid had entered Mecca as pilgrims (*ḥājjīs*) with the mission to kill the Imam during the rites of hajj with the arms they carried under their special pilgrimage dress (*iḥrāmī*).[61]

The Imam shortened the pilgrimage rites and decided to leave. Amidst the vast crowd of people he stood up and in a short speech announced that he was setting out for Iraq.[62] In this short speech he also declared that he would be martyred and asked Muslims to help him in attaining the goal he had in view and to offer their lives in the path of God. On the next day he set out with his family and a group of his companions for Iraq.

Imam Husayn was determined not to give his allegiance to Yazid and knew full well that he would be killed. He was aware that his death was inevitable in the face of the awesome military power of the Umayyads, supported as it was by corruption in certain sectors, spiritual decline, and lack of will power among the people, especially in Iraq. Some of the outstanding people of Mecca stood in the way of Imam Husayn and warned him of the danger of the move he was making. But he answered that he refused to pay allegiance and give his approval to a government of injustice and tyranny. He added that he knew that wherever he turned or went he would be killed.[63] He would leave Mecca in order to preserve the respect for the house of God and not allow this respect to be destroyed by having his blood spilled there.

While on the way to Kufa and still a few days' journey away from the city, he received news that the uncle of Yazid in Kufa had put to death the representative of the Imam in that city and also one of the Imam's determined supporters who was a well-known man in Kufa. Their feet had been tied and they had been dragged through the streets.[64] The city and its surroundings were placed under strict observation and countless soldiers of the enemy were awaiting him. There was no way open to him but to march ahead and to face death. It was here that the Imam expressed his definitive determination to go ahead and be martyred; and so he continued on his journey.[65]

Approximately seventy kilometres from Kufa, in a desert named Karbala, the Imam and his entourage were surrounded by the army of Yazid. For eight days they stayed in this spot during which the circle narrowed and the number of the enemy's army increased. Finally the Imam, with his household and a small number of companions were encircled by an army of thirty thousand soldiers.[66] During these days the Imam fortified his position and made a final selection of his companions. At night he called his companions and during a short speech stated that there was nothing ahead but death and martyrdom. He added that since the enemy was concerned only with his person he would free them from all obligations so that anyone who wished could escape in the darkness of the night and save his life. Then he ordered the lights to be turned out and most of his companions, who had joined him for their own advantage, dispersed. Only a handful of those who loved the truth—about forty of his close aides—and some of the Banu Hashim remained.[67]

Once again the Imam assembled those who were left and put them to a test. He addressed his companions and Hashimite relatives, saying again that the enemy was concerned only with his person. Each could benefit from the darkness of the night and escape the danger. But this time the faithful companions of the Imam answered each in his own way that they would not deviate for a moment from the path of truth of which the Imam was the leader and would never leave him alone. They said they would defend his household to the last drop of their blood and as long as they could carry a sword.[68]

On the ninth day of the month the last challenge to choose between "allegiance or war" was made by the enemy to the Imam. The Imam asked for a delay in order to worship overnight and became determined to enter battle on the next day.[69]

On the tenth day of Muḥarram of the year 61/680 the Imam lined up before the enemy with his small band of followers, less than ninety persons consisting of forty of his companions, thirty some members of the army of the enemy that joined him during the night and day of war, and his Hashimite family of children, brothers, nephews, nieces and cousins. That day they fought from morning until their final breath, and the Imam, the young Hashimites and the companions were all martyred. Among those killed were two children of Imam Hasan, who were only thirteen and eleven years old; and a five-year-old child and a suckling baby of Imam Husayn.

The army of the enemy, after ending the war, plundered the *ḥaram* of the Imam and burned his tents. They decapitated the bodies of the martyrs, denuded them and threw them to the ground without burial. Then they moved the members of the haram, all of whom were helpless women and girls, along with the heads of the martyrs, to Kufa.[70] Among the prisoners there were three male members: a twenty-two year old son of Imam Husayn who was very ill and unable to move, namely Ali ibn Husayn, the fourth Imam; his four year old son, Muhammad ibn Ali, who became the fifth Imam; and finally Hasan Muthannā, the son of the second Imam who was also the son-in-law of Imam Husayn and who, having been wounded during the war, lay among the dead. They found him near death and through the intercession of one of the generals did not cut off his head. Rather, they took him with the prisoners to Kufa and from there to Damascus before Yazid.

The event of Karbala, the capture of the women and children of the Household of the Prophet, their being taken as prisoners from town to town and the speeches made by the daughter of Ali, Zaynab, and the fourth Imam who were among the prisoners, disgraced the Umayyads. Such abuse of the Household of the Prophet annulled the propaganda which Muʿawiyah had carried out for years. The matter reached such proportions that Yazid in public disowned and condemned the actions of his agents. The event of Karbala was a major factor in the overthrow of Umayyad rule although its effect was delayed. It also strengthened the roots of Shiʿism. Among its immediate results were the revolts and rebellions combined with bloody wars which continued for twelve years. Among those who were instrumental in the death of the Imam not one was able to escape revenge and punishment.

Anyone who studies closely the history of the life of Imam Husayn and Yazid and the conditions that prevailed at that time, and analyzes this chapter of Islamic history, will have no doubt that in those circumstances there was no choice before Imam Husayn but to be killed. Swearing allegiance to Yazid would have meant publicly showing contempt for Islam, something which was not possible for the Imam, for Yazid not only showed no respect for Islam and its injunctions but also made a public demonstration of impudently treading under foot its basis and its laws. Those before him, even if they opposed religious injunctions, always did so in the guise of religion, and at least formally respected religion. They took pride in being companions of the Holy Prophet and the other religious figures in whom people believed. From this it can be concluded that the claim of some interpreters of these events is false when they say that the two brothers, Hasan and Husayn, had two different tastes and that one chose the way of peace and the other the way of war, so that one brother made peace with Mu'awiyah although he had an army of forty thousand while the other went to war against Yazid with an army of forty. For we see that this same Imam Husayn, who refused to pay allegiance to Yazid for one day, lived for ten years under the rule of Mu'awiyah, in the same manner as his brother who also had endured for ten years under Mu'awiyah, without opposing him.

It must be said in truth that if Imam Hasan or Imam Husayn had fought Mu'awiyah they would have been killed without there being the least benefit for Islam. Their deaths would have had no effect before the righteous-appearing policy of Mu'awiyah, a competent politican who emphasized his being a companion of the Holy Prophet, the "scribe of the revelation," and "uncle of the faithful" and who used every stratagem possible to preserve a religious guise for his rule. Moreover, with his ability to set the stage to accomplish his desires he could have had them killed by their own people and then assumed a state of mourning and sought to revenge their blood, just as he sought to give the impression that he was avenging the killing of the third caliph.

The Fourth Imam

Imam Sajjād (Ali ibn Husayn entitled Zayn al-'ābidīn and Sajjad) was the son of the third Imam and his wife, the queen among women, the daughter of Yazdigird the king of Iran. He was the only son of Imam Husayn to survive, for his other three brothers Ali Akbar, aged twenty-five, five year old Ja'far and Ali Asghar (or 'Abdallāh) who was a suckling baby were martyred during the event of Karbala.[71] The Imam had also accompanied his father on the journey that terminated fatally in Karbala, but because of severe illness and the inability to carry arms or participate in fighting he was prevented from taking part in the holy war and being martyred. So he was sent with the womenfolk to Damascus. After spending a period in imprisonment he was sent with honor to Medina because Yazid wanted to conciliate public opinion. But for a second time, by the order of the Umayyad caliph, 'Abd al-Malik, he was chained and sent from Medina to Damascus and then again returned to Medina.[72]

The fourth Imam, upon returning to Medina, retired from public life completely, closed the door of his house to strangers and spent his time in worship. He was in contact only with the elite among the Shi'ites such as Abū Ḥamzah Thumālī, Abū Khālid Kābulī and the like. The elite disseminated among the Shi'ah the religious sciences they learned from the Imam. In this way Shi'ism spread considerably and showed its effects during the imamate of the fifth Imam. Among the works of the fourth Imam is a book called *Ṣaḥīfah sajjādīyah.* It consists of fifty-seven prayers concerning the most sublime Divine sciences and is known as "The Psalm of the Household of the Prophet."

The fourth Imam died (according to some Shi'ite traditions poisoned by Walīd ibn 'Abd al-Malik through the instigation of the Umayyad caliph Hishām[73]) in 95/712 after thirty-five years of imamate.

The Fifth Imam

Imam Muhammad ibn Ali Bāqir (the word *bāqir* meaning he who cuts and dissects, a title given to him by the Prophet)[74] was the son of the fourth Imam and was born in 57/675. He was present at the event of Karbala when he was four years old. After his father, through Divine Command and the decree of those who went before him, he became Imam. In the year 114/732 he died, according to some Shi'ite traditions poisoned by Ibrahim ibn Walid ibn 'Abdallah, the nephew of Hisham, the Umayyad caliph.

During the imamate of the fifth Imam, as a result of the injustice of the Umayyads, revolts and wars broke out in some corner of the Islamic world every day. Moreover, there were disputes within the Umayyad family itself which kept the caliphate busy and to a certain extent left the members of the Household of the Prophet alone. From the other side, the tragedy of Karbala and the oppression suffered by the Household of the Prophet, of which the fourth

Imam was the most noteworthy embodiment, had attracted many Muslims to the Imams.[75] These factors combined to make it possible for people and especially the Shi'ites to go in great numbers to Medina and to come into the presence of the fifth Imam. Possibilities for disseminating truths about Islam and the sciences of the Household of the Prophet, which had never existed for the Imams before him, were presented to the fifth Imam. The proof of this fact is the innumerable traditions recounted from the fifth Imam and the large number of illustrious men of science and Shi'ite scholars who were trained by him in different Islamic sciences. These names are listed in books of biographies of famous men in Islam.[76]

The Sixth Imam

Imam Ja'far ibn Muhammad, the son of the fifth Imam, was born in 83/702. He died in 140/757, according to Shi'ite tradition, poisoned and martyred through the intrigue of the Abbasid caliph Manṣūr. After the death of his father he became Imam by Divine Command and decree of those who came before him.

During the imamate of the sixth Imam greater possibilities and a more favorable climate existed for him to propagate religious teachings. This came about as a result of revolts in Islamic lands, especially the uprising of the Muswaddah to overthrow the Umayyad caliphate, and the bloody wars which finally led to the fall and extinction of the Umayyads. The greater opportunities for Shi'ite teachings were also a result of the favorable ground the fifth Imam had prepared during the twenty years of his imamate through the propagation of the true teachings of Islam and the sciences of the Household of the Prophet.

The Imam took advantage of the occasion to propagate the religious sciences until the very end of his imamate, which was contemporary with the end of the Umayyad and beginning of the Abbasid caliphates. He instructed many scholars in different fields of the intellectual and transmitted sciences, such as Zarārah, Muhammad ibn Muslim, Mu'min Ṭāq, Hisham ibn

Ḥakam, Abān ibn Taghlib, Hisham ibn Sālim, Ḥurayz, Hisham Kalbī Nassābah, and Jābir ibn Ḥayyān, the alchemist. Even some important Sunni scholars such as Sufyān Thawrī, Abu Hanifah, the founder of the Hanafi school of law, Qāḍī Sukūnī, Qadi Abu'l-Bakhtarī, and others, had the honor of being his students. It is said that his classes and sessions of instruction produced four thousand scholars of hadith and other sciences.[77] The number of traditions preserved from the fifth and sixth Imams is more than all the hadith that have been recorded from the Prophet and the other ten Imams combined.

But toward the end of his life the Imam was subjected to severe restrictions placed upon him by the Abbasid caliph Mansur, who ordered such torture and merciless killing of many of the descendants of the Prophet who were Shiʿite that his actions even surpassed the cruelty and heedlessness of the Umayyads. At his order they were arrested in groups, some thrown into deep and dark prisons and tortured until they died, while others were beheaded or buried alive or placed at the base of or between walls of buildings, and walls were constructed over them.

Hisham, the Umayyad caliph, had ordered the sixth Imam to be arrested and brought to Damascus. Later, the Imam was arrested by Saffāḥ, the Abbasid caliph, and brought to Iraq. Finally, Mansur had him arrested again and brought to Samarrah where he had the Imam kept under supervision, was in every way harsh and discourteous to him, and several times thought of killing him.[78] Eventually the Imam was allowed to return to Medina where he spent the rest of his life in hiding, until he was poisoned and martyred through the intrigue of Mansur.[79]

Upon hearing the news of the Imam's martyrdom, Mansur wrote to the governor of Medina instructing him to go to the house of the Imam on the pretext of expressing his condolences to the family, to ask for the Imam's will and testament and read it. Whoever was chosen by the Imam as his inheritor and successor should be beheaded on the spot. Of course the aim of Mansur was to put an end to the whole question of the imamate and to Shiʿite aspirations. When the governor of Medina, following orders, read the last will and testament, he saw that the Imam had chosen four people rather than one to administer his last will and testament: the caliph himself, the governor of Medina, ʿAbdallāh Aftaḥ, the Imam's older son, and Musa, his younger son. In this way the plot of Mansur failed.[80]

The Seventh Imam

Imam Mūsā ibn Jaʿfar Kāẓim, the son of the sixth Imam, was born in 128/744 and was poisoned and martyred in prison in 183/799.[81] He became Imam after the death of his father, through Divine Command and the decree of his forefathers. The seventh Imam was contemporary with the Abbasid caliphs, Mansur, Hādī, Mahdi and Harun. He lived in very difficult times, in hiding, until finally Harun went on the hajj and in Medina had the Imam arrested while praying in the Mosque of the Prophet. He was chained and imprisoned, then taken from Medina to Basra and from Basra to Baghdad where for years he was transferred from one prison to another. Finally he died in Baghdad in the Sindī ibn Shāhak prison through poisoning[82] and was buried in the cemetery of the Quraysh which is now located in the city of Kazimayn.

The Eighth Imam

Imam Riḍā (Ali ibn Musa) was the son of the seventh Imam and according to well-known accounts was born in 148/765 and died in 203/817.[83] The eighth Imam reached the imamate, after the death of his father, through Divine Command and the decree of his forefathers. The period of his imamate coincided with the caliphate of Harun and then his sons Amīn and Ma'mūn. After the death of his father, Ma'mun fell into conflict with his brother Amin which led to bloody wars and finally the assassination of Amin, after which Ma'mun became caliph.[84] Until that day the policy of the Abbasid caliphate toward the Shiʿites had been increasingly harsh and cruel. Every once in a while one of the supporters of Ali

(*ʿalawīs*) would revolt, causing bloody wars and rebellions which were of great difficulty and consequence for the caliphate.

The Shiʿite Imams would not cooperate with those who carried out these rebellions and would not interfere with their affairs. The Shiʿites of that day, who comprised a considerable population, continued to consider the Imams as their religious leaders to whom obedience was obligatory and believed in them as the real caliphs of the Holy Prophet. They considered the caliphate to be far from the sacred authority of their Imams, for the caliphate had come to seem more like the courts of the Persian kings and Roman emperors and was being run by a group of people more interested in worldly rule than in the strict application of religious principles. The continuation of such a situation was dangerous for the structure of the caliphate and was a serious threat to it.

Ma'mun thought of finding a new solution for these difficulties which the seventy-year old policy of his Abbasid predecessors had not been able to solve. To accomplish this end he chose the eighth Imam as his successor, hoping in this way to overcome two difficulties: first of all to prevent the descendants of the Prophet from rebelling against the government since they would be involved in the government themselves, and secondly, to cause the people to lose their spiritual belief and inner attachment to the Imams. This would be accomplished by having the Imams become engrossed in wordly matters and the politics of the caliphate itself, which had always been considered by the Shiʿites to be evil and impure. In this way their religious organization would crumble and they would no longer present any dangers to the caliphate. Obviously, after accomplishing these ends, the removal of the Imam would present no difficulties to the Abbasids.[85]

In order to have this decision put into effect, Ma'mun asked the Imam to come to Marw from Medina. Once he had arrived there, Ma'mun offered him first the caliphate and then the succession to the caliphate. The Imam made his apologies and turned down the proposal, but he was finally induced to accept the successorship, with the condition that he would not interfere in governmental affairs or in the appointment or dismissal of government agents.[86]

This event occurred in 200/814. But soon Maʿmun realized that he had committed an error, for there was a rapid spread of Shi'ism, a growth in the attachment of the populace to the Imam and an astounding reception given to the Imam by the people and even by the army and government agents. Ma'mun sought to find a remedy for this difficulty and had the Imam poisoned and martyred. After his death the Imam was buried in the city of Tus in Iran, which is now called Mashhad.

Ma'mun displayed great interest in having works on the intellectual sciences translated into Arabic. He organized gatherings in which scholars of different religions and sects assembled and carried out scientific and scholarly debates. The eighth Imam also participated in these assemblies and joined in the discussions with scholars of other religions. Many of these debates are recorded in the collections of Shi'ite hadiths.[87]

The Ninth Imam

Imam Muhammad (ibn Ali) Taqī (sometimes called Jawād and Ibn al-Riḍā) was the son of the eighth Imam. He was born in 195/809 in Medina and according to Shi'ite traditions was martyred in 220/835, poisoned by his wife, the daughter of Ma'mun, at the instigation of the Abbasid caliph Mu'taṣim. He was buried next to his grandfather, the seventh Imam, in Kazimayn. He became Imam after the death of his father through Divine Command and by the decree of his forefathers. At the time of the death of his father he was in Medina. Ma'mun called him to Baghdad which was then the capital of the caliphate and outwardly showed him much kindness. He even gave the Imam his daughter in marriage and kept him in Baghdad. In reality he wanted in this way to keep a close watch upon the Imam from both outside and within his own household. The Imam spent some time in Baghdad and then with the consent of Ma'mum set out for Medina where he remained until Ma'mun's death. When Mu'tasim became the caliph he called the Imam back to Baghdad and, as we have seen, through the Imam's wife had him poisoned and killed.[88]

The Tenth Imam

Imam Ali ibn Muhammad Naqī (sometimes referred to by the title of Hādī), was the son of the ninth Imam. He was born in 212/827 in Medina and according to Shi'ite accounts was martyred through poisoning by Mu'tazz the Abbasid caliph, in 254/868.[89]

During his lifetime the tenth Imam was contemporary with seven of the Abbasid caliphs: Ma'mun, Mu'tasim, Wāthiq, Mutawakkil, Muntaṣir, Musta'īn and Mu'tazz. It was during the rule of Mu'tasim in 220/835 that his noble father died through poisoning in Baghdad. At that time Ali ibn Muhammad Naqi was in Medina. There he became the Imam through Divine Command and the decree of the Imams before him. He stayed in Medina teaching religious sciences until the time of Mutawakkil. In 243/857, as a result of certain false charges that were made, Mutawakkil ordered one of his government officials to invite the Imam from Medina to Samarrah which was then the capital. He himself wrote the Imam a letter full of kindness and courtesy asking him to come to the capital where they could meet.[90] Upon arrival in Samarrah the Imam was also shown certain outward courtesy and respect. Yet at the same time Mutawakkil tried by all possible means to trouble and dishonor him. Many times he called the Imam to his presence with the aim of killing or disgracing him and had his house searched.

In his enmity toward the Household of the Prophet Mutawakkil had no equal among the Abbasid caliphs. He was especially opposed to Ali, whom he cursed openly. He even ordered a clown to ridicule Ali at voluptuous banquets. In the year 237/850 he ordered the mausoleum of Imam Husayn in Karbala and many of the houses around it to be torn down to the ground. Then water was turned upon the tomb of the Imam. He ordered the ground of the tomb to be plowed and cultivated so that any trace of the tomb would be forgotten.[91] During the life of Mutawakkil the condition of life of the descendants of Ali in the Hijaz had reached such a pitiful state that their womenfolk had no veils with which to cover themselves. Many of them had only one old veil which they wore at the time of the daily prayers. Pressures of a similar kind were put on the descendants of Ali who lived in Egypt.[92] The tenth

Imam accepted in patience the tortures and afflictions of the Abbasid caliph Mutawakkil until the caliph died and was followed by Muntasir, Mustaʿin and finally Muʿtazz, whose intrigue led to the Imam's being poisoned and martyred.

The Eleventh Imam

Imam Hasan ibn Ali ʿAskarī, the son of the tenth Imam, was born in 232/845 and according to some Shiʿite sources was poisoned and killed in 260/872 through the instigation of the Abbasid caliph Muʿtamid.[93] The eleventh Imam gained the imamate, after the death of his noble father, through Divine Command and through the decree of the previous Imams. During the seven years of his imamate, due to untold restrictions placed upon him by the caliphate, he lived in hiding and dissimulation (*taqīyah*). He did not have any social contact with even the common people among the Shiʿite population. Only the elite of the Shiʿah were able to see him. Even so, he spent most of his time in prison.[94]

There was extreme repression at that time because the Shiʿite population had reached a considerable level in both numbers and power. Everyone knew that the Shiʿah believed in the imamate, and the identity of the Shiʿite Imams was also known. Therefore, the caliphate kept the Imams under its close supervision more than ever before. It tried through every possible means and through secret plans to remove and destroy them. Also, the caliphate had come to know that the elite among the Shiʿah believed that the eleventh Imam, according to traditions cited by him as well as his forefathers, would have a son who was the promised Mahdi. The coming of the Mahdi had been foretold in authenticated hadiths of the Prophet in both Sunni and Shiʿite sources.[95] For this reason the eleventh Imam, more than other Imams, was kept under close watch by the caliphate. The caliph of the time had decided definitely to put an end to the imamate in Shiʿism through every possible means and to close the door to the imamate once and for all.

Therefore, as soon as the news of the illness of the eleventh Imam reached Muʿtamid, he sent a physician and a few of his trusted agents and judges to the house of the Imam to be with him and observe his condition and the situation within his house at all times. After the death of the Imam, they had the house investigated and all his female slaves examined by the midwife. For two years the secret agents of the caliph searched for the successor of the Imam until they lost all hope.[96] The eleventh Imam was buried in his house in Samarrah next to his noble father.

Here it should be remembered that during their lifetimes the Imams trained many hundreds of scholars of religion and hadith, and it is these scholars who have transmitted to us information about the Imams. In order not to prolong the matter, the list of their names and works and their biographies have not been included here.[97]

The Twelfth Imam

The promised Mahdi, who is usually mentioned by his title of Imām-i 'Aṣr (the Imam of the "Period") and Ṣāḥib al-Zamān (the Lord of the Age), is the son of the eleventh Imam. His name is the same as that of the Holy Prophet. He was born in Samarrah in 256/868 and until 260/872 when his father was martyred, lived under his father's care and tutelage. He was hidden from public view and only a few of the elite among the Shi'ah were able to meet him.

After the martyrdom of his father he became Imam and by Divine Command went into occultation (*ghaybat).* Thereafter he appeared only to his deputies (*nā'ib*) and even then only in exceptional circumstances.[98]

The Imam chose as a special deputy for a time Uthman ibn Sa'īd 'Umarī, one of the companions of his father and grandfather who was his confidant and trusted friend. Through his deputy the Imam would answer the demands and questions of the Shi'ah. After Uthman ibn Sa'id, his son Muhammad ibn Uthman Umari was appointed the deputy of the Imam. After the death of Muhammad ibn Uthman, Abu'l Qāsim Husayn ibn Rūḥ Nawbakhtī was the special deputy, and after his death Ali ibn Muhammad Simmarī was chosen for this task.[99]

A few days before the death of Ali ibn Muhammad Simmari in 329/939 an order was issued by the Imam stating that in six days Ali ibn Muhammad Simmari would die. Henceforth the special deputation of the Imam would come to an end and the major occultation (*ghaybat-i kubrā*) would begin and would continue until the day God grants permission to the Imam to manifest himself.

The occultation of the twelfth Imam is, therefore, divided into two parts: the first, the minor occultation (*ghaybat-i ṣughrā*) which began in 260/872 and ended in 329/939, lasting about seventy years; the second, the major occultation which commenced in 329/939 and will continue as long as God wills it. In a hadith upon whose authenticity everyone agrees, the Holy Prophet has said, "If there were to remain in the life of the world but one day, God would prolong that day until He sends in it a man from my community and my household. His name will be the same as my name. He will fill the earth with equity and justice as it was filled with oppression and tyranny."[100]

On the Appearance of the Mahdi

In the discussion on prophecy and the imamate it was indicated that as a result of the law of general guidance which governs all of creation, man is of necessity endowed with the power of receiving revelation through prophecy, which directs him toward the perfection of the human norm and the well-being of the human species. Obviously, if this perfection and happiness were not possible for man, whose life possesses a social aspect, the very fact that he is endowed with this power would be meaningless and futile. But there is no futility in creation.

In other words, ever since he has inhabited the earth, man has had the wish to lead a social life filled with happiness in its true sense and has striven toward this end. If such a wish were not to have an objective existence it would never have been imprinted upon man's inner nature, in the same way that if there were no food there would have been no hunger. Or if there were to be no water there would be no thirst and if there were to be no reproduction there would have been no sexual attraction between the sexes.

Therefore, by reason of inner necessity and determination, the future will see a day when human society will be replete with justice and when all will live in peace and tranquillity, when human beings will be fully possessed of virtue and perfection. The establishment of such a condition will occur through human hands but with Divine succor. And the leader of such a society, who will be the savior of man, is called in the language of the hadith, the Mahdi.

In the different religions that govern the world such as Hinduism, Buddhism, Judaism, Christianity, Zoroastrianism and Islam there are references to a person who will come as the savior of mankind. These religions have usually given happy tidings of his coming, although there are naturally certain differences in detail that can be discerned when these teachings are compared carefully. The hadith of the Holy Prophet upon which all Muslims agree, "The Mahdi is of my progeny," refers to this same truth.

There are numerous hadiths cited in Sunni and Shi'ite sources from the Holy Prophet and the Imams concerning the appearance of the Mahdi, such as that he is of the progeny of the Prophet and that his appearance will enable human society to reach true perfection and the full realization of spiritual life.[101] In addition, there are numerous other traditions concerning the fact that the Mahdi is the son of the eleventh Imam, Hasan al-'Askari. They agree that after being born and undergoing a long occultation the Mahdi will appear again, filling with justice the world that has been corrupted by injustice and iniquity.

As an example, Ali ibn Musa al-Rida (the eighth Imam) has said, in the course of a hadith, "The Imam after me is my son, Muhammad, and after him his son Ali, and after Ali his son, Hasan, and after Hasan his son Ḥujjat al-Qā'im, who is awaited during his occultation and obeyed during his manifestation. If there remain from the life of the world but a single day, Allah will extend that day until he becomes manifest, and fill the world with justice in the same way that it had been filled with iniquity. But when? As for news of the 'hour,' verily my father told me, having heard it from his father who heard it from his father who heard it from his ancestors who heard it from Ali, that it was asked of the Holy Prophet, 'Oh Prophet of God, when will the "support" (qa'im) who is from thy family appear?' He said, 'His case is like that of the Hour (of the Resurrection). "He alone will manifest it at its proper time. It is heavy in the heavens and the earth. It cometh not to you save unawares" (Quran, VII, 187).' "[102]

Ṣaqr ibn Abī Dulaf said, "I heard from Abu Ja'far Muhammad ibn Ali al-Rida [the ninth Imam] who said, 'The Imam after me is my son, Ali; his command is my command; his word is my word; to obey him is to obey me. The Imam after him is his son, Hasan. His command is the command of his father; his word is the word of his father; to obey him is to obey his father.' After these words the Imam remained silent. I said to him, 'Oh son of the Prophet, who will be the Imam after Hasan?' The Imam cried hard, then said, 'Verily after Hasan his son is the awaited Imam who is "al-qā'im bi'l-ḥaqq" (He who is supported by the Truth).' "[103]

Musa ibn Ja'far Baghdādī said, "I heard from the Imam Abu Muhammad al-Hasan ibn Ali [the eleventh Imam] who said, 'I see that after me differences will appear among you concerning the Imam after me. Whoso accepts the Imams after the Prophet of God but denies my son is like the person who accepts all the prophets but denies the prophethood of Muhammad, the Prophet of God, upon whom be peace and blessing. And whoso denies [Muhammad] the Prophet of God is like one who has denied all the prophets of God, for to obey the last of us is like obeying the first and to deny the last of us is like denying the first. But beware! Verily for my son there is an occultation during which all people will fall into doubt except those whom Allah protects."[104]

The opponents of Shi'ism protest that according to the beliefs of this school the Hidden Imam should by now be nearly twelve centuries old, whereas this is impossible for any human being. In answer it must be said that the protest is based only on the unlikelihood of such an occurrence, not its impossibility. Of course such a long lifetime or a life of a longer period is unlikely. But those who study the hadiths of the Holy Prophet and the Imams will see that they refer to this life as one possessing miraculous qualities.

Miracles are certainly not impossible nor can they be negated through scientific arguments. It can never be proved that the causes and agents that are functioning in the world are solely those that we see and know and that other causes which we do not know or whose effects and actions we have not seen nor understood do not exist. It is in this way possible that in one or several members of mankind there can be operating certain causes and agents which bestow upon them a very long life of a thousand or several thousand years. Medicine has not even lost hope of discovering a way to achieve very long life spans. In any case such protests from "peoples of the Book" such as Jews, Christians and Muslims are most strange for they accept the miracles of the prophets of God according to their own sacred scriptures.

The opponents of Shiʿism also protest that, although Shiʿism considers the Imam necessary in order to expound the injunctions and verities of religion and to guide the people, the occultation of the Imam is the negation of this very purpose, for an Imam in occultation who cannot be reached by mankind cannot be in any way beneficial or effective. The opponents say that if God wills to bring forth an Imam to reform mankind He is able to create him at the necessary moment and does not need to create him thousands of years earlier. In answer it must be said that such people have not really understood the meaning of the Imam, for in the discussion on the imamate it became clear that the duty of the Imam is not only the formal explanation of the religious sciences and exoteric guidance of the people. In the same way that he has the duty of guiding men outwardly, the Imam also bears the function of walayat and the esoteric guidance of men. It is he who directs man's spiritual life and orients the inner aspect of human action toward God. Clearly, his physical presence or absence has no effect in this matter. The Imam watches over men inwardly and is in communion with the soul and spirit of men even if he be hidden from their physical eyes. His existence is always necessary even if the time has not as yet arrived for his outward appearance and the universal reconstruction that he is to bring about.

The Spiritual Message of Shi'ism

The message of Shi'ism to the world can be summarized in one sentence: "To know God." Or in other words, it is to instruct man to follow the path of Divine realization and the knowledge of God in order to gain felicity and salvation. And this message is contained in the very phrase with which the Holy Prophet commenced his prophetic mission when he said: "Oh men! Know God in His Oneness (and acknowledge Him) so that you will gain salvation."[105]

As a summary explanation of this message we will add that man is attached by nature to many goals in this worldly life and to material pleasures. He loves tasty food and drink, fashionable dress, attractive palaces and surroundings, a beautiful and pleasing wife, sincere friends and great wealth. And in another direction he is attracted to political power, position, reputation, the extension of his rule and dominion and the destruction of anything that is opposed to his wishes. But in his inner and primordial, God-given nature man understands that all these are means created for man, but man is not created for all these things. These things should be subservient to man and follow him and not vice versa. To consider the stomach and the region below it as a final end of life is the logic of cattle and sheep. To tear up, cut and destroy others is the logic of the tiger, the wolf and the fox. The logic inherent in human existence is the attainment of wisdom and nothing else.

This logic based upon wisdom with the power which it possesses to discern between reality and the unreal, guides us toward the truth and not toward things our emotions demand or toward passions, selfishness and egoism. This logic considers man as a part of the totality of creation without any separate independence or the possibility of a rebellious self-centeredness. In contrast to the current belief that man is the master of creation and tames rebellious nature and conquers it to force it to obey his wishes and desires, we find that in reality man himself is an instrument in the hand of Universal Nature and is ruled and commanded by it.

This logic based upon wisdom invites man to concentrate more closely upon the apprehension he has of the existence of this world until it becomes clear to him that the world of existence and all that is in it does not issue from itself but rather from an Infinite Source. He will then know that all this beauty and ugliness, all these creatures of the earth and the heavens, which appear outwardly as independent realities, gain reality only through another Reality and are manifested only in Its Light, not by themselves and through themselves. In the same way that the "realities" as well as the power and grandeur of yesterday have no greater value than tales and legends of today, so are the "realities" of today no more than vaguely remembered dreams in relation to what will appear as "reality" tomorrow. In the last analysis, everything in itself is no more than a tale and a dream. Only God is Reality in the absolute sense, the One Who does not perish. Under the protection of His Being, everything gains existence and becomes manifested through the Light of His Essence.

If man becomes endowed with such vision and power of apprehension, then the tent of his separative existence will fall down before his eyes like a bubble on the surface of water. He will see with his eyes that the world and all that is in it depend upon an Infinite Being who possesses life, power, knowledge and every perfection to an infinite degree. Man and every other being in the world are like so many windows which display according to their capacity the world of eternity which transcends them and lies beyond them.

It is at this moment that man takes from himself and all creatures the quality of independence and primacy and returns these qualities to their Owner. He detaches himself from all things to attach himself solely to the One God. Before His Majesty and Grandeur he does nothing but bow in humility. Only then does he become guided and directed by God so that whatever he knows he knows in God. Through Divine guidance he becomes adorned with moral and spiritual virtue and pure actions which are the same as Islam itself, the submission to God, the religion that is in the primordial nature of things.

This is the highest degree of human perfection and the station of the perfect man (the Universal Man, insān-i kāmil), namely the Imam who has reached this rank through Divine grace. Furthermore, those who have reached this station through the practice of spiritual methods, with the different ranks and stations that they possess, are the true followers of the Imam. It becomes thus clear that the knowledge of God and of the Imam are inseparable in the same way that the knowledge of God is inextricably connected to the knowledge of oneself. For he who knows his own symbolic existence has already come to know the true existence which belongs solely to God who is independent and without need of anything whatsoever.

NOTES

CHAPTER VII

1. *Tārīkh-i Ya'qūbī*, vol. III, pp. 60–61; *Sīrah* of Ibn Hishām, vol. IV, p. 197.
2. *Tārīkh-i Ya'qūbī*, vol. II, pp. 52–59; *Sīrah* of Ibn Hishām, vol. II, p. 223.
3. *Tārīkh-i Ya'qūbī*, vol. II, pp. 59–60 and p. 44; *Sirāh* of Ibn Hishām, vol. II, p. 251, vol. IV, p. 173 and p. 272.
4. *Tārīkh-i Ya'qūbī*, vol. II, p. 29; *Tārīkh-i Abi'l-Fidā'*, vol. I, p. 126; *Sīrah* of Ibn Hishām, vol. II, p. 98.
5. *Ghāyat al-marām*, p. 664, from the *Musnad* of Ahmad and others.
6. *Editor's note:* These refer to different sayings of the Prophet in which the question of the Imam is discussed. The most famous of these, Hadith-i ghadir, as mentioned above is the traditional basis for the celebration of the "Feast of Ghadir." Since the Safavid period this feast has acquired a particular political significance in Iran, since it marks the formal transfer of political power to Ali under whose aegis all Shi'ite kings have ruled.
7. Ṭabarī, *Dhakhā'ir al-'uqbā*, Cairo, 1356, p. 16. This hadith has been recorded with a slight variation in *al-Durr al-manthūr*, vol. II, p. 293. In his *Ghāyat al-marām*, p. 103, Baḥrānī cities 24 hadiths from Sunni sources and nineteen from Shi'ite sources concerning the conditions and reasons for the revelation of this Quranic verse.
8. Baḥrānī, *Ghāyat al-marām*, p. 336, where six Sunni and fifteen Shi'ite hadiths concerning the occasion and reason for the revelation of the above Quranic verse are cited.
9. For further explanation see 'Allāmah Ṭabāṭabā'ī, *Tafsīr al-mīzān*, vol. V, Tehran, 1377, pp. 177–214, and vol. VI, Tehran, 1377, pp. 50–64.
10. *al-Bidāyah wa'l-nihāyah*, vol. V, p. 208 and vol. VII, p. 346; *Dhakhā'ir al-'uqbā*, p. 67; *al-Fuṣūl al-muhimmah* of Ibn Ṣabbāgh, Najaf, 1950, vol. II, p. 23; *Khaṣā'iṣ* of Nasā'ī, Najaf, 1369, p. 31. In his *Ghāyat al-marām*, p. 79, Baḥrānī has cited eighty-nine different chains of transmission for this hadith from Sunni sources and forty-three from Shi'ite sources.
11. *Dhakhā'ir al-'uqbā*, p. 20; *al-Ṣawā'iq al-muḥriqah* of Ibn Ḥajar, Cairo, 1312, pp. 150 and 184; *Ta'rīkh al-khulafā'* of Jalāl al-Dīn Suyūṭī, Cairo, 1952, p. 307; *Nūr al-abṣār* of Shiblanjī, Cairo, 1312, p. 114. In his *Ghāyat al-marām*, p. 237, Baḥrānī cites eleven chains of transmission for this hadith from Sunni sources and seven from Shi'ite sources.
12. *al-Bidāyah wa'l-nihāyah*, vol. V, p. 209; *Dhakhā'ir al-'uqbā*, p. 16; *al-Fuṣūl al-muhimmah*, p. 22; *Khaṣā'iṣ*, p. 30; *al-Ṣawā'iq al-muḥriqah*, p. 147. In *Ghāyat al-marām* thirty-nine versions of this hadith have been recorded from Sunni sources and eighty-two from Shi'ite sources.

13. *Yanābī' al-mawaddah* of Sulaymān ibn Ibrāhīm Qundūzī, Tehran, 1308, p. 311.
14. *Yanābī' al-mawaddah*, p. 318.
15. *Ghāyat al-marām*, p. 539, where the substance of this hadith has been recounted in fifteen versions from Sunni sources and eleven from Shi'ite sources.
16. *al-Bidāyah wa'l-nihāyah*, vol. VII, p. 339; *Dhakhā'ir al-'uqbā*, p. 63; *al-Fuṣūl al-muhimmah*, p. 21; *Kifāyat al-ṭālib* of Kanjī Shāfi'ī, Najaf, 1356, pp. 148–154; *Khaṣā'iṣ*, pp. 19–25; *Ṣawā'iq al-muḥriqah*, p. 177. In *Ghāyat al-marām*, p. 109, one hundred versions of this hadith have been recounted from Sunni sources and seventy from Shi'ite sources.
17. *Tārikh Abi'l-Fidā'*, vol. I, p. 116.
18. *Ḥilyat al-awliyā'* of Abū Nu'aym Iṣfahānī, vol. I, Cairo, 1351, p. 64; *Kifāyat al-ṭālib*, p. 67.
19. *Muntakhab kanz al-'ummāl*, on the margin of *Musnad-i Aḥmad*, Cairo, 1368, vol. V, p. 94.
20. *al-Bidāyah wa'l-nihāyah*, vol. V, p. 227; *al-Kāmil*, vol. II, p. 217; *Tārīkh-i Ṭabarī*, vol. II, p. 436; *Sharḥ* of Ibn Abi'l-Ḥadīd, vol. I, p. 133.
21. *al-Kāmil*, vol. II, p. 292; *Sharḥ* of Ibn Abi'l-Ḥadīd, vol. I, p. 54.
22. *Sharḥ* of Ibn Abi'l-Ḥadīd, vol. I, p. 134.
23. *Tārīkh-i Ya'qūbī*, vol. II, p. 137.
24. *al-Bidāyah wa'l-nihāyah*, vol. VI, p. 311.
25. *Editor's note:* In this context of course imamate refers to the specific Shi'ite conception of Imam and not to the general Sunni usage of the term which in most instances is the same as caliph.
26. *Editor's note:* The translation of this Qurʾanic verse is that of A. J. Arberry, *The Quran Interpreted*, London, 1964, which corresponds more closely to the Arabic original than Pickthall's, which is as follows: "But if these disbelieve therein, then indeed We shall entrust it to a people who will not be disbelievers therein."
27. For example: "By the Scripture which maketh plain, Lo! We have appointed it a Lecture in Arabic that haply ye may understand. And lo! in the Source of Decrees, which We possess, it is indeed sublime, decisive" (Quran, XLIII, 2–4).
28. Such as these verses: "And every soul cometh, along with it a driver and a witness. (And unto the evildoers it is said): Thou wast in heedlessness of this. Now We have removed from thee thy covering, and piercing is thy sight this day" (Quran, L, 21–22). "Whosoever doeth right, whether male or female, and is a believer, him verily We shall quicken with good life . . ." (Quran, XVI, 97). "Obey Allah, and the messenger when He calleth you to that which quickeneth you . . ." (Quran, VIII, 24). "On the day when every soul will find itself confronted with all that it hath done of good and all that it hath done of evil . . ." (Quran, III, 30). "Lo! We it is Who bring the dead to life. We record that which they send before (them), and their footprints. And all things We have kept in a clear register" (Quran, XXXVI, 12).
29. *Biḥār al-anwār*, vol. XVII, p. 9.
30. *al-Wāfī* by Mullā Muḥsin Fayḍ Kāshānī, Tehran, 1310–14, vol. III, p. 33.
31. "Is He who leadeth to the Truth more deserving that He should be followed, or he who findeth not the way unless he (himself) be guided. What aileth you? How judge ye?" (Quran, X, 36).
32. "And We made them chiefs [Imams] who guide by Our command, and We inspired in them the doing of good deeds . . ." (Quran, XXI, 73). "And when they became steadfast and believed firmly in Our revelations, We appointed from among them leaders [Imams] who guided by Our command" (Quran, XXXII, 24). One can conclude from these that, besides being an outward leader and guide, the Imam possesses also a kind of spiritual power to guide and attract which belongs to the

world of the Spirit. He influences and conquers the hearts of people of capability through the Truth, the light, and the inner aspect of his being and thus guides them toward perfection and the ultimate goal of existence.

33. "Jābir ibn Samurah has said that the he heard the Prophet of God say, 'Until the time of twelve vicegerents (khalifah) this religion will continue to be powerful.' Jabir said, 'The people repeated the formula "Allah is Great" and cried. Then the Prophet said something softly. I asked my father, 'Oh Father, what did he say?' My father answered, 'The Prophet said, "All the vicegerents will be from Quraysh."''' *Ṣaḥīḥ* of Abū Dā'ūd, Cairo, 1348, vol. II, p. 207; *Musnad-i Aḥmad*, vol. V, p. 92. Several other hadiths resembling this are also found. And "Salmān Fārsī said, 'I came upon the Prophet and saw Husayn—upon whom be peace—on his knees as he was kissing his eyes and mouth and saying "Thou art a noble man, son of a noble man, an Imam, son of an Imam, a 'proof' (hujjah), son of a 'proof,' the father of the nine 'proofs' of which the ninth is their 'support' (*qā'im*)."''' *Yanābī' al-mawaddah*, p. 308.

34. See *al-Ghadīr; Ghāyat al-marām; Ithbāt al-hudāt* of Muhammad ibn Ḥasan Ḥurr al-'Āmilī, Qum, 1337–39; *Dhakhā'ir al-'uqbā; Manāqib* of Khwārazmī, Najaf, 1385; *Tadhkirat al-khawāṣṣ* of Sibṭ ibn Jawzī, Tehran, 1285; *Yanābī' al-mawaddah*; *al-Fuṣūl al-muhimmah*; *Dalā'il al-imāmah* of Muhammad ibn Jarīr Ṭabarī, Najaf, 1369; *al-Naṣṣ wa'l-ijtihād* of Sharaf al-Dīn Mūsā, Najaf, 1375; *Uṣūl al-kāfī*, vol. I; and *Kitāb al-irshād* of Shaikh-i Mufīd, Tehran, 1377.

35. *Editor's note:* As mentioned above in Shi'ite Islam the title Amīr al-mu'minīn is preserved for Ali and is never used in the case of others.

36. *al-Fusūl al-muhimmah*, p. 14; *Manāqib* of Khwārazmī, p. 17.

37. *Dhakhā'ir al-'uqbā*, p. 58; *Manāqib* of Khwārazmī, pp. 16–22; *Yanābī' al-mawaddah*, pp. 68–72.

38. *Irshād* of Mufīd, p. 4; *Yanābī' al-mawaddah*, p. 122.

39. *al-Fuṣūl al-muhimmah*, pp. 28–30; *Tadhkirat al-khawāṣṣ*, p. 34; *Yanābī' al-mawaddah*, p. 105; *Manāqib* of Khwārazmī, pp. 73–74.

40. *al-Fuṣūl al-muhimmah*, p. 34.

41. *al-Fuṣūl al-muhimmah*, p. 20; *Tadhkirat al-khawāṣṣ*, pp. 20–24; *Yanābī' al-mawaddah*, pp. 63–65.

42. *Tadhkirat al-khawāṣṣ*, p. 18; *al-Fuṣūl al-muhimmah*, p. 21; *Manāqib* of Khwārazmī, p. 74.

43. *Manāqib Āl Abī Ṭālib*, by Muhammad ibn Ali ibn Shahrāshūb, Qum, n.d., vol. III, pp. 62 and 218; *Ghāyat al-marām*, p. 539; *Yanābī' al-mawaddah*, p. 104.

44. *Editor's note:* The Khawarij, literally those who stand "outside," refers to a group who opposed both Ali and Mu'awiyah after the Battle of Siffin and later formed an extremist group that disobeyed established authority and was adamantly opposed to both the Sunnis and the Shi'ites.

45. *Manāqib Āl Abī Ṭālib*, vol. III, p. 312; *al-Fuṣūl al-muhimmah*, pp. 113–123; *Tadhkirat al-khawāṣṣ*, pp. 172–183.

46. *Tadhkirat al-khawāṣṣ*, p. 27.

47. *Ibid.*, p. 27; *Manāqib* of Khwārazmī, p. 71.

48. *Manāqib Āl Abī Ṭālib*, vol. III, p. 221; *Manāqib* of Khwārazmī, p. 92.

49. *Nahj al-balāghah*, part III, book 24.

50. *Manāqib* of Ibn Shahrāshūb, vol. IV, pp. 21 and 25; *Dhakhā'ir al-uqbā*, pp. 67 and 121.

51. *Manāqib* of Ibn Shahrāshūb, vol. IV, p. 28; *Dalā'il al-imāmah*, p. 60; *al-Fuṣūl al-muhimmah*, p. 133; *Tadhkirat al-khawāṣṣ*, p. 193; *Tārīkh-i Ya'qūbī*, vol. II, p. 204; *Uṣūl-i kāfī*, vol. I, p. 461.

52. *Irshād*, p. 172; *Manāqib* of Ibn Shahrāshūb, vol. IV, p. 33; *al-Fuṣūl al-muhimmah*, p. 144.

53. *Irshād*, p. 172; *Manāqib* of Ibn Shahrāshūb, vol. IV, p. 33; *al-Imāmah wa'l-*

siyāsah of 'Abdallāh ibn Muslim ibn Qutaybah, Cairo, 1327–31, vol. I, p. 163; *al-Fuṣūl al-muhimmah*, p. 145; *Tadhkirat al-khawāṣṣ*, p. 197.

54. *Irshād*, p. 173; *Manāqib* of Ibn Shahrāshūb, vol. IV, p. 35; *al-Imāmah wa'l-siyāsah*, vol. I, p. 164.

55. *Irshād*, p. 174; *Manāqib* of Ibn Shahrāshūb, vol. IV, p. 42; *al-Fuṣūl al-muhimmah*, p. 146; *Tadhkirat al-khawāṣṣ*, p. 211.

56. *Irshād*, p. 181; *Ithbāt al-hudāt*, vol. V, pp. 129 and 134.

57. *Irshād*, p. 179; *Ithbāt al-hudāt*, vol. V, pp. 168–212; *Ithbāt al-waṣīyah* of Mas'ūdī, Tehran, 1320, p. 125.

58. *Irshād*, p. 182; *Tārīkh-i Ya'qūbī*, vol. II, pp. 226–228; *al-Fuṣūl al-muhimmah*, p. 163.

59. *Manāqib* of Ibn Shahrāshūb, vol. IV, p. 88.

60. *Ibid*., p. 88; *Irshād*, p. 182; *al-Imāmah wa'l-siyāsah*, vol. I, p. 203; *Tārīkh-i Ya'qūbī*, vol. II, p. 229; *al-Fuṣūl al-muhimmah*, p. 163; *Tadhkirat al-khawāṣṣ*, p. 235.

61. *Irshād*, p. 201.

62. *Manāqib* of Ibn Shahrāshūb, vol. IV, p. 89.

63. *Irshād*, p. 201; *al-Fuṣūl al-muhimmah*, p. 168.

64. *Irshād*, p. 204; *al-Fuṣūl al-muhimmah*, p. 170; *Maqātil al-ṭālibīn* of Abu'l-Faraj Iṣfahānī, second edition, p. 73.

65. *Irshād*, p. 205; *al-Fuṣūl al-muhimmah*, p. 171; *Maqātil al-ṭālibīn*, p. 73.

66. *Manāqib* of Ibn Shahrāshūb, vol. IV, p. 98.

67. *Ibid.*

68. *Manāqib* of Ibn Shahrāshūb, vol. IV, p. 99; *Irshād*, p. 214.

69. *Manāqib* of Ibn Shahrāshūb, vol. IV, p. 98; *Irshād*, p. 214.

70. *Biḥār al-anwār*, vol. X, pp. 200, 202, 203.

71. *Maqātil al-ṭālibīn*, pp. 52 and 59.

72. *Tadhkirat al-khawāṣṣ*, p. 324; *Ithbāt al-hudāt*, vol. V, p. 242.

73. *Manāqib* of Ibn Shahrāshūb, vol. IV, p. 176; *Dalā'il al-imāmah*, p. 80; *al-Fuṣūl al-muhimmah*, p. 190.

74. *Irshād*, p. 246; *al-Fuṣūl al-muhimmah*, p. 193; *Manāqib* of Ibn Shahrāshūb, vol. IV, p. 197.

75. *Uṣūl al-kāfī*, vol. I, p. 469; *Irshād*, p. 245; *al-Fuṣūl al-muhimmah*, pp. 202 and 203; *Tārīkh-i Ya'qūbī*, vol. III, p. 63; *Tadhkirat al-khawāṣṣ*, p. 340; *Dalā'il al-imāmah*, p. 94; *Manāqib* of Ibn Shahrāshūb, vol. IV, p. 210.

76. *Irshād*, pp. 245–253. See also *Kitāb rijāl al-Kashshī* by Muhammad ibn Muhammad ibn 'Abd al-'Azīz Kashshī, Bombay, 1317; *Kitāb rijāl al-Ṭūsī* by Muhammad ibn Hasan Ṭūsī, Najaf, 1381; *Kitāb-i fihrist* of Ṭūsī, Calcutta, 1281; and other books of biography.

77. *Uṣūl-i kāfī*, vol. I, p. 472; *Dalā'il al-imāmah*, p. 111; *Irshād*, p. 254; *Tārīkh-i Ya'qūbī*, vol. III, p. 119; *al-Fuṣūl al-muhimmah*, p. 212; *Tadhkirat al-khawāṣṣ*, p. 346; *Manāqib* of Ibn Shahrāshūb, vol. IV, p. 280.

78. *Irshād*, p. 254; *al-Fuṣūl al-muhimmah*, p. 204; *Manāqib* of Ibn Shahrāshūb, vol. IV, p. 247.

79. *al-Fuṣūl al-muhimmah*, p. 212; *Dalā'il al-imāmah*, p. 111; *Ithbāt al-waṣīyah*, p. 142.

80. *Uṣūl al-kāfī*, vol. I, p. 310.

81. *Ibid*., p. 476; *Irshād*, p. 270; *al-Fuṣūl al-muhimmah*, pp. 214–223; *Dalā'il al-imāmah*, pp. 146–148; *Tadhkirat al-khawāṣṣ*, pp. 348–350; *Manāqib* of Ibn Shahrāshūb, vol. IV, p. 324; *Tārīkh-i Ya'qūbī*, vol. III, p. 150.

82. *Irshād*, pp. 279–283; *Dalā'il al-imāmah*, pp. 148 and 154; *al-Fuṣūl al-muhimmah*, p. 222; *Manāqib* of Ibn Shahrāshūb, vol. IV, pp. 323 and 327; *Tārīkh-i Ya'qūbī*, vol. III, p. 150.

83. *Uṣūl al-kāfī*, vol. I, p. 486; *Irshād*, pp. 284–295; *Dalā'il al-imāmah*, pp. 175–177; *al-Fusūl al-muhimmah*, pp. 225–246; *Tārīkh-i Ya'qūbī*, vol. III, p. 188.

84. *Uṣūl al-Kāfī*, vol. I, p. 488; *al-Fuṣūl al-muhimmah*, p. 237.
85. *Dalā'il al-imāmah*, p. 197; *Manāqib* of Ibn Shahrāshūb, vol. IV, p. 363.
86. *Uṣūl-i kāfī*, vol. I, p. 489; *Irshād*, p. 290; *al-Fuṣūl al-muhimmah*, p. 237; *Tadhkirat al-khawāṣṣ*, p. 352; *Manāqib* of Ibn Shahrāshūb, vol. IV, p. 363.
87. *Manāqib* of Ibn Shahrāshūb, vol. IV, p. 351; *Kitāb al-iḥtijāj* of Aḥmad ibn Ali ibn Abī Ṭālib al-Ṭabarsī, Najaf, 1385, vol. II, pp. 170–237.
88. *Irshād*, p. 297; *Uṣūl al-kāfī*, vol. I, pp. 492–497; *Dalā'il al-imāmah*, pp. 201–209; *Manāqib* of Ibn Shahrāshūb, vol. IV, pp. 377–399; *al-Fuṣūl al-muhimmah* pp. 247–258; *Tadhkirat al-khawāṣṣ*, p. 358.
89. *Uṣūl-i kāfī*, vol. I, pp. 497–502; *Irshād*, p. 307; *Dalā'il al-imāmah*, pp. 216–222; *al-Fuṣūl al-muhimmah*, pp. 259–265; *Tadhkirat al-khawāsṣ*, p. 362; *Manāqib* of Ibn Shahrāshūb, vol. IV, pp. 401–420.
90. *Irshād*, pp. 307–313; *Uṣūl-i kāfī*, vol. I, p. 501; *al-Fuṣūl al-muhimmah*, p. 261; *Tadhkirat al-khawāṣṣ*, p. 359; *Manāqib* of Ibn Shahrāshūb, vol. IV, p. 417; *Ithbāt al-waṣīyah*, p. 176; *Tārīkh-i Ya'qūbī*, vol. III, p. 217.
91. *Maqātil al-ṭālibīn*, p. 395.
92. *Ibid.*, pp. 395–396.
93. *Irshād*, p. 315; *Dalā'il al-imāmah*, p. 223; *al-Fuṣūl al-muhimmah*, pp. 266–272; *Manāqib* of Ibn Shahrāshūb, vol. IV, p. 422; *Uṣūl al-kāfī*, vol. I, p. 503.
94. *Irshād*, p. 324; *Uṣūl al-kāfī*, vol. I, p. 512; *Manāqib* of Ibn Shahrāshūb, vol. IV, pp. 429–430.
95. *Ṣaḥīḥ* of Tirmidhī, Cairo, 1350–52, vol. IX, chapter "*Mā jā'a fi'l-hudā*"; *Ṣaḥīḥ* of Abū Dā'ūd, vol. II, *Kitāb al-Mahdī*; *Ṣaḥīḥ* of Ibn Mājah, vol. II, chapter "*khurūj al-Mahdī*"; *Yanābī' al-mawaddah*; *Kitāb al-bayān fī akhbār Ṣahib al-zamān* of Kanjī Shāfi'ī, Najaf, 1380; *Nūr al-abṣār*; *Mishkāt al-maṣābīḥ* of Muhammad ibn 'Abdallāh al-Khaṭīb, Damascus, 1380; *al-Ṣawā'iq al-muḥriqah*, *Is'āf al-rāghibīn* of Muhammad al-Ṣabbān, Cairo, 1281; *al-Fuṣūl al-muhimmah*; *Ṣaḥīḥ* of Muslim; *Kitāb al-ghaybah* by Muhammad ibn Ibrāhīm al-Nu'mānī, Tehran, 1318; *Kamāl al-dīn* by Shaykh Ṣadūq, Tehran, 1301; *Ithbāt al-hudāt*; *Biḥār al-anwār*, vol. LI and LII.
96. *Uṣūl-i kāfī*, vol. I, p. 505; *Irshād*, p. 319.
97. See *Kitāb al-rijāl* of Kashshī; *Rijāl* of Ṭūsī; *Fihrist* of Ṭūsī, and other works of biography (rijāl).
98. *Biḥār al-anwār*, vol. LI, pp. 2–34 and pp. 343–366; *Kitāb al-ghaybah* of Muhammad ibn Hasan Ṭūsī, Tehran, 1324, pp. 214–243; *Ithbāt al-hudāt*, vol. VI and VII.
99. *Biḥār al-anwār*, vol. LI, pp. 360–361; *Kitāb al-ghaybah* of Ṭūsī, p. 242.
100. This particular version is related from 'Abdallāh ibn Mas'ūd, *al-Fuṣūl al-muhimmah*, p. 271.
101. Abu Ja'far (the fifth Imam) has said, "When our 'support' (qa'im) rises, Allah will place his hand upon the heads of His servants. Then through him their minds will come together and through him their intellect will become perfected." (*Biḥār al-anwār*, vol. LII, pp. 328 and 336.) And Abū 'Abdallāh (the sixth Imam) has said, "Knowledge is comprised of twenty-seven letters, and all that has been brought by the prophets is comprised of two letters; and men have not gained knowledge of anything but these two letters. When our 'support' (qa'im) comes forth, he will make manifest the other twenty-five letters and will spread them among the people. He will add the two letters to them so that they become propagated in the form of twenty-seven letters." (*Biḥār al-anwār*, vol. LII, p. 336.)
102. *Ibid.*, vol. LI, p. 154.
103. *Ibid.*
104. *Ibid.*, p. 160.
105. *Editor's note:* Salvation (from the root falaḥa) in this sense does not mean only salvation in the current, purely exoteric sense it has acquired, but also means deliverance and spiritual realization in the highest sense of the word.

APPENDIX I TAQIYAH OR DISSIMULATION

'Allāmah Ṭabāṭabā'ī

One of the most misunderstood aspects of Shi'ism is the practice of dissimulation or taqiyah. With the wider meaning of taqiyah, "to avoid or shun any kind of danger," we are not concerned here. Rather, our aim is to discuss that kind of taqiyah in which a man hides his religion or certain of his religious practices in situations that would cause definite or probable danger as a result of the actions of those who are opposed to his religion or particular religious practices.

Among followers of the different schools of Islam, Shi'ites are well known for their practice of taqiyah. In case of danger they dissimulate their religion and hide their particular religious and ritual practices from their opponents.

The sources upon which the Shi'ites base themselves in this question include the following verse of the Holy Quran: "Let not the believers take disbelievers for their friends in preference to believers. Whoso doeth that hath no connection with Allah unless (it be) that ye but guard yourselves against them [*tattaqū minhum*, from the same root as *taqīyah*], taking (as it were) security [*tuqātan*, again from the same root as *taqīyah*]. Allah biddeth you beware (only) of Himself. Unto Allah is the journeying" (III, 28). As is clear from this sacred verse, God, the Most Exalted, forbids with the utmost emphasis wilayah (meaning in this case friendship and amity to the extent that it affects one's life) with unbelievers and orders man to be wary and have fear in such a situation.

In another place He says, "Whoso disbelieveth in Allah after his belief—save him who is forced thereto and whose heart is still content with Faith—but whoso findeth ease in disbelief: On them is wrath from Allah. Theirs will be an awful doom" (Quran, XVI, 106). As mentioned in both Sunni and Shi'ite sources this verse was revealed concerning 'Ammār ibn Yāsir. After the migration (hijrah) of the Prophet the infidels of Mecca imprisoned some of the Muslims of that city and tortured them, forcing them to leave Islam and to return to their former religion of idolatry. Included in this group who were tortured were Ammar and his father and mother. Ammar's parents refused to turn away from Islam and died under torture. But Ammar, in order to escape torture and death, outwardly left Islam and accepted idol worship, thereby escaping from danger. Having become free, he left Mecca secretly for Medina. In Medina he went before the Holy Prophet—upon whom be blessings and peace—and in a state of penitence and distress concerning what he had done asked the Prophet if by acting as he did he had fallen outside the sacred precinct of religion. The Prophet said that his duty was what he had accomplished. The above verse was then revealed.

The two verses cited above were revealed concerning particular cases but their meaning is such that they embrace all situations in which the outward expression of doctrinal belief and religious practice might bring about a dangerous situation. Besides these verses, there exist many traditions from the members of the Household of the Prophet ordering taqiyah when there is fear of danger.

Some have criticized Shi'ism by saying that to employ the practice of taqiyah in religion is opposed to the virtues of courage and bravery. The least amount of thought about this accusation will bring to light its invalidity, for taqiyah must be practiced in a situation where man faces a danger which he cannot resist and against which he cannot fight. Resistance to such a danger and failure to practice taqiyah in such circumstances shows rashness and foolhardiness, not courage and bravery. The qualities of courage and bravery can be applied only when there is at least the possibility of success in man's efforts. But before a definite or probable danger against which there is no possibility of victory—such as drinking water in which there is probably poison or throwing oneself before a cannon that is being fired or lying down on the tracks before an onrushing train—any action of this kind is nothing but a form of madness contrary to logic and common sense. Therefore, we can summarize by saying that taqiyah must be practiced only when there is a definite danger which cannot be avoided and against which there is no hope of a successful struggle and victory.

The exact extent of danger which would make permissible the practice of taqiyah has been debated among different mujtahids of Shiʿism. In our view, the practice of taqiyah is permitted if there is definite danger facing one's own life or the life of one's family, or the possibility of the loss of the honor and virtue of one's wife or of other female members of the family, or the danger of the loss of one's material belongings to such an extent as to cause complete destitution and prevent a man from being able to continue to support himself and his family. In any case, prudence and the avoidance of definite or probable danger which cannot be averted is a general law of logic accepted by all people and applied by men in all the different phases of their lives.

APPENDIX II MUTʿAH OR TEMPORARY MARRIAGE

ʿAllāmah Ṭabāṭabā'ī
and
Seyyed Hossein Nasr

Another of the misunderstood practices of Shiʿism that has often been criticized, especially by some of the moderns, is temporary marriage or mutʿah.

It is a definitely established historical fact that at the beginning of Islam, namely between the commencement of the revelation and the migration of the Holy Prophet to Medina, temporary marriage, called mutʿah, was practiced by Muslims along with permanent marriage. As an example one can cite the case of Zubayr al-Ṣaḥābī, who married Asmā', the daughter of Abu Bakr, in a temporary marriage; from this union were born ʿAbdallāh ibn Zubayr and ʿUrwah ibn Zubayr. These figures were all among the most famous companions of the Holy Prophet. Obviously if this union were to have been illegitimate and categorized as adultery, which is one of the most grievous sins in Islam and entails heavy punishments, it would never have been performed by people who were among the foremost of the companions.

Temporary marriage was also practiced from the time of the migration until the death of the Holy Prophet. And even after that event during the rule of the first caliph and part of the rule of the second, Muslims continued to practice it until it was banned by the second caliph, who threatened those who practiced it with stoning. According to all of the sources the second caliph made the following statement: "There are two mutʿahs which existed in the time of the Prophet of God and Abu Bakr which I have banned, and I will punish those who disobey my orders. These two mutʿahs are the mutʿah concerning the pilgrimage[1] and the mutʿah concerning women."

Although at first some of the companions and their followers were opposed to this ban by the second caliph, since that time the Sunnis have considered mutʿah marriage to be unlawful. The Shiʿites, however, following the teachings of the Imams of the Household of the Prophet, continued to consider it legitimate as it was during the lifetime of the Prophet himself.

In the Quran, God says concerning the believers: "And who guard their modesty—Save from their wives or the (slaves) that their right hands possess, for then they are not blameworthy, But whoso craveth beyond that, such are the transgressors—" (Quran, XXIII, 5–7). Also, "And those who preserve their chastity Save with their wives and those whom their right hands possess, for thus they are not blameworthy; But whoso seeketh more than that, those are they who are transgressors" (Quran, LXX, 29–31). These verses were revealed in Mecca and from the time of their revelation until the Hijrah, it is well known that mutʿah marriage was practiced by Muslims. If mutʿah marriage had not been a true marriage and women who had married according to it had not been legitimate wives, certainly according to these Quranic verses they would have been considered to be transgressors of the law and would have been forbidden to practice mutʿah. It is thus clear that since temporary marriage was not forbidden by the Prophet it was a legitimate marriage and not a form of adultery.

The legitimacy of the mutʿah marriage continued from the time of the hijrah until the death of the Holy Prophet as this verse, revealed after the hijrah, proves, "And those of whom ye seek content [*istamtaʿtum*, from the same root as *mutʿah*] (by marrying them), give unto them their portions as a duty" (Quran, IV, 24). Those opposed to Shiʿism contend that this verse from the "Chapter on Women" was later abrogated, but the Shiʿah do not accept this view. In fact, the words of the second caliph cited above are the best proof that up to the time of his ban such marriages were still practiced. It is inconceivable that if mutʿah had been abrogated and forbidden it would have continued to be commonly practiced by Muslims during the lifetime of the Holy Prophet and after his death until the time of the second caliph; that if mutʿah had been abrogated no action would have been taken to forbid it. We cannot accept the claim that the only thing that the second caliph did was to put into action an order of prohibition and abrogation of mutʿah given by the Holy Prophet, for such a possibility is negated by the clear words of the second caliph, "There are two mutʿahs which existed in the time of the Prophet of God and Abu Bakr which I have banned, and I will punish those who disobey my orders."

From the point of view of legislation and the preservation of public interest also we must consider the legitimacy of temporary marriage, like that of divorce, one of the noteworthy features of Islam. It is obvious that laws and regulations are executed with the aim of preserving the vital interests of the people in a society and providing for their needs. The legitimization of marriage among mankind from the beginning until today is an answer to the instinctive urge for sexual union. Permanent marriage has been continuously practiced among the different peoples of the world. Yet despite this fact, and all the campaigns and efforts at public persuasion that are carried out against it, there exist throughout the countries of the world, in large and small cities, both hidden and public places where illegitimate sexual union or fornication takes place. This in itself is the best proof that permanent marriage cannot fulfill the instinctive sexual desires of everyone and that a solution must be sought for the problem.

Islam is a universal religion and in its legislation takes all types of human beings into consideration. Considering the fact that permanent marriage does not satisfy the instinctive sexual urge of certain men and that adultery and fornication are according to Islam among the most deadly of poisons, destroying the order and purity of human life, Islam has legitimized temporary marriage under special conditions by virtue of which it becomes distinct from adultery and fornication and free of their evils and corruptions. These conditions include the necessity for the woman to be single, to become married temporarily to only one man at one time, and after divorce to keep a period during which she cannot be remarried (*ʿiddah*), half of the time that is required after the permanent marriage. The legitimizing of temporary marriage in Islam is done with the aim of allowing within the sacred law possibilities that minimize the evils resulting from the passions of men, which if not channeled lawfully manifest themselves in much more dangerous ways outside the structure of religious law.

1. The hajj al-mutʿah is a kind of pilgrimage which was legislated at the end of the lifetime of the Prophet.

APPENDIX III RITUAL PRACTICES IN SHIʿISM

Seyyed Hossein Nasr

The religious rites practiced by Twelve-Imam Shiʿites are essentially the same as those of the Sunnis with certain minor modifications of posture and phrasing which are little more than the differences that are to be found among the Sunni schools (madhhabs) themselves, except in the addition of two phrases in the call to prayer. For Shiʿism, like Sunnism, the major rite consists of the daily prayers (*ṣalāt* in Arabic, *namāz* in Persian and Urdu), comprised of the prayers of sunrise, noon, afternoon, evening and night. Altogether they consist of seventeen units (*rakʿahs*) divided in the ratio of 2, 4, 4, 3 and 4 for the respective five prayers. The only singular quality of Shiʿite practice in this respect is that instead of performing the five prayers completely separately, usually Shiʿites say the noon and afternoon prayers together, as well as the evening and the night prayers.

Shiʿites also perform supererogatory prayers and prayers on special occasions such as moments of joy, fear and thanksgiving, or when visiting a holy place of pilgrimage. In these practices also there is little difference between Shiʿism and Sunnism. However, we can sense a distinction in the Friday congregational prayers. Of course these prayers are performed in both worlds but they definitely have a greater social and political significance in the Sunni world. In Shiʿism, although these prayers are performed in at least one mosque in every city and town, in the absence of the Imam, who according to Shiʿism is the true leader of these prayers, their importance is somewhat diminished and more emphasis is placed upon individual prescribed prayers.

As for the second basic Islamic rite of fasting, it is practiced by

Shiʿites in a manner that is nearly identical with that of Sunnis and differs only in the fact that Shiʿites break their fast a few minutes later than Sunnis, when the sun has set completely. All those capable of fasting and above the age of puberty must abstain from all drinking and eating during the month of Ramadan from the first moments of dawn until sunset. The moral and inward conditions that accompany the fast are also identical for the two branches of Islam. Likewise, many Shiʿites, like Sunnis, fast on certain other days during the year, especially at the beginning, middle and end of the lunar month, following the example of the Holy Prophet.

Also, for the pilgrimage (hajj), Shiʿite and Sunni practices have only very minor differences. It is the pilgrimage to other holy places that is emphasized more in Shiʿism than in Sunnism. The visit to the tombs of Imams and saints plays an integral role in the religious life of Shiʿites, one which in fact is compensated for in a way in the Sunni world by visits to the tombs of saints or what in North Africa are called tombs of marabouts. Of course these forms of pilgrimage are not obligatory rites such as the prayers, fasting and hajj, but they play such an important religious role that they can hardly be overlooked.

There are certain religious practices besides the basic rites which are specifically Shiʿite, yet curiously enough found also in certain parts of the Sunni world. There is the *rawḍah-khānī*, that combination of sermon, recitation of poems and Quranic verses and drama which depicts the tragic life of the different Imams, particularly Imam Husayn. Although the rawdah began to be practiced widely only during the Safavid period, it has become one of the most widespread and influential of religious acts in the Shiʿite world and leaves a profound mark upon the whole community. The rawdah is performed most of all during the Islamic months of Muharram and Safar, during which the tragedy of Karbala and its aftermath took place. The rawdah does not exist in Sunni Islam in the exact form it has taken in Shiʿism but other forms of elegy (*marāthī*) and dramas depicting the tragedy of Karbala are seen during Muharram as far away as Morocco.

Connected with the rawdah during Muharram is the passion

play (*taʿziyah*), which has become an elaborate art in both Persia and the Indo-Pakistani world. It is no longer directly a religious rite in the sense of the prayers, yet it too is a major manifestation of religious life as it traverses the depth and breadth of society. There are also at this time elaborate street processions in which people chant, cry and sometimes beat themselves in order to participate in the passion of the Imam. In this matter also, equivalences in the Sunni world must be sought in the Sufi processions which have become rarer in many Muslim countries during the past few years.

On the popular level there are certain Shiʿite religious practices which must be mentioned because of their wide popularity. These include almsgiving, in addition to the religious tax (zakat) promulgated by the Shariʿah, petitioning God for the acceptance of something asked in a prayer by giving to the poor, arranging special religious tables whose food is given to the poor, and many other practices of the kind which carry religion to the intimate activities of everyday life.

The recitation of the Holy Quran is a rite *par excellence* and it is a basic Shiʿite practice as much as a Sunni one. The Quran is chanted during special occasions such as weddings, funerals and the like, as well as at different moments of the day and night during one's daily routine. In addition the Shiʿites place much emphasis upon the reading of prayers of great beauty in Arabic from the prophetic hadith and from the sayings of Imams as contained in the *Nahj al-balāghah*, *Ṣaḥīfah sajjādīyah*, *Uṣūl al-kāfī*, etc. Some of these prayers, like the *Jawshan-i kabīr* and *Kumayl*, are long and take several hours. They are recited only by the especially pious, on certain nights of the week, particularly Thursday night and the nights of Ramadan. Other believers remain satisfied with shorter prayers. But the whole practice of reciting litanies and prayers of different kinds constitutes an important aspect of the rites of Muslims and their religious devotions in both the Shiʿite and Sunni worlds. And in both worlds these devotional prayers and litanies come from the works of the saints, who in the Shiʿite world are identified with the Imams and the Household of the Prophet and in the Sunni world with Sufism in general.

APPENDIX IV A NOTE ON THE JINN

Seyyed Hossein Nasr

One of the least understood aspects of Islamic teachings in the modern world concerns that class of beings called the jinn and referred to several times in the Quran. The reason for misunderstanding comes from the post-Cartesian materialistic conception of the Universe, which excludes the subtle and psychic world, where in fact the beings called jinn belong in the traditional schemes of cosmology. To understand the meaning of jinn one must therefore go beyond a conception of reality which includes only the world of matter and the mind (this paralyzing dualism which makes an understanding of traditional doctrines impossible) to an awareness of a hierarchic reality made up of the three worlds of spirit, psyche, and matter. The jinn can then be identified as beings that belong to the psychic or intermediary world, the barzakh, situated between this world and the world of pure Spirit.

In Quranic terminology and the hadith literature the jinn are usually coupled with *ins* or mankind and often the phrase *al-jinn wa'l-ins* (the jinn and men) is used as referring to that class of creatures to which God's commands and prohibitions address themselves. Man was made of clay into which God breathed (*nafakha*) His Spirit. The jinn in Islamic doctrines are that group of creatures which was made of fire rather than earth, and into which God also breathed His Spirit. Hence like man they possess a spirit and consciousness and have Divine commands revealed to them. On their own level of existence they are central creatures just as men are central creatures in this world. But in contrast to men they possess a volatile and "unfixed" outer form and so can take on many shapes. This means that they are essentially creatures of the psychic rather than the physical world and that they can appear to man in different forms and shapes.

Having been endowed with a spirit, the jinn, like men, possess responsibility before God. Some are "religious" and "Muslim." These are intermediate angels, the psychic forces that can lead man from the physical to the spiritual world through the labyrinth of the intermediate world or barzakh. Others are malefic forces that have rebelled against God, in the same way that some men rebel against the Divinity. Such jinn are identified with "the armies of Satan" (*junūd al-Shayṭān*) and are the evil forces which by inducing the power of apprehension (*wahm*) and imagination (khayāl) in its negative aspect lead man away from the Truth which his intelligence perceives by virtue of the innate light that dwells within him.

In the religious cosmos of the traditional Muslim, which is filled with material, psychic, and spiritual creatures of God, the jinn play their own particular role. By the elite they are taken for what they are, namely, psychic forces of the intermediate world of both a beneficent and an evil nature. On the popular level, the jinn appear as concrete physical creatures of different shapes and forms against which men seek the aid of the Spirit, often by chanting verses of the Quran. The jinn and all that pertains to them hence enter on the popular level into the domain of demonology, magic, etc., and are a vivid reality for men whose minds are still open towards the vast world of the psyche in its cosmic aspect. The Muslim of this type of mentality lives in a world in which he is aware of God and also of both the angelic forces representing the good and the demonic forces representing the evil. He sees his life as a struggle between these two elements within him and about him. Although the jinn are of both kinds, the good and the evil, most often in his thought he identifies them with the demonic forces that lead men astray. They are personifications of psychic forces that work within his mind and soul. On the theological and metaphysical level of Islam, the order of the jinn becomes understood as a necessary element in the hierarchy of existence, an element which relates the physical world to higher orders of reality. The jinn are, moreover, especially akin to men in that, as was mentioned above, into them also was breathed the Spirit of God. And some of God's prophets, like Solomon, ruled over both men and jinn, as attested to by the Holy Quran.

For the Western student of Islam, the meaning of the jinn cannot be understood except through an understanding of traditional metaphysics, cosmology and psychology. Only through this understanding do these beings and their function, which in fact have their correspondences in other religions, become meaningful. We cannot reduce the belief in jinn to superstition simply because we no longer understand what they signify.

If a traditional Muslim were asked to give his opinion concerning all the interest in the modern world in psychic phenomena, the exploration of the psychic world through drugs and other means, and the phenomena of a psychic origin that become ever more recurrent nowadays, he would answer that much of this is connected to what he would understand by the jinn. He would add that most of the jinn involved in these cases are, alas, of the malefic and demonic kind before whom there is no means of protection save the grace that issues forth from the world of pure Spirit.

BIBLIOGRAPHY

The Writings of 'Allāmah Ṭabāṭabā'ī

al-Mīzān (*The Balance*). 'Allāmah's most important single work, a monumental commentary upon the Quran of which nineteen of the projected twenty volumes have been completed, and fourteen volumes already printed, in the original Arabic as well as in Persian translation.

Uṣūl-i falsafah wa rawish-i ri'ālīsm (*The Principles of Philosophy and the Method of Realism*) in five volumes, with the commentary of Murtaḍā Muṭahharī, of which the first three volumes have been published twice and one volume has appeared in Arabic.

Ḥāshiyah bar Asfār (*Glosses upon the Asfār*). Glosses upon the new edition of the *Asfār* of Ṣadr al-Dīn Shīrāzī (Mullā Ṣadrā) appearing under the direction of 'Allāmah Ṭabāṭabā'ī, of which seven volumes have appeared. This edition will not include the third book (or rather "journey," *safar*) on substances and accidents (*al-jawāhir wa'l-a'rāḍ*).

Muṣāhabāt bā Ustād Kurban (*Dialogues with Professor Corbin*). Two volumes based on conversations carried out between 'Allāmah Ṭabāṭabā'ī and Henry Corbin, of which the first volume was printed as the yearbook of *Maktab-i tashayyu'*, 1339 (A.H. solar).

Risālah dar ḥukūmat-i islāmī (*Treatise on Islamic Government*) printed in both Persian and Arabic.

Ḥāshiyah-i kifāyah (*Glosses upon al-Kifāyah*).

Risālah dar quwwah wa fi'l (*Treatise on Potentiality and Actuality*).

Risālah dar ithbāt-i dhāt (*Treatise on the Proof of the Divine Essence*).

Risālah dar ṣifāt (*Treatise on the Divine Attributes*).

Risālah dar af'āl (*Treatise on the Divine Acts*).

Risālah dar wasā'iṭ (*Treatise on Means*).

Risālah dar insān qabl al-dunyā (*Treatise on Man before the World*).

Risālah dar insān fi'l-dunyā (*Treatise on Man in the World*).

Risālah dar insān baʿd al-dunyā (*Treatise on Man after the World*).

Risālah dar nubuwwat (*Treatise on Prophecy*).

Risālah dar walāyat (*Treatise on Initiation*).

Risālah dar mushtaqqāt (*Treatise on Derivatives*).

Risālah dar burhān (*Treatise on Demonstration*).

Risālah dar mughālaṭah (*Treatise on Sophism*).

Risālah dar taḥlīl (*Treatise on Analysis*).

Risālah dar tarkīb (*Treatise on Synthesis*).

Risālah dar iʿtibārāt (*Treatise on Contingents*).

Risālah dar nubuwwāt wa manāmāt (*Treatise on Prophecy and Dreams*).

Manẓūmah dar rasm-i khaṭṭ-i nastaʿlīq (*Poem on the Method of Writing the* Nastaʿlīq *Style of Calligraphy*).

ʿAlī waʾl-falsafat al-ilāhīyah (*ʿAlī and Metaphysics*).

Qur'ān dar islām (*The Quran in Islam*), the English translation of which will form the second volume of the present series.

Shīʿah dar islām (*Shiʿite Islam*), the present book.

ʿAllāmah Ṭabāṭabā'ī is also the author of many articles, which have appeared during the past twenty years in such journals as *Maktab-i tashayyuʿ*, *Maktab-i islām*, *Maʿārif-i islāmī*, and in such collections as *The Mullā Ṣadrā Commemoration Volume* (ed. by S. H. Nasr, Tehran, 1340) and *Marjaʿīyat wa rūḥānīyat*, Tehran, 1341.

GENERAL BIBLIOGRAPHY

'Abaqāt: see *'Abaqāt al-anwār.*

'Abaqāt al-anwār, Ḥāmid Ḥusayn Mūsawī, India, 1317.

Abu'l-Fidā': see *Tārīkh-i Abi'l-Fidā.*

al-Aghānī, Abu'l-Faraj Iṣfahānī, Cairo, 1345–51.

Akhbār al-ḥukamā', Ibn al-Qifṭī, Leipzig, 1903.

al-Ashbāh wa'l-naẓā'ir, Jalāl al-Dīn 'Abd al-Raḥmān Suyūṭī, Hyderabad, 1359.

A'yān al-shī'ah, Muḥsin 'Āmilī, Damascus, 1935 onward.

al-Bidāyah wa'l-nihāyah, Ibn Kathīr Qurashī, Cairo, 1358.

Biḥār al-anwār, Muḥammad Bāqir Majlisī, Tehran, 1301–15.

Dalā'il al-imāmah, Muḥammad ibn Jarīr Ṭabarī, Najaf, 1369.

Dhakhā'ir al-'uqbā, Muḥibb al-Dīn Aḥmad ibn 'Abdallāh Ṭabarī, Cairo, 1356.

al-Durr al-manthūr, Jalāl al-Dīn 'Abd al-Raḥmān Suyūṭī, Cairo, 1313.

al-Fuṣūl al-muhimmah, Ibn Ṣabbāgh, Najaf, 1950.

al-Ghadīr, Mīrzā 'Abd al-Ḥusayn ibn Ahmad Tabrīzī Amīnī, Najaf, 1372.

Ghāyat al-marām, Sayyid Hāshim Baḥrānī, Tehran, 1272.

Ḥabīb al-siyar, Ghiyāth al-Dīn Khwānd Mīr, Tehran, 1333, A.H. solar.

al-Haḍārat al-islāmīyah, Arabic translation of Adam Mez's *Die Renaissance des Islams* by 'Abd al-Hādī Abū Rīdah, Cairo, 1366.

Ḥāḍir al-'ālam al-islāmī, Arabic translation of Lothrop Stoddard's *The New World of Islam* by 'Ajjāj Nuwayhiḍ, Cairo, 1352.

Ḥilyat al-awliyā', Abū Nu'aym Iṣfahānī, Cairo, 1351.

Ibn Abi'l-Ḥadīd: see *Sharḥ Nahj al-Balāghah* of Ibn Abi'l-Ḥadīd.

Ibn Mājah: see *Sunan* of Ibn Mājah.

al-Imāmah wa'l-siyāsah, 'Abdallāh ibn Muslim ibn Qutaybah Dīnawarī, Cairo, 1327–31.

Irshād: see *Kitāb al-irshād.*

al-Iṣābah, Ibn Ḥajar 'Asqalānī, Cairo, 1323.

Is'āf al-rāghibīn, Muḥammad al-Ṣabbān, Cairo, 1281.
Ithbāt al-hudāt, Muḥammad ibn Ḥasan Ḥurr al-'Amilī, Qum, 1337–39.
Ithbāt al-waṣīyah, 'Alī ibn Ḥusayn Mas'ūdī, Tehran, 1320.
I'tiqādāt (*al-'Aqā'id*), Abū Ja'far Muḥammad ibn 'Alī Shaykh Ṣadūq ibn Bābūyah, Tehran, 1308.
al-Itqān fī 'ulūm al-Qur'ān, Jalāl al-Dīn 'Abd al-Raḥmān Suyūṭī, Cairo, 1342.
Kamāl al-dīn, Shaykh Ṣadūq, Tehran, 1378–79.
al-Kāmil (*al-Kāmil fi'l-tārīkh*), 'Izz al-Dīn 'Alī ibn al-Athīr Jazarī, Cairo, 1348.
Kanz al-'ummāl, Shaykh 'Alā al-Dīn 'Alī al-Muttaqī Ḥusām al-Dīn al-Burhān Pūrī, Hyderabad, 1364–73.
Khaṣā'iṣ (*Kitāb al-Khaṣā'iṣ fī faḍl 'Alī ibn Abī Ṭālib*), Abū 'Abd al-Raḥman Aḥmad ibn 'Alī Nasā'ī, Najaf, 1369.
al-Khiṣāl, Shaykh Ṣadūq, Tehran, 1302.
Kifāyat al-ṭālib, Kanjī Shāfi'ī, Najaf, 1356.
Kitāb al-iḥtijāj, Aḥmad ibn 'Alī ibn Abī Ṭālib al-Ṭabarsī, Najaf, 1385.
Kitāb al-bayān fī akhbār sāḥib al-zamān, Kanjī Shāfi'ī, Najaf, 1380.
Kitāb al-fihrist, Shaykh Abū Ja'far Muḥammad ibn Ḥasan Ṭūsī, Calcutta, 1281.
Kitāb al-ghaybah, Muḥammad ibn Ibrāhīm al-Nu'mānī, Tehran, 1318.
Kitāb al-ghaybah, Shaykh Ṭūsī, Tehran, 1324.
Kitāb al-ghurar wa'l-durar, Sayyid 'Abd al-Wāḥid Āmidī, Sidon, 1349.
Kitāb al-irshād, Shaykh Mufīd, Tehran, 1377.
Kitāb rijāl al-Kashshī, Muḥammad ibn Muḥammad ibn 'Abd al-'Azīz al-Kashshī, Bombay, 1317.
Kitāb rijāl al-Ṭūsī, Shaykh Ṭūsī, Najaf, 1381.
Ma'ānī al-akhbār, Shaykh Ṣadūq, Tehran, 1379.
Manāqib Āl Abī Ṭālib, Muḥammad ibn 'Alī ibn Shahrāshūb, Qum, n.d.
Manāqib, Khwārazmī, Najaf, 1385.
Manāqib of Ibn Shahrāshūb: see *Manāqib Āl Abī Ṭālib*.
Maqātil al-ṭālibīn, Abu'l-Faraj Iṣfahānī, Najaf, 1353.
al-Milal wa'l-niḥal, 'Abd al-Karīm Shahristānī, Cairo, 1368.
Mishkāt al-maṣābīḥ, Muḥammad ibn 'Abdallāh al-Khaṭīb, Damascus, 1380–83.
Mu'jam al-buldān, Yāqūt Ḥamawī, Beirut, 1957.
Murūj al-dhahab, 'Alī ibn Ḥusayn Mas'ūdī, Cairo, 1367.
Musnad-i Aḥmad, Aḥmad ibn Ḥanbal, Cairo, 1368.
Naḥw (*al-Bihjat al-marḍīyah fī sharḥ al-alfīyah*), Jalāl al-Dīn 'Abd al-Raḥmān Suyūṭī, Tehran, 1281, etc.

Nahj al-balāghah, ʿAlī ibn Abī Ṭālib, Tehran, 1302, etc.
al-Naṣā'iḥ al-kāfīyah, Muḥammad ibn al-ʿAlawī, Baghdad, 1368.
al-Naṣṣ wa'l-ijtihād, Sharaf al-Dīn Mūsā, Najaf, 1375.
Nūr al-abṣār, Shaykh Shiblanjī, Cairo, 1312.
Rabīʿal-abrār, Zamakhsharī, mss.
Rayḥānat al-adab, Muḥammad ʿAlī Tabrīzī, Tehran, 1326–32 A.H. solar.
Rawḍāt al-ṣafā, Mīr Khwānd, Lucknow, 1332.
Rijāl: see *Kitāb al-rijāl* of Ṭūsī.
Safīnat al-Biḥār, Ḥājj Shaykh ʿAbbās Qumī, Najaf, 1352–55.
Ṣaḥiḥ of Abū Dā'ūd: see *Sunan* of Abū Dā'ūd.
Ṣaḥīḥ of Ibn Mājah: see *Sunan* of Ibn Mājah.
Ṣaḥīḥ, Bukhārī, Cairo, 1315.
Ṣaḥīḥ, Muslim, Cairo, 1349.
Ṣaḥīḥ, Tirmidhī, Cairo, 1350–52.
al-Ṣawāʿiq al-muhriqah, Ibn Ḥajar Makkī, Cairo, 1312.
Sharḥ of Ibn Abi'l-Ḥadīd: see *Sharḥ Nahj al-balāghah*, Ibn Abi'l-Ḥadīd.
Sharḥ Nahj al-balāghah, Ibn Abi'l-Ḥadīd, Cairo, 1329.
Sharḥ Nahj al-balāghah, Ibn Maytham al-Baḥrānī, Tehran, 1276.
Sīrah (*Insān al-ʿuyūn fi'l-amīn al-ma'mūn*) of Ḥalabī, Cairo, 1320.
Sīrah, Ibn Hishām, Cairo, 1355–56.
Sunan, Abū Dā'ūd, Cairo, 1348.
Sunan, Ibn Mājah, Cairo, 1372.
Sunan, Nasā'ī, Cairo, 1348.
Ṭabaqāt (*al-Ṭabaqāt al-kubrā*), Ibn Saʿd, Beirut, 1376.
Ṭabarī: see *Tārīkh-i Ṭabarī.*
Tadhkirat al-awliyā', Farīd al-Dīn ʿAṭṭār Nīshābūrī, Tehran, 1321 A.H. solar.
Tadhkirat al-khawāṣṣ, Sibṭ ibn Jawzī, Tehran, 1285.
Tafsīr al-mizān, ʿAllāmah Ṭabāṭabā'ī, Tehran, 1375 on.
Tafsīr al-ṣāfī, Mullā Muḥsin Fayḍ Kāshānī, Tehran, 1269.
Tamaddun-i islām wa ʿarab, Gustave Le Bon, translated into Persian by Fakhr Dā'ī Gīlānī, Tehran, 1334 A.H. solar.
Ṭarā'iq al-ḥaqā'iq, Maʿṣūm ʿAlī Shāh, Tehran, 1318.
al-Tārīkh: see *Tārīkh-i Abu'l-Fidā'*, *Tārīkh-i Ṭabarī.*
Tārīkh-i Abi'l-Fidā' (*al-Mukhtaṣar*), ʿImād al-Dīn Abu'l-Fidā' Ṣāḥib Ḥamāt, Cairo, 1325.
Tārīkh-i ʿālam ārāy-i ʿabbāsī, Iskandar Bayk Munshī, Tehran, 1334 A.H. solar.
Tārīkh-i Aqā Khānīyah (*Fī tārīkh firqat al-āghākhānīyah wa'l-buhrah*), Muḥammad Riḍā al-Maṭbaʿi, Najaf, 1351.

Tārīkh al-khulafā', Jalāl al-Dīn 'Abd al-Raḥmān Suyūṭī, Cairo, 1952.
Tārīkh-i Ṭabarī (Akhbār al-rusul wa'l-mulūk), Muḥammad ibn Jarīr Ṭabarī, Cairo, 1357.
Tārīkh-i Ya'qūbī, Ibn Wāḍiḥ Ya'qūbī, Najaf, 1358.
Tawḥīd, Shaykh Ṣadūq, Tehran, 1375.
Usd al-ghābah, 'Izz al-Dīn 'Alī ibn al-Athīr Jazarī, Cairo, 1280.
Uṣul al-kāfī, Muḥammad ibn Ya'qūb Kulaynī, Tehran, 1375.
'Uyūn al-akhbār, Ibn Qutaybah, Cairo, 1925–35.
Wafayāt al-a'yān, Ibn Khallakān, Tehran, 1284.
al-Wāfī, Mullā Muḥsin Fayḍ Kāshānī, Tehran, 1310–14.
Yanābī' al-mawaddah, Sulaymān ibn Ibrāhīm Qandūzī, Tehran, 1308.
Ya'qūbī: see *Tārīkh-i Ya'qūbī.*

INDEX